D1761030

Understanding Special Educational Needs and Disability in the Early Years

This key text provides essential tools for understanding legislation, policy, provision and practice for children in the early years, particularly young children with special educational needs and disability (SEND). Based on extensive research and the four areas of need as defined in the *Special Educational Needs and Disability Code of Practice: 0 to 25 Years* (DfE, 2015a), the book charts the development of young children and their growing constructions of learning, communication, language, motor movement and emotion.

Providing material that translates into practice in a straightforward and practical way, this text is packed full of personal accounts and case studies, enabling readers to appreciate what the experience of SEND in the early years means for families and professionals, and also to learn more about how they might understand and respond appropriately to a child's needs.

Understanding Special Educational Needs and Disability in the Early Years will be of interest to students studying Early Years courses, families, SENDCOs, teachers and other staff supporting young children with a range of special educational needs and disabilities.

Janice Wearmouth is Professor of Education at the University of Bedfordshire. She has previously published a range of books in the area of special educational needs and disability, including *Special Educational Needs and Disability: The Basics, Second Edition* (Routledge).

Abigail Gosling is Senior Lecturer in Early Years at the University of Bedfordshire.

Julie Beams is Senior Lecturer in Early Years at the University of Bedfordshire.

Stephanie Davydaitis is Senior Lecturer in Early Years at the University of Bedfordshire.

Gower College Swansea
Library
Coleg Gŵyr Abertawe
Llyrfgell

Understanding Special Educational Needs and Disability in the Early Years

Principles and Perspectives

Janice Wearmouth, Abigail Gosling, Julie Beams and Stephanie Davydaitis

ACC. No: GCS040078

GOWER COLLEGE SWANSEA
LEARNING RESOURCE CENTRE

CLASS No: 371·9 WEA

Routledge
Taylor & Francis Group

LONDON AND NEW YORK

First published 2018
by Routledge
2 Park Square, Milton Park, Abingdon, Oxon OX14 4RN

and by Routledge
711 Third Avenue, New York, NY 10017

Routledge is an imprint of the Taylor & Francis Group, an informa business

© 2018 Janice Wearmouth, Abigail Gosling, Julie Beams and Stephanie Davydaitis

The right of Janice Wearmouth, Abigail Gosling, Julie Beams and Stephanie Davydaitis
to be identified as authors of this work has been asserted by them in accordance
with sections 77 and 78 of the Copyright, Designs and Patents Act 1988.

All rights reserved. No part of this book may be reprinted or reproduced or
utilised in any form or by any electronic, mechanical, or other means, now
known or hereafter invented, including photocopying and recording, or in any
information storage or retrieval system, without permission in writing from the
publishers.

Trademark notice: Product or corporate names may be trademarks or registered
trademarks, and are used only for identification and explanation without intent
to infringe.

British Library Cataloguing in Publication Data
A catalogue record for this book is available from the British Library

Library of Congress Cataloging in Publication Data
A catalog record for this book has been requested

ISBN: 978-1-138-20100-2 (hbk)
ISBN: 978-1-138-20101-9 (pbk)
ISBN: 978-1-315-51337-9 (ebk)

Typeset in Bembo
by Deanta Global Publishing Services, Chennai, India

Printed in the United Kingdom
by Henry Ling Limited

Contents

Preface

This book provides the grounding for an understanding of legislation, policy, provision and practice for children in the early years, from birth to 8 years, specifically for those young children with special educational needs and disabilities, the way in which this has developed and changed over the years and what it comprises today. It is a key text for students studying early years courses at various levels, for newly appointed SENDCos[1] and more experienced teachers dealing with the arrival of two-year-olds in schools and for families and others with an interest in SEND in the early years sector.

Revised legislation related to provision for special educational needs and disabilities for young people from birth to 25 years was introduced in England in September, 2014: Part 3 of the Children and Families Act (2014) together with associated regulations and documents with the status of 'statutory advice'. This new legislation functions to strengthen and extend the legal requirement to ensure the availability and effectiveness of high-quality provision for young children with SEND in the early years. Under the terms of Section 19(d) of Part 3 of this Act, simply to ensure that children with SEND have access to an appropriate education is no longer sufficient. Instead, it specifies access that enables young people to 'achieve the best possible' educational and other outcomes. This reflects a new and higher level of outcome required by law. At the time of writing, legislation elsewhere in the UK is currently under revision.

All those working in early years educational institutions of various kinds are bound, at some time or another, to come across young children who experience SEND. These children's families want to know that their learning and general welfare needs are being met appropriately. This book, therefore, includes material that is clearly theorised and translates theorising into practice in a straightforward, intelligible and practical way, and points to sources of information for those wishing to pursue their interest in the area further. In addition, we have included personal accounts to enable readers both to appreciate what the experience of SEND in the early years means for families and professionals, and also to learn more about how they, the readers, might understand and respond appropriately to needs.

In order to set the context within which provision and practice for SEND in the early years can be understood, the book opens with a brief history of the development of provision, culminating in discussion of current legislation, policy and curriculum structures. This is followed by an outline of various understandings of the development of young children: growing constructions of learning, including communication, language, motor movement and emotional aspects. Subsequent chapters include discussion of:

- theory, research, methods of assessment and commonly used interventions in each of the four areas of need as defined in the *Special Educational Needs and Disability Code of Practice: 0 to 25 Years* (DfE, 2015a) (communication and interaction, cognition and learning, social, emotional and mental health and sensory and/or physical needs);

- the rights and entitlements of families in decision-making about SEND provision for young children and experiences in practice;
- inclusion in classrooms: effective practices and challenges;
- requirements relating to, and experiences of, multi-agency working.

Chapter 1, *Historical and current perspectives on legislation and provision*, comprises two parts. Part 1 takes a chronological approach in weaving together an overview of the history of provision for children seen as 'different' from peers on account of the learning or physical difficulties they experienced, or the behaviour they displayed, with that of the growth and development of provision for children in the early years. This account, time period by time period, is contextualised with discussion of societal changes and changes in thinking about learning, behaviour and children's rights over time. A major focus in Part 2 is discussion of the development of the concept of 'special educational needs' and children's rights under disability equality legislation that leads to an overview of current law and practice across the four countries of the UK. Interwoven in this discussion is a consideration of further growth in the early years sector in the past four decades which includes an overview of, and reflection on, the development of non-statutory and statutory frameworks and regulations relating to provision for children from birth.

Chapter 2, *Understanding and responding to the developing learning needs of young children*, comprises reflection on a range of understandings of the development of young children. This includes growing constructions of learning and development:

- the impact on development and learning of the pre-birth context, especially the physical and emotional health and well-being of the mother;
- the nature of early human development including the individually unique developmental pathways and timelines of babies and young children;
- the impact of secure/insecure primary attachments on development and learning and the setting's role, for example, the Key Person;
- the human urge to play, including varieties of rough and tumble, and the need for physical first-hand experiences indoor and outdoor and the impact that has on children's behaviour when it is limited e.g. suppressed natural human needs leading to frustration and unwanted behaviour;
- how babies and young children develop concepts of the world and the role of language in that conceptual development;
- the critical role of practitioner interactions, observations and reflections on babies' and young children's learning and development;
- the imperative for highly effective practitioner training programmes to be developed that reflect current knowledge and understanding.

Following this account is a discussion of early childhood curricula seen as appropriate to meeting young children's needs at different points in time.

Chapters 3–6 focus on understanding and addressing a number of issues in each of the four areas of need outlined in the *Special Educational Needs and Disability Code of Practice: 0 to 25 years* (DfE, 2015a), whilst acknowledging that these areas have considerable overlap. These issues relate to: difficulties in communication and interaction; difficulties in cognition and learning, social, emotional and mental health needs; and sensory and/or physical difficulties and needs. There is discussion of current research and practice related to identifying and making effective provision for needs within each area, including difficulties in receptive and expressive language, autism, profound and multiple difficulties in learning, dyslexia, AD/HD, Tourette's, visual, auditory and multi-sensory impairments and physical difficulties, in particular muscular dystrophy.

The discussion in each chapter includes:

- what is known about these delays and disorders in the early years from rigorous, high quality research studies;
- the relationship between such delay, impairment and/or disorder and learning;
- ways that the difficulties can be assessed and addressed in the early years through attention to the learning environment, curriculum and teaching approaches;
- vignettes of experience and/or extended case studies of personal experiences from various perspectives, including those of teachers and SENDCos. Experiences of family members are included in the following chapter.

Chapter 7, *Family perspectives*, begins by outlining the background to current policies on families' rights and entitlements in decision-making about SEND provision for young children. It goes on to discuss legal requirements in relation to partnership work with families and carers and some of the challenges in meeting these, with examples of effective practical initiatives designed to enable more positive working relationships between professionals and home.

Included also in this chapter are personal accounts of what can happen in practice, both in a positive and less than positive sense, taken from interviews with families/carers, siblings and other family members, together with professionals experienced in working with families.

In Chapter 8, *Inclusion of young children with SEND*, we discuss the assumption in the various *Codes of Practice* across the UK that teachers will offer differentiated learning opportunities for all children, including those with special educational needs and disabilities. This chapter illustrates how the assess → plan → do → review framework as outlined in the *Special Educational Needs and Disability Code of Practice: 0 to 25 years* (DfE, 2015a) can and should be used to ensure that all young children are included in early years settings and schools.

Chapter 9, *Collaboration with other professionals*, sketches the range of people with whom educators in the early years might be expected to work to meet the needs of young children with SEND and their likely roles: teaching assistants (TAs), outside agencies (Health and Social Care in particular) and so on. It also includes the role of specialist external agencies in supporting provision for SEND in early years contexts, including consideration of the development of Education, Health and Care Plans for the children in most need of special or additional provision.

Note

1 Sometimes, as in the *Special Educational Needs and Disability Code of Practice: 0 to 25 years* (DfE, 2015a) in England, the term used is special educational needs co-ordinator (SENCo).

Acknowledgements

We would like to acknowledge the very valuable contributions made to this book by our colleagues, and, in particular, by:

- Alison Symonds, Inclusion lead, St Joseph's Catholic Lower School, Bedford
- Rosemary Abram, Vicky Thomson, Zoe Smith, Matthew, Joel and Esther
- Lesley Boyle, Deputy Head, Bedford Federation of Nursery Schools
- Mrs Alison Gardner and Mrs Veronica Lawrence, Specialist Senior Educational Psychologists – Early Years, Northamptonshire Educational Psychology Services
- Students of the University of Bedfordshire studying Early Years courses, in particular Rosie Gillett and Amber Jessop
- Anne Eadie, Early Years SEND Advisory Teacher, Early Years and SEND Service, Central Bedfordshire

Historical and current perspectives on legislation and provision

---

Major questions addressed in this chapter are:

- How did special educational, and additional support, provision and provision for children from birth to 8 years develop in the UK?
- What purposes did this provision serve?
- What was the nature of the national context that supported these developments?
- What are the current legislative frameworks across the UK that govern the area of:
    - special educational, or additional support, needs and disabilities?
    - provision for children in the early years?

Introduction

Chapter 1 comprises two parts. Part 1 begins by weaving together an overview of the growth and development of provision for children in the early years, that is, from birth to 8 years of age, with the history of special or additional provision for children seen as 'different' from peers on account of the learning, physical or behavioural difficulties they experienced. This account is chronological, time period by time period, and is contextualised with discussion of societal changes and changes in thinking about learning, behaviour and children's rights over time. Part 2 completes the chapter with an overview of, and reflection on, the development of statutory frameworks and regulations governing policy and practice related to special educational, or additional support, and disability needs of children across the UK, and a consideration of growth in the early years sector in the past four decades.

Part 1: A historical perspective

School curricula 'and even schools themselves are seen to be products of the social system in which they exist' (Broadfoot, 2011, p. 9). This system includes society's values, beliefs and political ideology (Wearmouth, 2009) and the question about what purpose the special education and early years sectors were developed to serve.

Reflective activity: Understanding the historical context of the special education sector and early years provision

Take a few moments to reflect on:

- What you know about the historical development of (1) the 'special' education sector; (2) educational provision for children in the early years;
- Why it may be important to be aware of the historical origins to understand current policy and practice.

National context for developments in provision in the eighteenth and nineteenth centuries

In the UK, the development of early special education provision and provision in the early years, beginning at the end of the eighteenth century, should be seen in a national context where industry was rapidly developing and expanding. This was an age of child labour in, for example, factories in towns and cities and on the land in the countryside. 'There could be no question of establishing a system of compulsory popular education when the new factory system was insistently demanding child labour' (Simon, 1974, p. 152). As recorded by the National Archives in Kew, London, it was not until the Factory Act of 1833 that it became illegal to employ children under 9 years of age. Even then, children between 9 and 13 could work up to 9 hours a day (National Archives, 1833 Factory Act). The minimum age of employment was not raised to 10 years until 1876, and to 11 in 1893.

Until the end of the nineteenth century, education was largely for the children of the wealthy. For all those children whose parents were unable to afford fees, education was minimal, and largely religious. Children of poor and lower-middle-class parents might attend a network of Sunday Schools, 'voluntary' (mostly church) schools and informal neighbourhood schools with low fees, but a significant proportion of the poorest children had no access to education at all.

Rationale for development of provision

Special education

In a national context of the growing industrialisation of society, we might see special education serving a number of purposes, for example, to:

- serve the economic and commercial interests of society, so that all children as far as possible should work and contribute to an industrial society. As Cole (1990, p. 101) notes, it was businessmen, not government, who 'played a part in the founding of pioneer establishments for the deaf and for the blind, and ... throughout the nineteenth century trade training took up much of the lives of the handicapped attending them'; and/or
- look after the needs and welfare of children who were different from others and unable to progress, academically, in the same way, from an essentially benevolent standpoint (Cole, 1989); and/or

- provide a formal means to exclude troublesome pupils from mainstream schooling, or pupils who require a lot of the teacher's time (Thomas and Loxley, 2007), for example, segregating mental defectives as defined under the Mental Deficiency Act of 1913.

Early years sector

There are a number of different ways of looking at the rationale for the emergence of early years provision in this context also. We might refer specifically to Robert Owen's reasons for the establishment of the first nursery-infant school in Britain for children as young as 1 year old long before elementary education for (almost) all became statutory. Owen (1771–1858) had made an enormous profit from his enterprises in the cotton industry in the early part of the Industrial Revolution. Subsequently, he became a social and educational reformer who set about trying to address some of the effects of rapid industrialisation on the workers and their children through education as well as poor law reform and reform of factories and the environment.

Owen drew on his own experiences as an industrialist to take a humanitarian and philanthropic position in viewing education as the most important instrument for social reform. He had a deterministic belief that 'the character of man is formed for him' (Owen, 1841, p. 40).

> It must be evident to those who have been in the practice of observing children with attention, that much of good or evil is taught to or acquired by a child at a very early period of its life; that much of temper or disposition is correctly or incorrectly formed before he attains his second year and that many durable impressions are made at the termination of the first twelve or even six months of his existence. The children, therefore, of the uninstructed and ill-instructed, suffer material injury in the formation of their characters during these and the subsequent years of childhood and of youth.

His schools were therefore established with a view to influencing character formation and social training of children from a very young age. As he wrote himself:

> It was to prevent, or as much as possible to counteract, these primary evils, to which the poor and working classes are exposed when infants, that the area [i.e. a playground] became part of the New Institution [i.e. school].
>
> Into this playground the children are to be received as soon as they can freely walk alone.
>
> (Owen, 1857, p. 288)

Given the societal context of the time, it is unsurprising that, despite Owen's humanitarian view, others took a more pragmatic view of the purpose of education for young children as it relates to employment. John Griscom, for example, an American visitor to Owen's schools, is cited in Donnachie and Hewitt (1993, p. 102) as saying:

> This baby school is of great consequence to the establishment, for it enables mothers to shut up their houses in security, and to attend to their duties in the factory, without concern for their families.

Types of special and early years provision prior to the advent of universal elementary education

Special provision

The earliest institutions providing any kind of training for children who experienced difficulties of any kind, learning, sensory or physical, were established in a societal context where child labour was the norm. Schools for blind and deaf children founded by individuals or by charities, not by government, came first (DES, 1978, ch. 2). When central government intervened subsequently, initially it was to supplement what voluntary agencies provided and, later on, to create a national system of special education provision. (Education for all children, however severe the difficulties they experienced, was not officially seen as an entitlement until the 1970s).

Early private foundations were designed to focus on training in work skills, moral improvement and the Christian religion (Oliphant, 2006), for example, the School of Instruction for the Indigent[1] Blind, established in 1791 in Liverpool, the School for the Indigent Blind in London founded in 1800 and the Asylum and School for the Indigent Blind at Norwich in 1805. The founding plan of the School of Industry in Liverpool included 'to furnish the blind with employment that may prevent them from being burdens to their family and community ...' (Oliphant, 2006, p. 58). As recipients of public charity, the inmates should form 'habits of industry', with men making baskets, tablecloths and whips while the women spun yarn, made sail cloths and picked oakum. Misdeeds could be punished severely, and most children's prospects were grim. In 1825, two boys were flogged for insolence and another for 'making away with his yarns', as the Liverpool School Visitors' Books records (Oliphant, ibid.). It was not for another 30 years that educational aspects were introduced, for example, in the London Society for Teaching the Blind to Read in 1838.

Other charitable institutions were similarly limited in what they offered. Attempts were made to teach a trade to girls with physical disabilities from poor homes in the Cripples' Home and Industrial School for Girls established in Marylebone in 1851, and to boys in the Training Home for Crippled Boys founded in Kensington in 1865. However, although the curriculum was predominantly training, ironically 'many of their inmates failed to find employment on leaving and had recourse to begging', as the Warnock Report (DES, 1978, p. 9) notes in relation to institutions for the deaf.

Apart from workhouses and infirmaries with secure care, there was little provision for those children who experienced serious difficulties in learning until the end of the nineteenth century. The first specific provision was a philanthropic asylum for 'idiot' children, the Earlswood Asylum for Idiots established at Highgate in 1847, in Britain. The National Archives records the aim of this asylum as:

> not merely to take the Idiot and Imbecile under its care, but especially, by the skilful and earnest application of the best means in his education, to prepare him, as far as possible, for the duties and enjoyments of life [Bye-laws 1857].
>
> (National Archives, The Royal Earlswood Hospital Records)

However, as Hall (2008, p. 1006) notes, the philanthropic optimism accompanying the founding of the Earlswood Asylum, that those with difficulties in learning could be educated, faded and was replaced by a eugenicist preoccupation with fears of national decline, because of what was seen to be a link between mental defectiveness and criminality (Thomson, 1998; Wright and Digby, 1996). Mental defectives were seen as genetically tainted; they should be both separated from society, and prevented from reproducing.

By 1870, there were five asylums. Parents had to agree to their children being certified as 'idiots' in order to have them admitted, a label that attracted much odium (Cole, 1989, p. 22).

One exception to provision restricted to a focus on training for work and religion was the foundation of the College for the Blind Sons of Gentlemen in 1866 in Worcester. (In its 1872 report, 'gentlemen' were described as 'belonging by birth or kinship to upper, the professional or the middle classes of society' [Bell, 1967, p. 16]). Worcester College remained the only route for blind boys to achieve higher qualifications and entry into the professions until after World War Two. (The equivalent for girls was not established until 1921, by the National Institute for the Blind [NIB] in Chorleywood.)

Early years sector

Britain's first nursery-infant school was established by Robert Owen in a community in New Lanark, Scotland, in 1816. This, as Bradburn (1966, p. 57) notes, was 21 years before Froebel opened his kindergarten in Germany. After spending time learning about the cotton spinning industry in Manchester, in 1800 he had taken over management of the cotton mills in New Lanark. Over the next 24 years he established a new system of industrial life based around communitarian philosophy and proto-socialist beliefs, with improved working conditions, housing, nutrition and the development of a community environment in opposition to the prevailing patterns found elsewhere in Britain:

> Owen was enlightened enough to advocate and provide schooling for the poor at a time when it was fashionable to scoff at the idea of educating the 'lower orders'. In a class-conscious society where mobility between the classes was neither envisioned nor encouraged, he said that, given the right education, 'infants of any one class in the world may be readily formed into men of any other class (Owen, 1857, p. 315).
>
> (Bradburn, 1966, p. 58)

Central to Owen's work was the belief that an individual's character was formed predominantly by their environment and aspects of the community in which they lived. In a healthy and happy environment individuals would flourish. He associated character defects with a 'lack of proper guidance and direction' (Owen, 1816, p. 14). He therefore encouraged children to attend his school from about 1 year of age, although in practice it tended to be from 2 or 3 years old (Owen, 1824). Owen did not subscribe to the common view that children were little adults, but instead recognised that childhood was a unique phase of growth for humans and had its own distinctive traits which needed to be accommodated for within the school environment. He paid little attention to the spiritual dimension of the child.

The underpinning principles for the infant school related to play in many respects and 'play' areas were set up within the school environment. Rich natural resources were presented within the classroom, copy books were used sparingly and secular stories were seen to be as important as the Bible. Children were encouraged to engage in discussion about their learning (Donnachie, 2000), to express themselves in words and images and later on in dancing, marching and singing. In terms of the curriculum, the subject base was broad, relevant and engaging for the young children who were encouraged to be tactile and learn through field studies in the outdoor environment around New Lanark.

In Owen's view, the family could potentially be a negative force on the child's character, and therefore to compensate for this the schools were there to counteract the family influences. Hence, he took a particularly stringent approach to the role of adults as teachers; teachers who were kind and enabling would foster happiness in the young children, which he considered would be indicative of a happy community. In fact, rather than educated scholars, he deliberately chose as teachers those individuals whose temperaments were gentle. He expected:

> increasing kindness in tone, look, word, and action, to all the children without exception, by every teacher employed, so as to create a real affection and full confidence between the teachers and the taught.
>
> (Owen, 1857, p. 319)

Much of this was in direct contrast to the tradition usually associated with education at this time, typified in Dickens's *Hard Times* where Thomas Gradgrind, school master of the school in Coketown, was portrayed as harsh, inflexible and concerned only with teaching 'facts':

> 'Now, what I want, is Facts. Teach these boys and girls nothing but Facts. Facts alone are wanted in life. Plant nothing else, and root out everything else. You can only form the minds of reasoning animals upon Facts; nothing else will ever be of any service to them'. ... The scene was a plain, bare, monotonous vault of a schoolroom, and the speaker's square forefinger emphasized his observations by underscoring every sentence with a line on the schoolmaster's sleeve. ... The emphasis was helped by the speaker's voice, which was inflexible, dry and dictatorial.
>
> (Dickens, 1910, p. 1)

Influence of Froebel

Alongside Owen's work in Scotland, the German educationalist Friedrich Froebel (1782–1852), one of the most influential thinkers of the nineteenth century, was pioneering a new view of early childhood education in Germany. Like Owen, Froebel believed that the pre-school period was a fundamentally important time for education and viewed childhood to have integrity in its own right.

> Even as a child, every human being should be viewed and treated as a necessary essential member of humanity.
>
> (Froebel, 1826, p. 16)

As a young man, Froebel was first apprenticed to a forester where he learnt about the value of the outdoors and nature. He later attended the University of Jena where, through studying general sciences, he began to think about the interconnection and unity of life and the soul.

In 1816, Froebel started his own school in Griesheimand, and in 1826 wrote *The Education of Man*, which outlined his aims and teaching methods based on the educational principles of wholeness, innate human goodness and activity – thinking and doing. For Froebel, the purpose of education is to guide children to become pure and perfect representations of God's divine inner law through personal choice:

> … the destiny of man as a child of God and of nature is to represent in harmony and unison the spirit of God and of nature, the natural and the divine, the terrestrial and the celestial, the finite and the infinite. Again, the destiny of the child as a member of the family is to unfold and represent the nature of the family, its spiritual tendencies and forces, in their harmony, all-sidedness and purity; and, similarly, it is the destiny and mission of man as a member of humanity to unfold and represent the nature, the tendencies and forces of humanity as a whole.
>
> (Froebel 1826/2005, p. 19)

In 1840, he coined the word 'kindergarten' for the Play and Activity Institute he had founded for young children in 1837 at Bad Blankenburg. Play and creativity were central integrating elements in development and learning in Froebel's thinking. He stressed the importance of experiences in the natural environments, and in his writing he praised the benefits of children exercising and developing 'powers in the open air' (1826, p. 114) to develop their primary understanding of their world and later develop their symbolic thinking:

> … modelling with paper and paste-board has its peculiar progressive course. Still more profitable, but only for those who have attained a certain degree of mental power, is the modelling of soft material in accordance indicated by the cubical form.
>
> (1826, p. 284)

Influence of Pestalozzi

A strong influence on Froebel's thinking about education was the work of Johann Heinrich Pestalozzi (1746–1827), born in Zurich, Switzerland. Pestalozzi's influence on thinking about teaching methods owes much to a book he published in 1801: *How Gertrude Teaches Her Children*. In it he stated that he wanted to establish a 'psychological method' of teaching (p. 132) 'to gain light for myself upon the mechanical formulas of instruction and their subordination to the eternal laws of human nature' (p. 129).

Instead of dealing with words, he argued, children should learn through activity and through things. To get rid of the meaningless with which new vocabulary was usually taught, Pestalozzi developed his principle of 'Anschauung' (Pestalozzi, 1801/1894): learning the meaning of a word through direct concrete observation. No word was to be used for any purpose until the thing or distinction had been sensed or observed in the concrete. Once perception had been gained through the Anschauung an appropriate action must follow. As a result, he placed a special emphasis on encouraging children's own powers of seeing, judging and reasoning, spontaneity and self-activity. 'I have given you threads from which I believe a general and psychological method of instruction might be woven' (p. 135). In his method the aim was to educate the whole child, and he looked to balance three elements: hands, heart and head. Intellectual education was only one part:

> I wish to wrest education from the outworn order of doddering old teaching hacks as well as from the new-fangled order of cheap, artificial teaching tricks, and entrust it

to the eternal powers of nature herself, to the light which God has kindled and kept alive in the hearts of fathers and mothers, to the interests of parents who desire their children grow up in favour with God and with men.

(Pestalozzi, quoted in Silber 1965, p. 134)

The 'Pestalozzi Method' came to fruition in his school at Yverdon that he established in 1805 following a number of unsuccessful experiments. It was here that Froebel and a number of other educators who became famous in their own right came to observe and learn from Pestalozzi's ideas.

Development of education for (almost) all, 1870–World War Two

For a whole variety of reasons pressure grew in the second half of the nineteenth century for a nationally organised system of universal elementary education that was to have a consequent effect on the organisation of special education provision. For example, the expansion of industry during the Industrial Revolution led some manufacturers to call for a greater pool of educated individuals from which to 'select the higher grades of work-ers, foremen and managers' (Simon, 1974, p. 360). A Reform Act of 1867 enfranchised the lower-middle class and better-off workers. The extension of voting rights under this Act led some politicians to argue that the lower classes must now be educated 'to qualify them for the power that has passed … into their hands', as a Liberal Party parliamentar-ian, Robert Lowe, (1867, pp. 31–2) cited in Simon (1974, p. 356) commented at the time. Then there was the question of the social control of children in cities and towns. Those under 9 years of age could not legally be employed under the terms of the 1833 Factory Act, as noted on page 2 and, in any case, fewer children were needed to work in factories once machinery became more complex. Deliberate moves were therefore made towards universal elementary education under the terms of the 1870 Forster Education Act in England and Wales, and the 1872 Education (Scotland) Act. School boards were charged with ensuring provision of elementary education in places where there were insufficient places through voluntary enterprise. In 1880, a further Act finally made school attendance compulsory in England between the ages of 5 and 10, although attendance until the age of 13 was compulsory for those who had not achieved the standard of education that was 'fixed by a byelaw in force in the district' (Elementary Education Act, 1880, chapter 23, §4).

Special education 1870–1944

The beginnings of compulsory elementary schooling from 1870 had a particular signifi-cance for the special education sector. It meant that large numbers of children who seemed to have poor intellectual ability came to school for the first time. This included those aged 5–8 years. The question was what to do with these children. Now that they were com-pelled to attend, their presence was felt to be holding others back in the large classes that existed in public elementary schools. Besides, national level funding for individual schools, including teachers' salaries, depended in part on the outcomes of examinations of pupils conducted by school inspectors. For example, the policy of payment by results was intro-duced into schools in England in 1863. It lasted until 1890 when it was abandoned.

In 1889, a Royal Commission recommended compulsory education for the blind from age 5 to 16 and for the deaf from age 7 to 16. In other words, education for blind children in the early years became compulsory for children from 5 years of age. Deaf children, generally considered slower to learn on account of difficulties in communication, were to be taught separately by teachers who should be specially qualified to do so.[2] Legislation in Scotland followed in 1890 with the Education of the Blind and Deaf Mute Children (Scotland) Act, and in England and Wales in 1893 with the Elementary Education (Blind and Deaf Children) Act.

The same 1889 Royal Commission distinguished between three groups of children seen as experiencing varying degrees of learning difficulties: 'feeble-minded', 'imbeciles' and 'idiots'. Again, this included children from 5 years of age. 'Feeble-minded' should be educated in 'auxiliary' schools away from other children; 'imbeciles' should be sent to institutions where education should concentrate on sensory and physical development and improved speech. 'Idiots' were not thought to be educable.

Formalising categories of difference

These days we would consider the use of these labels for children unacceptable. However, the new discipline of psychology made formal identification and assessment of 'deficiencies' in children seem more legitimate in the context of the time. A Mental Deficiency Act was passed in 1913 that defined four grades of Mental Defective. The archive of the National Association for the Feebleminded (Kirby, 1914) reads as follows in relation to this Act:

> It would be well for every public official and social worker to commit the wording of these definitions to memory, in order that the mentally defective may not pass unrecognized, and be, in consequence, committed to unsuitable institutions, submitted to inappropriate treatment, and discharged; his mental abnormality still remaining undiscovered and ignored.
> Definition.
> The four classes of mental defectives within the meaning of the Act are described as follows:

(1) Idiots; that is to say, persons so deeply defective in mind from birth or from an early age as to be unable to guard themselves against common physical dangers.
(2) Imbeciles; that is to say, persons in whose case there exists from birth or from an early age mental defectiveness not amounting to idiocy, yet so pronounced that they are incapable of managing themselves or their affairs, or, in the case of children, of being taught to do so.
(3) Feeble-minded Persons; that is to say, persons in whose case there exists from birth or from an early age mental defectiveness not amounting to imbecility, yet so pronounced that they require care, supervision, and control for their own protection, or for the protection of others, or, in the case of children, that they by reason of such defectiveness appear to be permanently incapable of receiving proper benefit from the instruction in ordinary schools.
(4) Moral Imbeciles; that is to say, persons who from an early age display some permanent mental defect coupled with strong vicious, or criminal propensities, on which punishment has had little or no deterrent effect.

> The scheme of provision under the Mental Deficiency Act is based upon the assumption that a defective person is one who remains mentally immature, and in need, therefore, of the permanent care and protection which should be the natural right of every child during immature years.
>
> (Internet Archive, Legislation for the feeble-minded)

Only three MPs voted against the Act. One, Josiah Wedgwood, is cited in Woodhouse (1982, p. 13) as saying, 'It is a spirit of the Horrible Eugenic Society which is setting out to breed up the working class as though they were cattle'. Local education authorities in England and Wales, and school boards in Scotland, were required to ascertain and certify which children aged 7 to 16 in their area were 'defective'. Those judged by the authority to be ineducable became the responsibility of parish councils for placement in an institution. One can only imagine what life would have been like for children so defined at a young age.

Early years provision, 1870–World War Two (1939)

Prior to 1870, young children sometimes attended 'dame schools'[3] and Sunday schools. However, as the teachers were often elderly women with little education of their own in reality they only loosely functioned as places of education and more pragmatically as a means of protection for poor children from the streets or fields. The effect of the 1870 Education Act was to make infant schools or departments, serving children aged 5 to 7, a part of public elementary schools. In some places new schools were built with separate infant classes, often in adjacent buildings.

Froebel's influence was felt in infant schools as several of the newly established school boards began to implement his methods and some had teachers trained in the principles of Froebel's kindergarten techniques. By 1888, the National Froebel Union was founded as an examining body for teaching staff. The use of Froebel's methods in some infant classes, however, was often in the form of mechanical instruction rather than embracing his coherent view of education practices (Board of Education, 1933).

The end of the nineteenth century saw some expansion in education for children below the age of 5. By 1893, children between 3 and 5 years of age often attended infant schools, for example. By the early 1900s, the importance of provision for children below the age of 5 was beginning to be aired by educationalists and the medical profession. A report by five of the Board of Education's women inspectors in 1905 provided clear primary research on the physical, moral and health development and attainment of young children in elementary schools across rural and urban England and Wales. Much of it reflects the ongoing debate on education today. The report suggested that children under 5 in 'baby' classes did not benefit from their current education:

> The Inspectors agree that the mechanical teaching in many infant schools seems to dull rather than awaken the little power of imagination and independent observation which these infants possess. Children say what they think the teacher would like them to say; if asked to draw anything they like, they attempt the reproduction of some school copy previously set; the wearisome iteration of the same work makes

them all of one pattern; they become apathetic; the actual knowledge acquired is not beneficial.

(Board of Education, 1905, p. i)

These inspectors understood that young children need oral language before they will be able to read, need to understand number-ness before they should learn to recite number names and need gross and fine motor skills before they should be expected to write:

There is little doubt in the minds of all these Inspectors that these little children should have no formal instruction in the three R's, but plenty of opportunities for free expression: they must learn to talk before they learn to read; to understand before they learn number by heart; and to use arms and fingers freely and boldly before they hold pen or pencil to trace letters.

(Board of Education, 1905, p. ii)

The report paid attention to the health and nutrition of the children with praise for 'certificated nurses' (1905, p. 9) supporting interventions for ailments of the skin, eyesight and so on, and noted the impact of poverty on young children's development and well-being. It suggested that a 'new form of school is necessary' especially for poor children where 'no formal instruction is the burden of all the recommendations, but more play, more sleep, more free conversation, story-telling and observation' (1905, p. iii).

The view of these inspectors was supported by the 1908 Acland *Report on School Attendance of Children Below the Age of Five* (Board of Education, 1908) that recommended the introduction of nursery schools with an adapted curriculum and environment, adjusted to suit the needs of the youngest children who were in need of education in infant schools due to impoverished home circumstances. Formal lessons in literacy and numeracy

should be rigidly excluded from the curriculum of younger infants, and also everything that requires prolonged complex operations of the nervous or muscular systems. Freedom of movement, constant change of occupation, frequent visits to the playground, and opportunities for sleep, are essential.

(Board of Education, 1908, p. 58)

In 1911, reflecting this view, and concerned for the health and well-being of poor working-class children, the McMillan sisters, Margaret and Rachel, established an open-air nursery in Deptford, East London. This nursery was predicated on the need for health care with proper nourishment, cleanliness, exercise and fresh air, access to play areas and gardens and no fixed time schedule (Kwon, 2002). Their approach to early years education that emphasised the need to nurture mind and body is reflected in what many experienced early years educators would recognise as the hallmark of high quality, appropriate, holistic practice for all young children today.

Slow growth in provision between the two World Wars, 1918–1939

The inter-war years were difficult for families and children. The depression caused unemployment to soar and the impact on the health of children living in poverty was considerable: illnesses such as scurvy and rickets and tuberculosis were common (Gillard, 2011).

In 1929, a joint circular was issued from the Ministry of Health and the Board of Education that the purpose of a nursery school was twofold: nurture and education (Parker-Rees and Willan, 2006). It was not until 2008, however, with the publication of the *Early Years Foundation Stage*, that these two areas were finally enshrined in statute as being co-dependent for young children's development and learning (DCSF, 2008).

It was around this time that interest in the work of some of the key thinkers in education grew. Dewey's (1902) essays stressed the importance of children learning by doing, and Montessori (1913) explored the importance of carefully prepared physical provision to enable children to construct their own experiences in a social environment. Both stressed the need to engage the child in active exploration, echoing Froebel and Pestalozzi. A British educationalist who expanded on the work of Froebel and Dewey was Susan Isaacs (1885–1948) with her strong belief that attendance at a nursery school should be a natural part of a young child's life. 'Experience has shown that it can be looked upon as a normal institution in the social life of any civilised community' (Isaacs, 1952, p. 31). Early years settings should reflect the love and warmth of the family, provide social experiences and relationships with peers and adults that are important to development as a social being and also extend the family's function through providing new opportunities and resources that will engage young children's interests. '... the nursery school is an extension of the function of the home, not a substitute for it' (ibid.).

Reflective activity: Learning about current early years provision from the past

At the beginning of this chapter we suggested that it is important to know the history of the development of both special education provision and also provision in the early years sector.

- Why do you think it is important for us to know about the work of key early years thinkers?
- How does it help to shape our current practice?
- What are the key points you have learnt from considering the work of the McMillan sisters and/or Susan Isaacs?

Isaacs contributed evidence towards the Hadow Report on infant and nursery education (Board of Education, 1933) that had an impact on thinking associated with early years education over the coming years. The report restated the 'recognised principles underlying the teaching and training of young children' (1933, p. xvii) that should guide practice, with the 'curriculum [being] thought of in terms of activity and experience rather than of knowledge to be acquired and facts to be stored' (1933, p. xviii). Hadow recommended that nursery schools become:

> a desirable adjunct to the national system of education ... where children below the age of five are admitted to infant schools or departments, nursery classes should eventually be the normal type of provision.
>
> (Board of Education, 1933, pp. 114–115)

The report also provided information on what a nursery or infant classroom should look like, the requirements of having a garden or play-space available, funding regulations, health and safety stipulations. It had, however, less impact on day-to-day practice at the time than it did on the general debate on what early years practice should be (Gillard, 2011), and there remained slow growth in nursery provision over the coming years.

In World War Two, R.A. Butler was appointed as Head of the Board of Education in 1941 and over the next few years planned social reform in the form of a new vision for education. The 1943 Board of Education White Paper prompted, once again, the need for nursery provision, and facilitated this by providing funding through grants to release women from work on the war effort to work in nursery settings. However, this did not survive the removal of the grants at the end of the war, even though the 1944 Act (Chapter 31, Section 2b) had stipulated:

> the need for securing that provision is made for pupils who have not attained the age of five years by the provision of nursery schools or, where the authority consider the provision of such schools to be inexpedient, by the provision of nursery classes in other schools.

Summary of provision from the early nineteenth to mid-twentieth century

To summarise, different views of the child as learner underpin the early development of the special education and early years sectors. The first assumed a model of defectiveness, a deficient child who must be trained for employment from an early age, the second an innate potential for growth, engagement and active interest in the world, a child who needs to play and learn by doing.

In special education, the earliest institutions were established to provide training in work skills and the Christian religion in a societal context where child labour was normal. Subsequently, legislation provided for education in separate institutions by category of difference from the norm, with the advent of the discipline of psychology making formal identification of 'deficiencies' seeming more legitimate in the contemporary context. The 1921 Act consolidated previous legislation, including the 1913 Mental Deficiency Act that defined four grades of Mental Defective. Following this Act, as Warnock (DES, 1978) comments, the statutory foundation of special education continued broadly until the end of World War Two.

Specific provision in the early years during this period began with nursery schools established for humanitarian purposes in an age of industrialisation, often founded to support the 'unfolding' of young children's abilities, 'mental and physical, by surrounding them with a suitable environment' and 'a happy wholesome spirit of freedom and activity' (Board of Education, 1905, p. 103). Over the years, a series of reports recommended the expansion of nursery provision, but for a variety of reasons this faltered, and access to it was challenging for poorer parents. Children from 5 years of age attended mainstream infant or primary schools unless they were deemed to require special provision.

Reorganisation of education after 1944

Between the introduction of compulsory elementary education and World War Two there were a number of developments in the education system. In particular, the age of compulsory attendance was extended to 14 in 1918 and to 15 in 1936. However, the expansion of secondary education consequent on this legislation was fragmented across the country. During World War Two, a coalition government therefore sought to reorganise the education system through the 1944 Education Act in England and Wales and develop a national framework

> ... in three progressive stages to be known as primary education, secondary education, and further education
>
> (Education Act, 1944, Part 11, §7)

A report by Sir William Spens in 1938, *Secondary Education with Special Reference to Grammar Schools and Technical High Schools*, had recommended that there should be three types of secondary school:

- grammar schools for the academically able;
- technical schools for those with a practical bent; and
- new 'modern' secondary schools for the rest.[4]

The 1944 Act never mentioned the words 'tripartite', 'grammar schools' or 'secondary modern schools'. It simply required that education should be provided at three levels: primary, secondary and further. However, central government advised local education authorities to 'think in terms of three types' of state secondary schools in circular No. 73 (12 December 1945). The tripartite system of secondary education was quickly adopted by many local education authorities, with grammar schools for the most able, secondary modern schools for the majority and secondary technical schools for those with a technical or scientific aptitude.[5]

Reorganisation of special education

The reorganisation of special education reflected the assessment into categories of mainstream education (1944 Education Act, Sections 33 and 34 and associated Regulations). Local education authorities' duties to ascertain which children required special educational 'treatment' was extended to all children from the age of 2 who 'suffer from any disability of mind or body'. Children seen as ineducable in school were to be reported for the purposes of the Mental Deficiency Act 1913. In Scotland, the Education (Scotland) Act (1945) repeated much of the content of the Education Act 1944.

The Handicapped Students and School Health Service Regulations (1945) in England and Wales developed a new framework of eleven categories of students: blind, partially sighted, deaf, partially deaf, delicate, diabetic, educationally subnormal, epileptic, maladjusted, physically handicapped and those with speech defects. Two categories were included for the first time: maladjustment and speech defects. Blind, deaf, epileptic, physically handicapped and aphasic[6] children were to be educated in special schools. Children with other disabilities could attend mainstream if there was adequate provision (DES, 1978: 2.46). Official guidance (Ministry of Education, 1946) estimated that the proportion of children who might be expected to require special educational treatment would range from between 14 per cent and 17 per cent of the school population.

During the years which followed, those students considered 'educationally sub-normal' (ESN) and those identified as 'maladjusted' were the two groups that continually expanded in numbers (DES, 1978). The number of children in ESN special schools nearly doubled between 1947 and 1955 from 12,060 to 22,639, with a further 12,000 children awaiting placement.

The system established after 1944 proved not as stable as it first seemed. In mainstream, many commentators began to see that the system of selection into grammar, technical and secondary modern schools was not as fair as had been assumed (Clark *et al.*, 1997). In special education, there was obvious overlap between the learning needs of students in mainstream and special schools (Wearmouth, 1986) that cast doubt on the validity of the process of identification and assessment, but movement between school types was difficult. Young children might therefore be placed in special provision on entry to school and remain there throughout their education. Further, many became concerned about the 32,000 children in institutions of various sorts together with an unknown number at home who were deemed ineducable. As a result, beginning in the 1960s and increasingly in the 1970s, a growing number of comprehensive schools were opened, increasingly special classes and 'remedial' provision were established in mainstream and some children were integrated from special into mainstream schools.

In terms of special provision, the Education (Handicapped Children) Act 1970 removed the power of health authorities to provide training for children who experienced the most serious difficulties in learning (deemed 'mentally handicapped') and required the staff and buildings of junior training centres to be transferred to the education service. In future, they were to be regarded as 'severely educationally sub-normal' (ESN(S)), and entitled to education. In Scotland, the 1974 Act also gave education authorities responsibility for the education of children who previously had been viewed as 'ineducable and untrainable'.

Development of the early years sector

World War Two shaped policy and practice in interesting ways across all sectors of education in the second half of the twentieth century. Post-war idealism led to the creation of the welfare state, of which education was seen as a central part, although expectations of a more equal society as a result of expansion of nursery and secondary schooling soon gave way to some disillusionment.

For nursery education, during the war a mixture of care and education had prevailed and indeed expanded, to meet the needs of mothers involved in long hours of working as a result of the war effort. The years post-war, however, were a time of financial constraint, and day nurseries became the place for children of needy families, and nursery provision, still a largely separate entity at this time, was reduced to more part time places.

This situation continued through to the early 1960s when Belle Tutaev, a mother wanting care, play and social experiences for her child, recognised the paucity of provision and began to take action. Thus, the Pre-School Playgroups Association (now the Pre-School Learning Alliance) was born, primarily designed for the benefit of children rather than to help mothers seek paid employment and return to work in some capacity.

Reflective activity: Growth of the playgroup movement

You might like to read the text below that outlines the inception of the playgroup movement in Britain, and then reflect on the questions that follow:

A report in the *Independent* newspaper 'Here's to the early years: The Pre-school Learning Alliance's playgroups are facing an uncertain future' gives a very clear outline of the chronological development of the playgroup movement from its inception more than five decades ago (Garner, 2010).

Since that time, the playgroup movement has gained in national repute. However, when this article was written in 2010 members of the playgroup association were very concerned at the significant decline in financial support from their Learning Alliances (LAs). They were contemplating a future of having to battle for provision once again in a time of national financial stringency.

Note down your responses to the following:

- In your own experience what effect does pre-school provision have on children in the early years?
- How do you think pre-school provision might assist the learning and development of children with SEND?
- How important do you feel it is to maintain these services?

State intervention and provision, therefore, at the point when the playgroup movement began, was limited, a situation that again prevailed through the remainder of the 1960s and into the 1970s, despite the Plowden Report (CACE, 1967) and changes of government.[7] However, the economic slump of the 1970s, in the wake of Plowden, fuelled by the oil crisis, labour disputes, uncertain prosperity and regular changes in government, meant that any hoped-for expansion within the state sector became lost. The private sector, however, in the form of childminders in particular, showed some increase (Baldock *et al.*, 2013), but this provision was largely unsupported and unregulated.

Summary of changes in the education system post-war

In terms of special education, Regulations in 1945 created further categories of difference between students, some of which led to placement in special schools, reflecting categories of difference in mainstream. However, in many areas there was a move towards adopting a comprehensive system to address concerns about flaws identified in the tripartite approach to secondary education. This was accompanied by a growth in the establishment of special classes and 'remedial' provision in mainstream schools, and the reintegration of some students from special to mainstream also.

During this period, state nursery provision in the early years sector was very limited, and private provision was mostly run through untrained staff.

Part 2: Developments in special educational provision and the early years sector from the 1970s

A number of significant developments took place in the education system increasingly from the mid-1970s, through the 1980s, 1990s and onwards, as a marketised approach took hold with a growing focus on high-stakes accountability mechanisms.

Introduction of the concept of special educational needs

In November 1973, Margaret Thatcher, then education secretary in the Conservative government, announced that she proposed to appoint a committee of enquiry chaired by Mary Warnock:

> to review educational provision in England, Scotland and Wales for children and young people handicapped by disabilities of body or mind, taking account of the medical aspects of their needs, together with arrangements to prepare them for entry into employment; to consider the most effective use of resources for these purposes; and to make recommendations.
>
> (DES, 1978, p. 1)

The very influential 1978 Warnock report of special educational provision in Great Britain replaced the previous categorisation 'disabilities of body or mind' with a new concept of 'special educational needs'. Rutter, Tizard and Whitmore's (1970) study had reported teachers' perceptions that, on average, 20 per cent of their students were experiencing difficulty of some kind. Since then, the figure of 20 per cent has been used to estimate the number of children nationally who might experience difficulties at some point. Approximately 2 per cent of the total number of students were seen by policy makers as likely to have difficulties which require additional or extra resources to be provided. This figure of 2 per cent is arbitrary and drawn from a count of students in special schools in 1944 (DES, 1978). Legally there are no official figures for the incidence of children likely to need statutory assessment. However, it is useful to resource-providers to estimate what proportion of their resources they may require to provide for individual students' educational needs.

Development of new legislation

In England and Wales, the 1981 Act is seen by many as the key piece of legislation concerned with children and young people who experience difficulties or have disabilities in education. The Act was based to a large extent on the Warnock Report's recommendations to replace the eleven categories of handicap with a new umbrella category of 'special educational needs' and an understanding that children's difficulties occur on a continuum. Local education authorities were given responsibilities to identify needs that required provision in addition to what was normally available in schools. The report introduced 'statements of special educational need', which set out an analysis of the difficulties students over the age of 2 years experience in settings and schools and the curricular and human and material resources needed to address them. It required that parents should be consulted about provision for their child, and could appeal against a local education authority's decisions and that all children should be educated in mainstream schools but with certain provisos:

- their needs should be met there and
- it was compatible with the education of other children and with the 'efficient use of resources'.

Two more Acts in 1993 and 1996 developed the legal basis of special educational needs provision in England and Wales, and, in England, a further Act in 2014.

Definition of special educational needs

In England, Wales and Northern Ireland, the definition of 'special educational needs' has remained largely constant since Warnock. A child[8] has special educational needs if he or she has a learning difficulty[9] which calls for special educational provision to be made for him or her (Education Act, 1996, Part 1V, §312(1), Education Order (Northern Ireland) 1996, Part 11, §3(1); (Children and Families Act, 2014, Part 3, §20 (1)). In law, learning difficulties do not in themselves constitute such a need. A young person only has 'special educational needs' when special provision is required to meet them.

To understand this definition clearly, we first need to know what is legally defined as a 'learning difficulty'. A child or young person has such a difficulty if s/he experiences:

a 'significantly greater difficulty in learning than the majority of' same-age peers or
b s/he has a disability which prevents him (or her) from making use of (educational) facilities 'of a kind generally provided for' same-age peers in mainstream educational institutions.
(Education Act 1996, Part 1V, §312 [2]; Education Order [Northern Ireland] 1996, Part 11, §3[1]; Children and Families Act 2014, Part 3, §20 [2])

In education law, a learning difficulty creates a need which is 'special' only if the provision required to address it is 'special'. The meaning of 'learning difficulty' as a difficulty to learn something is fairly obvious. However, legally, a child might also have a 'learning difficulty' if s/he has a physical disability that creates a barrier to moving around the school or classroom to participate in those activities with peers.

Reflective activity: Implications of legal definitions

Note down your responses to the following questions:

- How straightforward do you find this way of defining learning difficulties?
- You might like to note down any questions this definition raises for you.

This way of defining a learning difficulty raises major questions for those in the early years sector particularly when, as we know, young children's learning and progress may well be uneven and irregular, rather than linear. It may therefore be problematic, for example, to conceptualise:

- how to measure a young child's 'significantly greater difficulty in learning';
- how to compare one young child to the majority. If we try to compare individuals against a mean average of the rest of the child population of the same age, it is bound to lead to mistakes, leaving some children with, and others without support that might be needed;
- how to gauge the contexts in which a difficulty becomes significant;
- what is meant by a general level of provision. Some settings have specialist and space for particular activities, others do not, for example.

One of the outcomes of this lack of absolute clarity is that whether young children are identified as needing additional support is very variable across the country.

The second part of the definition refers to a 'disability' as causing learning difficulties. By law, then, a young child with a visual impairment has a learning difficulty if the individual cannot access the same facilities as their peers. The implication is that, if LAs, settings and schools generally provide appropriate learning opportunities, then no child would be prevented 'from making use of educational facilities generally provided' (Education Act 1996, S. 312, DENI, 1998, para. 1.4; Children and Families Act 2014, Part 3, §20 [2][b]), and therefore no child would have special educational needs.

The situation is different in Scotland. Here, the Education (Additional Support for Learning) (Scotland) Act (2004) established the concept of 'additional support needs'. Under this Act, a child or young person has such needs if 'for whatever reason', s/he is not likely to be able 'to benefit from school education provided or to be provided' for him/her 'without the provision of additional support' (Scottish Government, 2004, p. 18, §1). 'School education' here includes, in particular, 'such education that is directed to the development of the personality, talents and mental and physical abilities of the child or young person to their fullest potential'. (2004, §3)

'Additional support' is defined as:

> provision which is additional to, or otherwise different from, the educational provision made generally for children or, as the case may be, young persons of the same age in schools (other than special schools) under the management of the education authority for the area to which the child or young person belongs.
>
> (Scottish Government, 2004, p. 206)

Changes in the law

In the UK, until recently, there have been strong similarities in England, Wales and Northern Ireland in terms of education law. However, proposals have been made by the National Assembly for Wales (NAW) for revisions to legislation in Wales, and by the Department for Education (DENI) for revisions in Northern Ireland. New legislation that was introduced in England in 2014 may increase the differences between them. Education law in Scotland is regulated by the Scottish Government in Edinburgh and continues to be different.

Legislation in Wales

Education-related law in Wales at the time of writing is still based on the 1996 Act. However, the National Assembly of Wales set out a proposal to amend legislation related to SEND policy and provision in 2012 in a consultation document *Forward in partnership for children and young people with additional needs*. In summary, the proposal in this consultation document was to:

- Introduce the concept of 'additional needs'(AN), rather than 'special educational needs' (SEN).
- Replace statements of SEN with new integrated 'Individual Development Plans' (IDPs) that:
  - include assessment and provision involving agencies beyond education where appropriate for young people aged 0–25 years with the highest levels of need and

- require multi-agency panels, called 'Support Panels', to assess and agree upon the support services from education, social and health services that should be recorded in the IDP.
- Require relevant bodies to collaborate in respect of provision for additional needs.
- Set out the duties to be required of relevant bodies (such as LAs and health services).
- Set out the resolution process for any disputes.
- Require the Welsh Ministers to issue a code of practice related to the new statutory framework for AN.

At the time of writing the new legislation has not yet been approved by the National Assembly of Wales.

Legislation in Northern Ireland

In Northern Ireland, Part II of the Education Order (Northern Ireland) (1996), which remains the basis of legislation related to special educational needs in the province, bears a close similarity to the 1996 Act in England and Wales. The 1996 Education Order was amended by the Special Educational Needs and Disability (Northern Ireland) Order (SENDO), (2005) Part II, Articles 3 to 12 and Schedule 1 to take account, specifically, of disability legislation that had been introduced across the UK in 2001. Recently, a proposition to amend the law related to SEND was introduced in the Northern Ireland Assembly on 2nd March 2015 through the Special Educational Needs and Disability Bill (Bill 46/11–16). Among the proposals in the Bill:

> Clause 1 places a new duty on the Education Authority to have regard to the views of the child in relation to decisions affecting them;
>
> Clause 3 extends the existing duties of Boards of Governors in relation to SEN, including a requirement to maintain a personal learning plan (PLP) for each pupil with SEN and ensuring that a teacher is designated as a learning support coordinator (LSC).
>
> Clause 9 gives children with SEN who are over compulsory school age rights previously exercisable by parents, including the right to appeal and to request a statutory assessment.
>
> (Northern Ireland Assembly, 2015)

Legislation in Scotland

The Education (Additional Support for Learning) (Scotland) Act 2004 provides the legal framework for provision of additional support for learning. The Act places duties on education authorities, (and in certain circumstances health, social work and Skills Development Scotland) to make joint provision for all children and young people with additional support needs, including those with complex or multiple additional support needs. Where needs are significant and would last more than one year, they may require a statutory co-ordinated support plan to meet their learning needs. This Act also sets out rights for parents and establishes mechanisms for resolving differences for families and authorities through mediation and dispute resolution.

The legislation was amended by the Education (Additional Support for Learning) (Scotland) Act 2009. The amendments related, among other issues, to the provision of a new national advocacy service for parents and children. A 'co-ordinated support plan' is seen as needed if the child or young person has additional support needs arising from:

(i)   one or more complex factors, or
(ii) multiple factors,

and if the needs 'are likely to continue for more than a year' (2009, p. 74, §3), with the proviso that 'significant additional support' is required to address the needs. In this situation, a factor is defined as 'complex' if 'it has, or is likely to have, a significant adverse effect on the school education of the child or young person'.

Legislation in England

Since 1996 a further Act, the Children and Families Act (2014), has brought about a number of changes in the law in England that have a particular significance in the early years sector. Much of the new law is still the same as in 1996, including the definition of what constitutes a special educational need, as we noted above. However, the new system of supporting children and young people with SEND now applies to young people from birth to 25 years as long as they stay in education or training. This issue of age is important. A child with SEND is entitled to support that enables them to achieve the 'best possible educational and other outcomes', and it is the LA's duty to ensure they identify all children and young people in their geographical area who have or may have SEN and/or disabilities. If, following statutory assessment of need, an Education, Health and Care (EHC) plan is then issued, the LA has the legal duty to ensure that the educational provision is made. The setting or school that a child attends should put support in place to make sure this is happening, but, if it does not, the LA has the responsibility to ensure it does.

Under this Act, statements of special education need[10] are being replaced by Education Health and Care Plans (EHCs). Where there is health provision in an EHC plan, the local health commissioning body, usually the Clinical Commissioning Group, has the duty to provide.

Every LA must develop and publish a 'Local Offer' (§30) that sets out the services and provision it expects to be available both inside and outside the LA's area for children and young people with SEN and/or a disability (see Chapter 9 for further discussion of this).

Definitions of areas of need across the UK

Reasons why students might experience special or additional needs are conceptualised somewhat differently in the different countries of the UK. The *Special Educational Needs Code of Practice for Wales* (2004, §7.52), just as the previous *Code of Practice* in England, (DfES, 2001, §7.52) recommends that assessment and provision should focus on four broad 'areas of need': communication and interaction, cognition and learning, behaviour, emotional and social development and sensory and/or physical. More recently, the *Special Educational Needs and Disability Code of Practice: 0 to 25 Years* (DfE, 2015a, §5.32) in England has amended the conceptualisation of the third 'broad' area of need from 'behaviour, emotional and social development' to 'social, emotional and mental health'. Clearly there is a lot of overlap between these areas. For example, in terms of communication and inter-action, lack of facility with receptive and expressive language has important implications for cognition and learning. As the *Code* in Wales, cautions:

> Although needs and requirements can usefully be organised into areas, individual pupils may well have needs which span two or more areas. For example, a pupil with general learning difficulties may also have behavioural difficulties or a sensory impair-ment. Where needs are complex in this sense it is important to carry out a detailed assessment of individual pupils and their situations.
>
> (NAW, 2004, §7:53)

Teaching approaches suggested in the *Code* in Wales as appropriate for addressing the learning needs of students who experience difficulties in communication and interac-tion may also be appropriate to those who experience difficulties in cognition and learning.

However, in Scotland the approach is rather different. The revised *Supporting Children's Learning Code of Practice* (2010, p. 13) offers a (non-exhaustive) list of children or young people who may require additional support for a variety of reasons. A wide range of factors broadly grouped into four overlapping areas are identified as potentially creating barriers that may lead to the need for additional support:

- learning environment
- family circumstances
- disability or health need
- social and emotional factors.

The definition of additional support provided in the Act is broad and inclusive to reflect the rather broader concept about who might require additional provision. Forms of additional support identified in the *Code* in Scotland are categorised under three broad headings (2010, p. 21):

- approaches to learning and teaching
- support from personnel
- provision of resources.

Disability equality legislation across the UK

Disability law applies to education as well as to other aspects of public life, across all the countries of the UK. It does not, however, apply to Northern Ireland where the relevant disability equality legislation is the Disability Discrimination (Northern Ireland) Order 2006. Since 2000, a number of pieces of legislation relating to disability equality have been passed across the UK.[11] Most recently, the Equality Act, 2010, stresses planned approaches to eliminating discrimination and improving access and is nationwide (including private education), imposing duties on schools and LAs. This means that organisations such as set-tings and schools are expected to be proactive in anticipating and responding to the needs of disabled young children.

The 2010 Equality Act applies to all early years providers. Providers **must** give thought:

> in advance to what disabled children ... might require and what adjustments might need to be made to prevent that disadvantage.
>
> (DfE, 2015a, §5.10)

In other words, they have an 'anticipatory' duty to 'make reasonable adjustments, including the provision of auxiliary aids and services for disabled children, to prevent them being put at substantial disadvantage' (DfE, 2015).

Definition of 'disabled'

Reflective activity: Considering how to define 'disabled'

'Disabled' and 'disability' are terms that may, or may not, provoke strong reactions for reasons that may be similar to those discussed above in relation to connotations of the terms 'special educational' or 'additional support' needs.

In law, a young child is disabled under the Equality Act 2010 (Section 6) if s/he has a physical or mental impairment which has a substantial and long-term adverse effect on his/her ability to carry out normal day-to-day activities.

- How clear do you find that definition?
- Can you see any overlap between the definition of 'disabled' and that of 'special educational needs'?

Under the terms of the 2010 Act, 'substantial' means more than minor or trivial and 'long term' means lasting more than one year or likely to last more than one year. Not all children with special educational, or additional support, needs will be disabled and not all disabled children will have special educational, or additional support, needs. The vast majority, however, will fall under both legal definitions.

Early years settings, schools and LAs have clear legal duties to act to prevent unlawful discrimination, whether directly or indirectly. For example, Paragraph 85 of the Equality Act 2010 states that there must be no discrimination by a school, for example:

(2) (a)   in the way it provides education for the pupil;
    (b)   in the way it affords the pupil access to a benefit, facility or service;
    (c)   by not providing education for the pupil;
    (d)   by not affording the pupil access to a benefit, facility or service.

Settings and schools must therefore ensure that they do not treat children with disabilities less favourably than others. Settings and schools also have a duty to make reasonable adjustments, to change what they do or were proposing to do, to ensure a child is not disadvantaged. This includes the provision of aids and services to support a child.

The 2010 Equality Act gives parents the right of appeal to a Tribunal, if they feel their child has suffered discrimination. The Tribunal in England is the First-tier Tribunal, in

Wales the Special Educational Needs Tribunal for Wales and in Scotland an Additional Support Needs Tribunal for Scotland.

In Northern Ireland, the relevant disability equality legislation is the Disability Discrimination (Northern Ireland) Order 2006. This Order extends previous legislation, the Disability Discrimination Act, 1995, to bring the functions of public authorities within the scope of disability legislation and imposes a new duty to promote positive attitudes towards disabled people and encourage participation in public life (2006, §49A).

Development of early years provision from the mid-1970s

The implications for children in the early years of the strengthening and formalising of the SEND legislative framework from the 1978 Warnock Report onwards should be seen in relation to development of provision and changes in the curricular framework for the early years during this period. From the late 1970s and through the 1980s the Conservative government, under the leadership of Margaret Thatcher, sought to develop a more market driven economy with increased regulation. With the further expansion of the voluntary sector, the Rumbold Report (DES, 1990) and the Start Right Report (Ball, 1994) both called for a focus on quality in early years provision to include an appropriate early learning curriculum, the selection, training and continuity of staff, high staff-children ratios, buildings and equipment designed for early learning and a partnership role for parents. The introduction of the nursery voucher scheme to subsidise part time places for 4-year-olds in 1996 was linked to a set of guidelines for pre-school settings: *Desirable Outcomes for Children's Learning on Entering Compulsory Education* (DfEE, 1996). The voucher scheme and its subsequent incarnation, the Nursery Education Grant, offered 12 hours of 'free' provision. This provision of public money, however, required a mechanism to ensure that money was being well spent, hence the need for a new curriculum, the *Desirable Outcomes*, all held in place through Ofsted inspections. This first formalised curriculum paved the way for a period of unprecedented focus on early years, and expansion, both state and voluntary, was rapid. The Labour party, in government from 1997, began to see early childhood services as a priority, and early years provision was subject to new systems of regulation, greater support and advisory mechanisms in the form of Early Years Development and Childcare Partnerships (EYDCPs) and Early Excellence Centres and the advent of the initiative Sure Start. Initially, this was an intervention programme for deprived and disadvantaged children, focused on raising quality to help prevent poverty and offer a good start in life.

Developments since 2000

Strategies gave way to new curriculum developments, and further philosophical discussion about the respective statuses of care and education and the value of those working with the under-3s gave rise to *Birth to Three Matters* (DfES, 2002). This was a non-statutory framework designed to support children in their earliest years that fully recognised children's right to healthy and holistic development, play and learning opportunities and the environments and partnerships that best support this. The recognition that care and education cannot be separated was a welcome affirmation for many in the early years field and in part acted as a philosophical forerunner to the wider and far-reaching policy of *Every Child Matters* (ECM) (DfES, 2004).

The development of *Every Child Matters* and the Children and Childcare Acts of 2004 and 2006 gave rise to further changes in curriculum documentation in the form of the *Early Years Foundation Stage* (EYFS) (DCSF, 2008) that brought together care and education for under- and over-3s in a more unified way. It was underpinned by a principled approach, incorporating theoretical knowledge from founding pioneers in early childhood education and care, and emerging information from newer research into, for example, brain development. Whilst broadly welcomed by the field, there remained issues regarding the speed of change and development of policy and, more importantly, the tensions between ideas about the 'unique child' as described in the Early Years Foundation Stage and the outcomes focus of the Early Learning Goals. In the EYFS, for example, there is an assumption that children need to be allowed to develop at their own rate and in their own way:

> Children are born ready, able and eager to learn. They actively reach out to interact with other people, and in the world around them. Development is not an automatic process, however. It depends on each unique child having opportunities to interact in positive relationships and enabling environments.
>
> (www.early-education.org.uk)

The Early Learning Goals, however, chart development at certain ages and stages and culminate in achievement as assessed over the final year of the Early Years Foundation Stage (DfE, 2017) in particular by the *Early Years Foundation Stage Profile* (EYFSP) (STA, 2016).

A report on the first 18 months of the EYFS (Brooker *et al.*, 2010) largely offered positive feedback regarding the impact of the EYFS on practitioners' knowledge base and the influence it had on their practice. However, many practitioners were concerned that this document heralded an even more prescriptive approach to early years (see, for example, House, 2011) and the possibility of there being a 'tick list' mentality in operation towards the *Development Matters* statements in the EYFS (Early Education, 2012). They were concerned that the goals for literacy and numeracy were too closely aligned to those of the National Curriculum (DfE, 2013a) and developmentally unrealistic for too many young children, thus creating 'failure' so young in children's educational lives.

A change of government in 2010 coincided with a review of the EYFS (Tickell, 2011). Alongside a strengthening hold on policy by a Coalition and then Conservative government, and set against a backdrop of austerity and financial constraints on service, a revised EYFS was published in 2012, together with *Early Years Outcomes* (DfE, 2013a), signalling very clearly the government's emphasis on progress measures.

At the time of writing, developments in early years provision continue. One aspect that has a particular relevance to children with SEND is the proposed reversal of the year-long, formative information gathering process of the EYFSP in the final year of the Early Years Foundation Stage (DfE, 2017). This signals a return to the baseline assessment of the days of the *Desirable Learning Outcomes*, thus profiling children's achievement (and possibly potential) within the first six weeks of formal schooling in Reception classes in a brief snapshot. Whilst recognising that assessment and intervention at an early stage can be of great benefit in addressing barriers to learning and progress (DfE, 2015a, §5.4), such assessment should be comprehensive and take account of the rich picture of the child that should be garnered by professionals in other settings in collaboration with the child's parents/carers.

Across the UK, *Codes of Practice* offering statutory guidance to settings and schools about appropriate assessment, intervention and provision for young children with special or additional needs have been published to ensure that there is conformity to the law in each country, as outlined above.

Codes of Practice across the UK

When a teacher is seriously concerned about the progress made by a child in a classroom, it is very important to be aware of the legal process that should be followed to maintain the child's access to education. In 1994, the government published a *Code of Practice for the Identification and Assessment of Special Educational Needs* (DfE, 1994) with the status of 'statutory guidance' to schools in England and Wales on how to interpret the law to provide appropriate support to those with learning difficulties. A similar publication was produced later in Northern Ireland (DENI, 1998). In Scotland, the *Code* reflects the somewhat different legal framework.

Since that time, further *Codes* have been published reflecting changes in the law, firstly in relation to the 1996 Education Act and, most recently, to the Children and Families Act 2014 (DfES 2001; National Assembly of Wales, 2004; DfE, 2015a). Their statutory nature is reflected in Part IV of the 1996 Education Act, §313, in England and Wales:

> (1) The Secretary of State shall issue, and may from time to time revise, a code of practice giving practical guidance in respect of the discharge by [LAs] and the governing bodies of [maintained schools] [and maintained nursery schools] of their functions under this Part.
>
> …
>
> On any appeal under this Part to the Tribunal, the Tribunal shall have regard to any provision of the code which appears to the Tribunal to be relevant to any question arising on the appeal.

In the section below, we exemplify the content and implications for children in the early years by referring to the 2015 *Code* that relate specifically to children in England.

Code of Practice in England

In England, early years settings and schools have clear duties under the *Special Educational Needs and Disability Code of Practice: 0 to 25 Years* (DfE, 2015a). Chapter 5, 'Early Years Providers', of the *Code of Practice* (DfE, 2015a) outlines what early years providers must do to fulfil their duties in relation to identifying and supporting all children with special educational needs (SEND), whether or not they have an Education, Health and Care (EHC) plan. All early years providers in the maintained, private, voluntary and independent sectors that an LA funds are required to have regard to this Code. Their duties include those related to the Children and Families Act 2014, the Equality Act 2010, the Statutory Framework for the *Early Years Foundation Stage* and the Special Educational Needs and Disability Regulations 2014.

Before examining the requirements of the *Code*, it is important to set out young children's legal entitlements. All children have the right to an education that enables them to 'achieve the best possible educational and other outcomes' as well as 'become confident young children with a growing ability to communicate their own views and ready to make the transition into compulsory education' (DfE, 2015a, §5.1). Support can include 'specialist support from health visitors, educational psychologists, speech and language therapists or specialist teachers, such as a teacher of the deaf or vision impaired' (§5.16). Sometimes programmes can be carried out at home, such as Portage, which offers 'a carefully structured system to help parents support their child's early learning and development'. There is a principle of equity here. Without additional or special provision, some children will not be able to achieve the outcomes of which they would otherwise be capable.

Assessment

The (2015a) *Code of Practice* requires providers to 'have arrangements in place to support children with SEN or disabilities', including 'a clear approach to identifying and responding to SEN … at the earliest point' (§5.4). Early identification includes listening 'when parents express concerns about their child's development' and also addressing 'any concerns raised by children themselves' (§5.5). Children with more complex developmental and sensory needs may be identified at birth. Health assessments, for example, the screening test used to check the hearing of all newborns,

> enable very early identification of a range of medical and physical difficulties. Health services, including paediatricians, the family's general practitioner, and health visitors, should work with the family, support them to understand their child's needs and help them to access early support.
>
> (§5.14)

Where health professionals believe a young child may have special educational needs,

> they **must** inform the child's parents and bring the child to the attention of the appropriate local authority. The health body **must** also give the parents the opportunity to discuss their opinion and let them know about any voluntary organisations that are likely to be able to provide advice or assistance.
>
> (§5.15)

The *Early Years Foundation Stage* (EYFS) framework (DfE, 2017) requires providers to review children's progress and share this with the children's families. In assessing the progress of children in the early years, practitioners can use the non-statutory Early Years Outcomes guidance (DfE, 2013a) as a tool to assess the extent to which a young child is developing at the expected levels for his/her age. Referring to the Early Years Outcomes guidance, the Code (DfE, 2015a, §5.21) advises settings and schools:

> The guidance sets out what most children do at each stage of their learning and development. These include typical behaviours across the seven areas of learning:

- communication and language
- physical development
- personal, social and emotional development
- literacy
- mathematics

- understanding of the world
- expressive arts and design.

Within the EYFS framework there are two specific points, when the child is aged 2 and at the end of the reception year, where written assessments must be provided for parents and other professionals. The progress check when a child is aged between 2 and 3 focuses in particular 'on communication and language, physical development and personal, social and emotional development' (DfE, 2015a, §5.23). If there are significant concerns, providers should develop a plan to support the child, involving other professionals as appropriate. The summary **must** highlight areas of good progress as well as those where there is a concern that a child may have a developmental delay and where additional support might be needed. In many places the EYFS progress check has now been integrated with the health visitors' check on children's physical developmental milestones between ages 2 and 3, as was recommended in the 2015 *Code of Practice* (see further discussion in Chapter 9). The integrated review should identify the child's progress, strengths and needs, support appropriate intervention where progress is less than expected and provide information to inform the provision of appropriate services.

The EYFS Profile that should give a comprehensive picture of a child's knowledge, understanding and abilities is usually completed in the final term of the year in which s/he turns five. It 'should inform plans for future learning and identify any additional needs for support' (DfE, 2015a, §5.26).

In addition to the formal checks, early years providers should review the progress and development of all children regularly:

> From within the setting practitioners should particularly consider information on a child's progress in communication and language, physical development and personal, social and emotional development.
>
> (DfE, 2015a, §5.28)

Where a child's progress is of concern, providers should consider evidence from within and beyond the setting, from formal checks, from practitioner observations and from any more detailed assessment needs. Any specialist advice should also inform decisions about whether or not a child has a special need. All the information should be brought together with the observations of parents and considered with them. Where a child has a significantly greater difficulty in learning than peers, or a disability that prevents or hinders a child from making use of the facilities in the setting and requires special educational provision, the setting should make that provision (2015a, §5.31) and the provision should be matched to a clear identification of need.

We have noted above how, in England, children's special educational needs are generally thought of in four broad areas of need and support (DfE, 2015a, §5.32): communication and interaction; cognition and learning; social, emotional and mental health; sensory and/or physical.

> However, individual children often have needs that cut across all these areas and their needs may change over time. For instance speech, language and communication needs can also be a feature of a number of other areas of SEN, and children with an Autism Spectrum Disorder may have needs across all areas.
>
> (DfE, 2015a, §5.33)

Identifying and assessing the needs of young children for whom English is not the first language requires particular care. All aspects of a child's learning and development should be considered to establish whether any delay is associated with learning English as an additional language or if it arises from a particular learning difficulty or disability. 'Difficulties related solely to learning English as an additional language do not constitute special educational needs' (2015a, §5.30).

All early years settings are expected to adopt a graduated approach of assess → plan → do → review in organising special educational provision for young children. The initial assessment should be reviewed regularly to ensure that support is effective in matching need. More specialist assessment may be requested from specialist teachers or from health, social services or other agencies beyond the setting if the child makes no improvement. Following assessment, the practitioner and the SENDCo should consult with the parent/family and agree upon appropriate outcomes, what interventions and support should be put into place, what kind of progress might be anticipated as a result of the additional provision and a date for review. The views of the child should also be taken into account. With support from the SENDCo, the child's key person or other agreed practitioner should oversee the implementation of the interventions or programmes agreed as part of SEN support. Its effectiveness should be reviewed by the agreed date. Any changes to the outcomes and support for the child in light of the child's continuing need should be agreed on. Parents should be involved in planning next steps.

> This cycle of action should be revisited in increasing detail and with increasing frequency, to identify the best way of securing good progress … Intended outcomes should be shared with parents and reviewed with them, along with action taken by the setting, at agreed times.
>
> (DfE, 2015a, §5.44)

Before a child moves into another setting or school, information should be shared by the current setting with the receiving setting or school, with the agreement of the parents.

Practitioners 'should consider involving appropriate specialists, for example, health visitors, speech and language therapists, Portage workers, educational psychologists or specialist teachers' (DfE, 2015a, §5.48) if a child continues to make poor progress. If the child continues to make less than expected progress, despite additional relevant support and/or provision, the early years setting should consider requesting an Education, Health and Care needs assessment from the LA.

A record of children's progress must be kept as required in the EYFS framework. These records **must** be available to parents and **must** include how the setting makes provision for children with SEN and disabilities.

The role of the SENDCo in early years provision

The Code of Practice (DfE, 2015a) requires that all settings have arrangements in place to meet children's special needs. Maintained nursery settings and schools **must** ensure that there is a qualified teacher designated as the SENDCo to ensure that appropriate support is implemented. The EYFS (DfE, 2017) framework **requires** other early years providers to have a designated SENDCo, who is not necessarily a qualified teacher. The role of the SENDCo includes ensuring that all practitioners in the setting are aware of their responsibilities to children with SEN, advising and supporting colleagues, ensuring parents are closely involved with discussions and decision-making in relation to their children and liaising with external professionals or agencies.

LAs are responsible for ensuring that funded early years provision meets children's special educational needs and that funding arrangements reflect the need to provide suitable support.

Reflective activity: Usefulness of Codes of Practice

Like a number of other areas in the context of special educational, or additional support provision, the publication of *Codes of Practice* and the establishment of tribunals to hear parental appeals can be viewed in different ways.

- On the one hand they can be interpreted as divisive in setting families against schools and LAs.
- On the other they may be seen as protecting young people's entitlements to having their individual needs identified and assessed, and appropriate provision guaranteed.

What is your own view on this? Why do you think this?

Summary

Over the years, the conceptualisations of differences between people, the development of notions of equity, entitlements and human rights and the change in focus of, and on, education itself in the early years, have all contributed to the complexity and changing nature of the field of special educational needs as it relates to young children.

In terms of early years provision during this period, historically, in the UK, there was little government-funded early years provision. Two hundred years ago, a growing concern about the health and welfare of children in the context of the industrialisation of Britain led to the establishment of the first nursery schools by individuals with humanitarian aims and a focus on the individuality of the child, play, creativity, growth and activity in the open air. In recent years, however, availability of government funding has been accompanied by an increasing focus on implementing a framework of goal-oriented outcomes to be achieved by young children. In part, at least, this is to enable the measurement of children's progress and, thus, the accountability of early years institutions for the use of public funds. There is an ongoing debate between a national policy that focuses on the attainment of specific learning targets, and many early childhood specialists are concerned that this focus may lead to over-concentration on formal teaching instead of a developmentally appropriate curriculum.

In terms of special educational, or additional, needs, the focus on outcomes is multi-edged. Pressure to achieve targets that are unrealistic for the individual young child can lead to marginalisation and a growing sense of personal failure and the creation of need where there should be none if the curriculum were more inclusive. Without identification of negative difference between the individual child's achievement and the norm, however, it is difficult to make a case for equity and the provision of resources, including human, that may be needed for a child to make progress. As we discuss in later chapters, effective practice for individual children with particular needs is often effective practice for all children in the early years.

Notes

1 i.e. poor/destitute.
2 It is interesting to note that teachers in special schools for children with visual and auditory impairments still require specialist qualifications but those in some other kinds of special educational institutions do not.
3 'Dame schools … were private schools, generally kept by a single mistress in her own home or cottage … Unqualified she undertook to teach the alphabet, reading, and sometimes the simple rules of summing for a few pence a week …' (Burnett, 1994, p. 140).
4 A booklet, *The Nation's Schools*, explained that the new 'modern' schools would be for working-class children 'whose future employment will not demand any measure of technical skill or knowledge' (MoE 1945, quoted in Benn and Chitty 1996:5). Although this booklet was withdrawn, the policy remained the same and was restated in *The New Secondary Education* two years later (Wilkinson, 1947).
5 In Scotland, the 1918 Education (Scotland) Act had introduced the principle of universal free secondary education. The Education (Scotland) Act 1945 consolidated what had already been established.
6 Aphasia is an inability to understand and use language correctly.
7 The Plowden Report had argued for part time nursery education places to be available for children aged 3–5 with qualified teachers who would be required to staff and lead the provision, but the impact it had on the expansion of state nursery classes remained limited (Palaiologou, 2016).
8 Child or young person in England.
9 Or disability in England.
10 See pages 186–7 for an explanation of statutory assessment of special educational needs that previously might result in a Statement of SEN, but now may result in an EHC Plan.
11 This does not apply in Northern Ireland where policy related to disability is devolved to the Northern Ireland Assembly.

Chapter 2

Understanding and responding to the developing learning needs of young children

Major questions addressed in this chapter are:

- What models of the development of young children are crucial to our thinking about learning and what might constitute difficulties in learning?
- Are there any conflicts between developmental understandings and formal curriculum requirements in the early years that may create barriers to progress?
- What is the place of play in early childhood development and learning, and what opportunities for play should be made available to all young children?
- What is the role of language in conceptual development and learning?

Introduction

Almost a century ago, Susan Isaacs, a seminal theorist and practitioner in the field of early years, was clear that we need to understand very young children's development before we start them on the road of formal education.

> The important thing about this change in our belief as to what is best for children's bodies is that it is not simply a change of custom, nor the passing of one tradition in favour of another. It is that mothers and nurses have turned away from mere custom and blind tradition, to science. Hearsay and habit are no longer enough. Many practices that had been taken for granted for centuries have been found to be false guides when carefully tested; and we have now begun to base baby rearing on proved scientific knowledge about food and sleep and clothing, the effects of light and air, and ways of preventing disease.
>
> In the case of the child's mind this is also beginning to be true; but it is not yet by any means as true as it might be.
>
> (Isaacs, 1929, p. 2)

Recently, neuroscientists and educationalists have been working together to learn from one another concerning the development of the young human brain and what will best benefit its cognitive, social and emotional development, as was evident in the Teaching and Learning Research Programme (TLRP) in the UK that ran from 2000 to 2011 (James and Pollard, undated). Isaacs would recognise what contemporary neuroscientific research has to offer concerning such things as sufficient nutrition, the importance of sleep, the need for free large motor play and fresh air and the need for children to be understood by the adults who care for them. She also understood the role of love and affection.

In this chapter, we first consider a range of biological, psychological and cognitive neuroscientific understandings of the learning and development of young children that are crucial to our thinking about what might constitute difficulties in learning or barriers to progress that are significant enough to warrant special educational, or additional, support. We go on to discuss potential conflicts between developmental understandings and formal curriculum requirements in the early years. Next we outline the nature of early human development, and then reflect on the place of play in early childhood development and learning, and the kinds of play in which young children engage. We conclude the chapter with a discussion of the role of language in conceptual development and learning.

Biological understandings

The study of early human development tells us that the developmental pathways and timelines of babies and young children are unique to each individual. Sunderland (2016, pp. 18–19) states that we have three brains: the Rational Brain, the Mammalian Brain and the Reptilian Brain, and it is the co-ordination between the three that affects us as individuals.

- The Rational Brain, the frontal lobes, has to do with creativity and imagination, problem solving, reasoning and reflection, self-awareness and kindness, empathy and concern.
- The Mammalian Brain, the limbic system or lower brain, activates rage and fear, separation distress, caring and nurturing, social bonding, playfulness and the exploratory urge.
- The Reptilian Brain, the brain stem and cerebellum, is 'largely unchanged by evolution' and is the key to our survival instincts and controls bodily functions such as hunger, digestion/elimination, breathing, circulation, temperature, movement, posture and balance, territorial instincts and fight or flight.

The young human brain has about 200 billion brain cells at birth but only a few connections between them and over the next 2 years of life, cells in the rational brain will have developed many complex connections and synaptic pruning is underway. What is important for us to understand is that in a child's early years the rational brain is so incomplete that it is the lower brain, the emotional brain, that dominates much of the child's actions and understanding. So when young children throw a tantrum or refuse to do something we want them to do or become so frustrated that they throw things or hit out, they need our help to manage their distress. They do not need our admonishment. Acknowledging their feelings, 'Oh I can see that that has made you really cross …' and then showing them, through modelling, how to respond will help them understand what they need to be able to do to manage their own feelings. What they do **not** need and what is certainly not helpful is for us to shout orders at them, tell them off, ostracise them or for those very youngest children tell them to 'sit and think' about what they have done. The latter is virtually impossible for two year olds and they will only learn that the world is a harsh, unfair and painful place if this is consistently their experience. Sensitively scaffolding learning is vital for children's emotional lives as well as their cognitive lives.

Developmental cognitive neuroscientific understandings

Developmental cognitive neuroscientific research tells us that all experiences: physical, emotional, cognitive or social, take place in the brain. They shape the brain. Robinson (2003, p. 4) describes the brain as 'the great mediator of all experience'. The Allen Report (2011) notes, from studies conducted by researchers from the Child Trauma Academy (www.childtrauma.org) (Perry, 2002), the impact on the developing brain of neglect at an early stage:

> The images on the front cover [of the report] illustrate the negative impact of neglect on the developing brain. The CT scan on the left is from a healthy 3-year-old child with an average head size (50th percentile). The image on the right is from a series of three 3-year-old children following severe sensory-deprivation neglect in early childhood. The child's brain is significantly smaller than average and has abnormal development of cortex (cortical atrophy) and other abnormalities suggesting abnormal development of the brain.
>
> (Allen, 2011, p. ii)

The brain is plastic; it is flexible. When experiences have been mostly negative, we can make some kind of recovery, though it might be neither total nor override completely the impact of our earliest experiences. However, for this to have a beneficial effect, it demands that those of us working with very young children understand them as individuals, why they react as they do in certain situations and what actions and experiences will support their overall well-being and that we are carefully responsive to these needs.

Reflective activity: one SENDCo's experience

Read the recollections of one SENDCo about her experiences with a young child who had experienced a very difficult upbringing in the very earliest stages of his childhood.

Note down your reactions to what she relates:

'I've worked with children with special educational needs up to the point of and receiving a statement. So at various levels really throughout that with children what used to be at School Action and School Action Plus. ... we had one child with behavioural concerns, a little boy that had been placed with an adoptive family and was now in a very, very good situation. But unfortunately still had some bits and pieces that needed dealing with from his past. ...

'He was adopted into a lovely family, and I think sometimes perhaps the perception is that then therefore it's okay. Unfortunately when he was removed from his previous family he was only a year old ... he had numerous broken bones throughout his body. The head teacher turned around and said, "Well he won't remember that, so I don't know why that's having an impact on him right now!" ... we were also trying to engage with CAMHS or somebody to try and get some support because he had been at a child minder's and stamped a guinea pig to death.

'I remember once reading a story, I think off the top of my head, I can't remember the plot line, but it was about a lion basically that always wanted to win everything, and sometimes his friend the hippo wouldn't let him, or the elephant might win. And the little boy's response was, "Well he should kill him, he should be really cross with them". He had a completely different response to the story to everybody else in the group. Everybody else in the group showed a lot of empathy towards the other characters and could understand why they might not like the lion because he was always so keen to win and would do anything to win. But this little boy just couldn't see that side of it. He just thought, "Well that lion he should win, and he should do at all costs really". … perhaps in terms of neurological development how pathways and things develop, I should imagine it [his early experiences] might have quite an impact'.

Lack of awareness and understanding of the impact of very early experiences on children's emotional lives and general well-being is a real problem. The case above is particularly graphic, but it echoes many children's experiences and practitioners' knowledge. Lack of understanding of what will help a child such as this one to manage the memory which is deep seated and one which he would not be able to articulate must be addressed in training and qualifications for all of those working with young children. Children's emotional memories run very deep. As Maria Robinson, in conversation with one of the authors stated, they form the 'underground river which flows continuously through our lives'.

Practitioners should be aware and reflect on a child's individual, personal abilities and skills as well as their global norms if we are to be sensitive to their personal and particular pathways of development and learning.

Reflective activity: understanding and responding to individual differences

Think about some young children you know who are in the same age grouping in an early years setting.

- In what ways are they similar to each other?
- In what ways are they different?
- How would you explain the similarities and differences you have noticed?
- Should they all be treated in the same way? Why do you think this?
- Do any of them have special educational, or additional learning, needs? If so, should they be assessed using the same criteria as other children? Why do you think this?

We must not make assumptions about future capabilities and understanding on the basis of the time babies and children are in our care, for example, September to July in a Reception Class. We know that experiences shape the brain cognitively and emotionally, and we must understand that we should not expect exactly the same levels of understanding or skills or behaviours from a child whose birthday is in August and so is just 48 months when they enter the Reception year, and a child whose fifth birthday is in September as there is a time factor of 11 months of life experiences. However, the complexity is that for some children 48 months of life may be filled with love, security, wonderful experiences and plenty of attention combined with their inner developmental clock working at speed so that they appear to be 'more advanced' than a child who, whilst being alive longer, has had fewer or different experiences or has a developmental delay or disability which affects their emotional life, physical and/or cognitive abilities. Added to that are the personality, the gender and the individual traits and interests of each child. In other words, early human development is highly complicated and dependent on both internal and external processes and traits.

Reflective activity: responding to the needs of young children

Read the text below. Note down your responses to the following questions:

- What do you think might, or should, be done in early years settings to support the learning needs of the young children here?
- What might, or should, be done to support the learning needs of their mothers?

A GP in discussion with an early years lecturer is commenting on the need for loving and careful attention for babies in day care and the tensions between what a new/inexperienced parent might want and what the professionals might understand as appropriate. The discussion includes sleep patterns and breast feeding and the lecturer is astonished and dismayed when the GP reports that in one very small inner city GP practice in the UK the issue is neither about mothers moving from breast milk to formula, nor from formula to solids but from a popular carbonated drink which contains caffeine and other additives, to formula feeds. The producers of the drink state clearly that it may have an adverse effect on activity and attention in children as it contains a source of Phenylalanine, Sunset Yellow and Ponceau 4R. But this very small group of very young and vulnerable mothers were feeding this to their newborn babies because they perceived that it kept their babies quiet and undemanding so that their own lives were less stressful.

As individual human beings we can only imagine the adverse impact this is having on the babies' developing brains and what the consequences for this group of children will be. The Allen Report (2011) graphically highlights that severe deprivation has an enormous impact on later life chances unless interventions are made appropriately, effectively and successfully. If, as those babies grow into childhood and adulthood, this lack of appropriate nutrition continues, its impact on their lives will be adverse and considerable. We can add to that the fact that these young mothers are vulnerable themselves and need support which may not be readily available for them or which they may not wish, or know how to, access. Their own personal health is poor and they all smoked through pregnancy and beyond, and as Gerhardt (2015) tells us there are two aspects of pre-natal experience that have very strong links with future anti-social behaviour: the mother's stress and her smoking. So add to this, the extremely poor nutrition that these children are experiencing in their earliest days and months of life, as well as through their gestation period, and the picture is a very sad one in terms of those children's life chances.

The question for educationalists here is how much flexibility is there in the education and care system to allow for this in both provision of appropriate and effective experiences for ALL children and the assessment of their learning and development. Those children, from whatever socio-economic group, whose experiences have consistently been positive emotionally, cognitively, socially and physically are able to take the best from their educational experiences and therefore achieve more highly than those whose experiences have been consistently poor. And possibly their learning experiences in schools and settings may have less impact on their outcomes; they have the strength and resilience to take from it what they need. There is no doubt that individual health visitors, nursery staff, GPs, teachers, social workers, family support workers and all other professionals who come into contact with families, need to and are working extremely hard to give the support that is required to those children whose life chances are restricted because of family circumstances, including health and well-being (Allen, 2011). But the task is demanding.

- What do you think about all this?
- Who could, or should, do what?

Psychological understandings

Attachment theory

Isaacs, along with previous seminal workers in the early years field (Owen, 1824, 1841, 1857; Pestalozzi, 1801; Froebel, 1826) recognised that what happens in our earliest years plays a crucial role in who we become as adults and how we live our lives, and that it was not the role of formal schooling to undertake this as, for many, the seeds of their future lives are already sown, for good or otherwise by the time they meet a teacher. So there is a major question for us here: how far have we come since Isaacs recognised this in 1929?

One psychological theory of human development that does take account of the relationship between the emotions and behaviour and that has had considerable influence over educational provision for young children whose behaviour is of concern in settings and schools is that of attachment theory (Bowlby, 1952). Bowlby, who trained as a psychoanalyst, drew together two different traditions: child psychiatry and ethology, the study of animal behaviour. As a child psychiatrist, he made the connection between the lack of consistent and caring relationships in early childhood and later development and published an article called 'Forty-four juvenile thieves: their characters and home life' (Bowlby, 1944). Later, he was influenced by the work of the ethologist Lorentz, who had noted the significance of 'imprinting', that is the bonding processes between mother and young of a species, in his book *King Solomon's Ring* (Lorenz, 1952). In it he described how he gave signals to a clutch of hatching ducklings which persuaded them that he was their mother, so that they waddled after him in a line. Support for a view of the devastating effects on their later social relationships of being reared in social isolation was indicated in the work of other ethologists, for example, Harlow's famous study of rhesus monkeys (Harlow and Harlow, 1962).

Central to Bowlby's work is the view that:

> children deprived of maternal care … may be seriously affected in their physical, intellectual, emotional and social development … Bowlby asserts that 'prolonged separation of a child from his mother (or mother substitute) during the first five years of life stands foremost among the causes of delinquent character development' (Bowlby, 1944; Bowlby, 1952).
>
> (Holmes, 1993, p. 39)

Research confirms Bowlby's work on attachment theory, that:

- consistent, loving, attentive behaviours by adults will typically result in children developing a secure attachment with those adults whether their mother, other parent or caregivers and
- well-loved, emotionally secure children are more able to overcome problems, persist for longer, take risks in their learning and make secure long-term attachments as adults.

We now understand that where experiences have been consistently impoverished and children have developed insecure attachments with their main carers or have been neglected or abused emotionally, physically, sexually or socially (and in some cases all of these), there is the possibility for making secure attachments later and probably outside of the family circle, with the care and attention of loving adults.

Piaget, Vygotsky and Bruner

It is really important to have a clear grasp of the process of learning itself so that we can think about, and plan how to, support further learning and address difficulties in a principled way. Two of the foremost theorists are Jean Piaget (1896–1980) and Lev Vygotsky (1896–1934). Other leading educationalists, for example Jerome Bruner (1915–2016), have picked up and developed Vygotsky's ideas. And we shall look at these in the context of what neurological research over the past 30 years or so has to add to our understanding.

Jean Piaget

Jean Piaget, a Swiss psychologist, was one of the theorists who contributed a lot to the thinking that children learn from the experience of doing something. From his work with his own children, Piaget (1954, 1964, 1969) concluded that there were four universal stages of learning:

- Sensorimotor (0–2 years): At birth a child has a set of reflex movements and perceptual systems. Learning is, in general, through trial and error. At this stage, the child relates physical actions to perceived results of those actions and thus learns through direct knowledge of the world.

- Preoperational (2–7 years): The child develops the ability to represent events and objects mentally and to engage in symbolic play but, as is characteristic of 'egocentrism', is not yet able to see another's point of view.
- Concrete operational (7–11 years): The child develops the ability to use logical thought or operations (rules) but can only apply logic to physical objects, hence the term concrete operational. S/he starts to develop an understanding of conservation of number, area, volume, orientation and reversibility, but is not yet able to think abstractly or hypothetically. The child also becomes less egocentric and begins to be able to see things from the viewpoint of others.
- Formal operational (11+ years): The child acquires the ability to reason in the abstract and manipulate ideas in his/her head, without being dependent on concrete objects, for example, to combine and classify items or do mathematical calculations.

Piaget's work has been criticised in a number of respects. His work implies that child development occurs in discrete stages rather than continuing throughout adulthood. In addition, he took too little consideration of different social or cultural contexts in which children in general live and grow. Further, some of the methods for the research on which his conclusions were based have been questioned (Donaldson, 1984). However, despite the criticisms, Piaget's conclusions that learners construct knowledge by interacting with their environment and that they re-construct their thoughts in the light of new experiences, have made a strong contribution to practice in early years settings and primary schools particularly. Neuroscientific research confirms Piaget's theories of schematic behaviours and the role of play in learning; the need for active repetition of first hand experiences and for practice and revisiting ideas in the development of concepts. However, such research also provides a different view of Piaget's stages of learning to think:

> … it is no longer widely believed that there are different developmental stages in learning to think (Piaget's theory, CACE 1967, p. 50). Similarly, it is not believed that a child cannot be taught until she/he is cognitively 'ready' (CACE 1967, p. 75). Rather, it is important to assess how far a child can go under the guidance of a teacher (the 'zone of proximal development', Vygotsky 1978).
>
> (Goswami, 2015, p. 1)

Neuroscientific research confirms that it is sensory motor learning that lays the foundation of cognition but what Goswami explains is that sensory motor representations are not replaced by symbolic ones but 'are augmented by symbolic ones gained through *action, language, pretend play* and *teaching*' (current authors' emphasis).

Lev Vygotsky

Akin to Piaget's model of constructivism, but developed in Soviet Russia, is the social constructivist model of Lev Vygotsky. The distinctiveness of Vygotsky's (1978) work lay in the importance he placed on the social context in which learning takes place. Vygotsky (1978, p. 57) proposed that the learning process takes place at:

- the interpersonal, 'between people' level, mainly through interacting with others, especially a more informed other; and

- the intrapersonal, 'within the individual' level, as s/he thinks about and reflects on new concepts and learning and appropriates skills and knowledge.

In this view of learning, the development of a young child's thinking, reflection, problem-solving, reasoning and so on, what Vygotsky called 'higher mental processes', depends on the presence of 'mediators' to mediate learning during interactions between the child and the environment.

Mediators can be humans who prompt, guide, reward, punish or model the use of, particularly, language, signs, written texts and so on. Once their use has been appropriated by the learner, such use itself mediates new learning. One might take the example of language which, as Vygotsky (1962), suggested, is very important to a young child's sense-making process. It is through interacting with a more knowledgeable mediator that communication and language are developed. The meanings of both have to be learnt in a social context.

One of the most well-known concepts for which Vygotsky is famous is that of the zone of proximal development (ZPD) to explain the process of learning in a social context. The ZPD for a young child is, effectively, the next steps in learning and the range of knowledge and skills that s/he is not ready to learn alone but can learn in interaction with more informed and experienced others (Kozulin, 2003). A more informed/expert other may 'scaffold', that is provide structured support for, new learning (Wood, Bruner and Ross, 1976) through the ZPD based on his/her knowledge of the young child and his/her current level of knowledge and understanding of a topic. Very importantly, feelings are very powerful in supporting, or preventing, learning (Wearmouth, Glynn and Berryman, 2005). Getting the balance right is crucial. Young children's learning and behaviour are mediated through the kind of relationship s/he has with a practitioner. This relationship both develops over time and is influenced by the practitioner's sense of a child's value and worth. Obvious implications of this view of learning is that all young children, including those who experience difficulties, need a safe space and time for discussion between themselves and the more informed other(s), most often the practitioner(s) teacher(s), and themselves with peers to enable 'interthinking' (Littleton and Mercer, 2013). This is focused talk around new learning to clarify and consolidate their understanding of new concepts and knowledge.

From a Vygotskian perspective, there are implications for educational practice, including the way that settings are organised and managed. In many settings children are grouped into so called 'ability' groups and these are usually described as low, middle or high achievers or top, middle or bottom groups. This is really a group management tool which does not reflect Vygotsky's theory of the importance of the 'more experienced other' nor the understanding that learning is mediated between the wider society and the individual, for example, by a child who has mastered a problem. Placing children of perceived similar cognitive/social/emotional abilities in the same group means that they may have fewer opportunities to learn from one another. 'Interthinking', that is sharing ideas with peers and thus developing personal understandings of new concepts and constructing new knowledge, is very important to children's learning (Littleton and Mercer, 2013). Early years professionals tend to use the term 'more or less interested or experienced' rather than label children according to cognitive ability because they recognise that in their early years children are still developing and learning; their outcomes are not set in stone at such an early age, but they are affected by the consistent experiences they have had and continue to have. And being placed in the bottom, middle or top group is bound to have an effect on a child's sense of self for ill or for good.

We now understand the implications of Vygotsky's view that learning is a social activity in which the child is active in constructing his/her own understandings. As we implied in Chapter 1, and as Alexander (2011) comments, it can be argued that this model of children's learning is not truly reflected in the implementation of the current curriculum for early years in England, the *Early Years Foundation Stage* (DfE, 2017). We may well feel that the inspection of professional settings which provide education and care for birth to 5 year olds does not pay enough attention to this, focusing instead on externally imposed outcomes and goals.

Jerome Bruner

A different, but in some ways related, way to conceptualise young children's progress as they develop their conceptual understanding of the world is through Bruner's (1966) three modes of representation of reality: enactive, iconic and symbolic. Like Piaget's model outlined on page 38–9, these modes move from the concrete 'learn by doing' to the abstract:

- The 'enactive' mode of representation works through action: we 'do' and then we know. In their very early years, young children rely on enactive modes to learn. They learn to move through their own actions without the need for verbal, written and/or physical symbols. Children unable to move easily or to experience their world directly through sight, hearing, taste, touch or smell, will be less able to understand and know through 'doing' unless special efforts are made to enable alternative access to their world.
- The 'iconic' mode is a visual representation of the real object. Images stand for the physical object. Using this mode, children learn what pictures and diagrams are and what they mean. In mathematics, for example, children progress to doing mathematical calculations using numbers rather than counting objects.
- The 'symbolic' mode is an abstract representation of something. Abstract symbols are 'arbitrary'. They do not necessarily bear any resemblance to whatever it is that they represent. Commonly in spoken language, for example, the sound of a word does not usually reflect its meaning, unless it is onomatopoeic.

It is really important for practitioners to acknowledge that children may experience difficulty at any point in their developing conceptual understandings of the world. Some may take much longer than others to develop abstract representations of reality, and/or may never be able to do this, and may need much more experience of learning by doing than peers.

Importance of play

Play is a natural, innate human activity and is crucial for many areas of human development and learning: intellectual growth, physical health, emotional well-being and social development. Play provides the first hand, concrete experiences which lead to abstract thinking and symbolic action. One important issue is the current pressurised educational system which imposes external goals on children, not least our youngest and most vulnerable, and causes them and their families and teachers stress. Children cannot think well under stress; it narrows thinking rather than encouraging 'divergent responses' (Moyles, 2010, p. 23). The lack of understanding of the power of play is prevalent in twenty-first century classrooms in western society. As Paley puts it, we are in danger of 'delegitimizing mankind's oldest and best used learning tool' (2005, p. 8).

There is a persistent ambiguity about what constitutes 'play'. It can mean engaging in a pastime, a sport, a dramatic production, a leisurely activity such as playing a musical instrument, a restful experience; being playful is seen as joking with an idea, a person, teasing someone; being 'at play' is seen as not working and therefore not engaging in serious or useful activity. And so those who care for, and work with, young children must be clear not only about what we mean when we use the word play but about what human play actually is.

Concept of play

Primates and animals engage in play in order to find out about their world. Play develops their understanding of the world into which they are born; the rules of that society, for example, who is leader of the troop or pack, what their own place is in that society; it strengthens them physically, socially and emotionally. Groos (1898) explains that primates do not play because they are young; they have their youth **in order to play**. The longer a young being is dependent on the adults who care for it, the greater potential it has for intellectual growth, emotional well-being and physical health. But before trying to define play, we need to consider some explanations of play:

Lowenfeld (1935, p. 16) explained that:

> Play in childhood is an exceedingly complex phenomenon. It is an activity which combines into a single whole, very different strands of thought and experience.

Vygotsky (1978, p. 102) is clear about the central importance of play in human development and learning:

> thus play creates a zone of proximal development of the child. In play a child is always beyond his average age, above his daily behaviour; in play it is as though he is a head taller than himself. As in the focus of a magnifying glass, play contains all developmental tendencies in a condensed form and is a major source of development.

Vygotsky stressed the importance of the social context of play and the use of language as a semiotic tool, a meaning making tool. Through play children can develop their knowledge through what they can see to what they are able to understand. He made it clear that a child's actions arise from her own ideas about the world rather than from her experience of objects in it. And he stated that play itself fulfills not only a child's real desires and needs but also those things that the child cannot yet attain. In other words, in imaginative play a child can be the adult: the mum who puts her child to bed, the doctor who checks her baby's health, the superhero who can fly and make things better for others. Play provides a child with a window into the adult world and a different perspective from that of the powerless child who is 'done to'. It also helps with the development of theory of mind: the ability to understand that other people have beliefs, desires, perspectives and intentions of their own and that these may be different from theirs. Vygotsky (1978, pp. 102–3) goes on to state that:

> Action in the imaginative sphere, in an imaginary situation, the creation of voluntary intentions, and the formation of real life plans and volitional motives – all appear in play and make it the highest level of pre-school development.

Robinson (2008, p. 150) makes the connection between all aspects of human development and play:

> Play provides the bridge between all the different aspects of development. It is the medium by which the links between different aspects of learning embedded in a maturing brain become established.

As Moyles (2010) comments, in their play children are engaged in activities which, amongst other things, have the power to develop confidence and independence, creative thinking, flexibility and open mindedness; they are able to persist and concentrate, explore, experiment and investigate new ideas and materials; acquire and use new knowledge, skills and understandings.

As we noted above, science supports our assertion about the critical role of play in learning and development. Panksepp (1998, p. 145), an eminent neuroscientist and psychobiologist, describes the brain as having a natural 'seeking system' which comprises interest, curiosity and sensation-seeking. The developing brain requires places, things and events to explore; it requires other children and adults to interact with in an enriched environment. Through play, young children are able to understand, to make meanings about all that they experience in their world and to make sense of that world, social, emotional, physical, spiritual and intellectual, through their own eyes and experiences and to gain a developing understanding of what that world looks like to others.

Types of play

Object play

Very young children grasp objects and put them to their mouths to find out whether they can eat it. The question here is 'What is it and what can I do with it?' The use of heuristic play baskets was developed by Goldschmeid (Goldschmeid and Jackson, 2004) as she observed how young children enjoyed playing with things found in both the natural, outdoor world and objects found in the home. These baskets were primarily for babies from around 7 to 12 months and enabled them to reach out for objects and make choices, perhaps for the first time, and to use their senses to discover things about the world.

Reflective activity: use of heuristic play baskets

Heuristic play sessions involve the provision of plenty of similar everyday objects so that children can play easily alongside one another using open-ended materials, those which have no set outcome as a commercial toy would have. This gives the child the opportunity for exploration, creativity, persistence and belies the notion that very young children have limited concentration. As adults, few of us can concentrate when we are not interested or do not see the point of what is being asked of us, yet we expect young children to do so on a daily basis and then punish them when they tell us clearly the activity is not relevant to them.

- How might you consider providing heuristic play baskets to help satisfy a young brain's seeking system for children who lack mobility?
- What would you put into such a basket in a nursery setting, or for use at home?

Fantasy play

Paley (2005) describes 'fantasy play' as 'an astonishing invention' and one which must be protected. Pretend play occurs in all cultures although it varies in emphasis (Robinson, 2008). Engaging in fantasy play episodes helps children understand the real world and take risks without any real risk to them as the dangers, whether crocodiles, angry parents or nasty witches, are only pretend. They can develop their emotional lives, work out how conflicts can be resolved, who has the power in a given situation and work out why people behave as they do. In fantasy play, children's free flow of ideas can be extremely powerful, and they have the ability to go in and out of play to take stock of what is happening. The just-4-year-old granddaughter of one of the authors ran into her bedroom to hide under the bedcovers from the 'monsters' chasing her. The author got under the covers with her and 'shook with fear' as she was doing it, and said 'Oh, I hope he doesn't get us!!' She looked carefully at her grandmother and said, 'It's just 'tend, Nanny. Don't be worried'. The child was sustaining reality and pretence at the same time (Robinson, 2008) and there was a look in her eye that said whilst she thought her grandmother knew it was pretence, she needed to make sure there really was no danger. And she was able to come out of the pretence situation to check and then return immediately to the play scenario. Robinson suggests that it is often the adult's role to mediate the child's emotions as in fantasy play, emotions, whether of joy or fear or anger, can lead to real emotions beyond the child's developmental capacity to manage them.

Reflective activity: support for children who lack social imagination

Imaginative play is very important for the development of metacognition, that is a child's awareness of his/her own knowledge, what s/he does (not) know, and the ability to use prior knowledge to work out strategies for completing tasks, or problem solve. Some children experience a particular difficulty in the area of social imagination and take everything literally. One child might take pillows, lay them on the floor to form a rectangle and encourage her mother to get into the 'bus' to drive to America to have a picnic by the sea. This child has had to detach the whiteness, smoothness and shape of the pillow from the pretend representation that it is a part of a bus. This requires her to be able to understand thoughts as things themselves. Another child will see and understand only the literal 'pillowness' of the pillow.

How might you ensure you know whether:

- Any young children in your care experience difficulties in social imagination?
- They all understand everything that is being said to them?

Locomotor and rough and tumble play

Young children love to jump and twist, to clamber and climb, to roll over and over and they tend to do so with joy. What is happening here is that they are developing strength, balance and control over their bodies; they are finding out that their body remains the same whether they are upside down or the right way up. They are finding out about the terrain they are moving on and how to manage it. And these actions trigger a growth of synapses in the cerebellum – providing a link in how play supports quality of movement.

Panksepp (1998) describes rough and tumble play as the brain's sources of joy. Most children just love this. As they interact with other children this rough and tumble play helps children understand their own strength, how far to go without hurting each other; it is a very intimate social interaction creating social bonds and friendships. Sunderland (2016, p. 106) explains that there are many reasons why this form of play is important for us:

> Physical interactive play increases the activation of a very important 'fertilizer' in the higher brain (frontal lobes) called brain-derived neurotrophic factor (BDNF). This helps to programme the regions in the frontal lobes that are involved in emotional behaviour. Research shows that there is increased gene expression of BDNF after play.

Therefore, this type of play has the potential to impact on children's emotional regulation and ability to cope with stress in later life.

Reflective activity: enabling learning through rough and tumble play

There is a price to be paid for not providing enough opportunities for rough and tumble, socially interactive play:

'Lack of these experiences in childhood can lead to making up for it harder later on and often in inappropriate places and at inappropriate times' (Sunderland, 2016, p. 106).

As Sunderland (ibid.) notes, in orphanages where children have been deprived of physical stimulation, they have been seen to make dramatic progress after programmes of play.

- How might you enable young children who experience physical and/or sensory difficulties access to the kind of learning acquired by peers through rough and tumble play?
- What kind of resources might you need?

Role of schema in play and learning

Most practitioners working in the early years will be aware of schemas, the general psychological term for a mental structure: concrete concepts, complex abstract conceptual structures; the co-ordination of sensory-motor activity (Athey, 2007). The early schemas babies have include action patterns, for example, sucking and grasping. They then start to learn about the more concrete things in their world such as the people and objects closest to them: mummy, daddy, brother, sister, caregivers and objects such as ball and hand. And as their experiences increase and they go out into the community their schematic knowledge widens and deepens.

Children develop schema about how things can be: things can be living, dead, hard, soft, tall, round, fat, asleep, invisible, square, sticky, smooth. Children learn what things can do and how they move: roll, run, squash, stretch; and they learn how things relate to one another: on top of, in front of, underneath, next to, inside of; they learn about events: bedtime, snack time, going home, going to the doctor, having a play time with a friend and importantly about birthdays and babies being born. They learn about more abstract concepts, things that go beyond the here and now such as space and time and ideas: yesterday, tomorrow, in Scotland, on the moon; truth and justice and beauty. Every schema is an abstraction of all the experiences children have and even the most abstract conceptual schemas are rooted in sensory experiences of and motor activity with the outside world although they are the most detached from their origins. Importantly, in order to identify and understand these concepts multi-sensory learning is critical. Gerhardt (2015, p. 26) notes that the key is:

> incremental learning on the basis of exemplars. The brain is an iterative system – each step is built on the previous step from the bottom up. And all systems are connected.

Reflective activity: providing multi-sensory experiences

Read the text below that relates to early dynamic schemas, and note your responses to the following questions:

- Considering the importance of sensory experiences in children's learning and development and the role of BDNF, how can we ensure that children with disabilities have opportunities to have these experiences?
- What do you provide in your setting?

In early years settings, early dynamic schemas include:

- **Dynamic vertical:** jumping up and down, climbing up, rolling down, painting straight vertical lines, be interested throwing things up.
- **Dynamic back and forth:** run back and forth, back and forth; brush strokes may go over and over one another; taking things from one place and to another and back again.
- **Dynamic circular:** running around in circles; painting, drawing circles; moving toy cars around and around in circles; twirling around, swinging toys, scarves around; scattering objects in wide circles.

- **Going over or under:** being under tables, benches or chairs or on top of sofa backs; snaking along walls, being under a pile of scarves, blankets, books or other children.
- **Going a round a boundary:** painting around the edges of the paper; walking/running around the perimeter of the setting; driving toy cars around the edge of a play mat.
- **Enveloping and containing:** wrapping things and self up with whatever comes to hand; putting things or self in boxes, storage spaces.
- **Going through a boundary:** knocking down towers, bursting through doors, making holes in paper.

Practitioners need to understand that children's developing brains must have the experiences listed above in order to develop the complexity of concepts that they will need in the adult world. They need to observe children very carefully and with insight to identify any dominant schematic behaviour, they need to reflect carefully and make provisions which will support the schema development. Identifying children's current schematic interests can obviate perceived problems with behaviour: a child who needs to run around and around needs to be directed to an appropriate place to do so. A child who is interested in deconstruction which results in knocking down towers that another child has built needs to be provided with space and opportunities to engage in that type of activity without inflicting distress on other children. Regularly forcing children to stop and sit or 'play quietly' will only raise distress levels and lead to unwanted behaviour. Once again, it is important to understand the importance of a rich and varied learning environment that will support these important schematic behaviours.

Development of conceptual understandings and the role of language

As Goswami (2015, p. 4) comments, the prerequisites for cognitive development are in place in the new human being very early:

> All forms of learning important for human cognition are ... present in rudimentary form soon after birth. Statistical learning, learning by imitation, learning by analogy and causal learning underpin cognitive development. Developmental cognitive neuroscience is revealing how powerful these learning mechanisms are, for example in rapid learning about social stimuli (like faces, Farroni *et al.* 2002), physical events (like grasping actions, Tai *et al.*, 2004), and language (Dehaene-Lambertz *et al.*, 2006).

It is vital that early years practitioners understand this. Newly born human brains are not empty vessels waiting to be filled but a mass of 200 billion cells most of which are waiting to be connected by experiences after birth. And the important difference is that it is not the adults who decide what goes into the vessel (although they have a huge impact on what each child's experiences are of course), but it is the individual child's brain that will respond to those experiences and make sense of its world in its own unique way. We now need to consider what we mean by conceptual understandings.

A concept can be defined as being an internalised, abstract representation of objects, ideas and events. It is a mental structure that goes beyond sensory perceptual representations. If we were not able to put objects and ideas into categories then everything we experienced would be unique and we would be overwhelmed by the information. So on first encountering a soft ball that is attached to her buggy or cot side and hearing it referred to as a 'ball' a network of neurons is activated in the child's brain in many areas. The child will begin to connect the word with the object through her perceptual knowledge of the roundness of the ball and the sound of the word consistently attached to it by adults. As her experiences of balls grows: beach balls, small balls that bounce very high, very hard cricket balls, light plastic pool balls and the differently shaped rugby balls (even a dance!), she will be able to recognise it as a ball because of the perceptual qualities of the ball – its roundness; its causal structure or how it behaves. For example, most balls roll. In Piagetian terms, the child will go through a process of assimilation and accommodation as they make sense of and refine their knowledge of the world. Sometimes this process has the potential to be embarrassing and funny. A couple were strolling along a river bank and two young women came towards them with a young child in a buggy. The child pointed at the husband and shouted loudly 'Daddy!!' There was a lot of laughter with the child's mother saying 'No! No! Daddy is at home'. This was an instance of a child generalising from her limited experience of men. She knew that 'Daddy' is a man and coming across a man she did not know she used the word she had at her disposal. As this child has incremental experiences of men she will learn that there are men who are brothers, fathers, uncles, footballers, bus drivers, nurses, teachers and so on. She will then learn that not all are men; some are women. And so the concept of man and maleness becomes refined because of all the experiences she has. This ability to categorise experiences is essential for developing memory, for thinking and for predicting how things will behave; an important skill as babies and young children experience more and more new objects, people and events. However, this level of categorisation is problematic for some young children.

Goswami (2015, p. 4) explains that neural studies show that the child's and the adult's brains have essentially the same structures and perform the same functions using the same mechanisms:

> Hence cognitive development is largely a matter of neural enrichment. The learning environments of home, school and the wider culture enable experience-dependent learning, and lay the basis for the cognitive and emotional functioning of the adult system.

So much of conceptual development critically depends upon language, and language is also critical to imaginative play which itself is important for cognitive development. Language is important for episodic memory development, it aids the development of theory of mind, of understanding that others may have a different view or understanding from one's own and it provides the basis for working memory (Goswami, 2015). Words themselves are symbolic – they are not the actual thing or person, but represent that thing or person, object, event or feeling.

Children's experiences and language skills vary greatly from child to child:

> For example, at 2 years, the range in word production is from 0 words to more than 500.
>
> (Goswami, 2015, p. 12)

Gesture, which precedes vocabulary and continues afterwards, is also important for concept development and communication and is also symbolic. We can often understand more about a child's understanding through the gestures she makes than through her use of vocabulary.

Therefore, our understanding of the crucial role of talk, conversation, explanations and careful questioning and of the language experiences of the child is vitally important in the early years. The way in which we interact with children is so important. Goswami (2015) explains that how adults talk to children can influence motivation to learn, as well as learning, memory and understanding. She agrees with Wolf (2007) that reading and interaction around books is one of the best ways to help children develop more complex language. And importantly she suggests (2015, p. 10) that language and conversation should remain the focus in the reception year:

> Adapting our dialogue with young children leads to more organised and detailed learning and memory. These findings suggest that using elaboration in classroom dialogues will aid retention and understanding.

It is a combination of experiences and the richness and frequency of those experiences and the quality of the learning environment which is important for children's learning. It is cumulative learning (Goswami, 2015) that has the greatest beneficial effect on children's cognitive development and so we argue that policy makers and early years settings must ensure that they embrace a multi-sensory approach to children's learning. Unisensory approaches such as those that focus on visual or auditory or kinaesthetic learning ignore the knowledge we now have that the brain works through the development of neural networks across multiple areas of the brain. Importantly, Goswami (ibid) states that where a network is not strong enough, gaps can appear in children's learning. So in providing experiences that help strengthen neural pathways we might be able to support those children with perceived gaps in their learning. And this must have implications for those of us working with children with sensory impairments.

Reflective activity: providing for conceptual development of children with impairments and disabilities

Look back at the discussion above on the development of conceptual understandings and the role of language. Note down your response to the following question:

- If these experiences are what is required for typical development, what experiences do you, or might you, provide for those children with impairments and disabilities in order to maximise their ability to form a conceptual understanding of the world?

As the Allen report (2011) concluded, it is an impoverished experience that affects the brain adversely: the consistent lack of natural, everyday experiences including love and security has a detrimental effect on children's healthy development. We must be aware that it is the rich, natural environment that provides enriched learning experiences; one that supports early learning. So people who are interested in us and care about us matter; as do exciting and novel experiences which we as young children can choose to explore in any way that is interesting to us: in our own time and alone or with whom we choose.

Unfortunately, the Allen report's findings on the case for early intervention to alleviate the impact of neglectful early experiences on later life whilst widely acknowledged, do not seem to be widely implemented. Gerhardt (2015, p. 222) reports that Allen himself in July 2013 at a Westminster Social Policy Forum said that it is like 'having the cure for cancer and keeping it up your jumper'. The two-year-old review probably comes too late for many children, considering what we now know about the brain and what it needs to develop healthily and especially the critical importance of experiences in the first year of life (Robinson, 2003).

We might think of Paley's exhortation (2009, p. 129) here:

> The unkind voices that surround us are shrill, demanding our thoughtful, truthful attention. All the more reason, then, to listen for the soft breath of friendship and carry our reassuring stories above the din. They are the beacons that help illuminate the moral universe. And we are required, even as is the great blue heron, to capture our prize and fly with it.

Summary

Isaacs' voice speaking clearly to us from the past resonates with the current understanding of how young human beings develop and learn. Neuroscientific research with babies and young children confirms the need for those of us who are responsible for their care and education to ensure that we are thoughtful and patient, that we show love and kindness and that we ensure that our own understanding of children is based not on what Isaacs calls 'mere custom and blind tradition', but on what the great theorists, philosophers and contemporary science have to tell us.

We live in times which present us with a dichotomy: developmental cognitive neuroscientific research overwhelmingly supports the view that children in their early years require personal and unique attention, alongside potentiating physical environments that reflect the natural environment that is rich, but not necessarily enriched. It acknowledges children's need for space and choice and agency as well as secure and caring emotional environments; it reflects major and influential theoretical perspectives of child development and learning such as those of Vygotsky, Piaget, Bowlby and Bruner. Yet whilst the curriculum model currently in place in England for children's care and education, the *Early Years Foundation Stage* (DfE, 2017) was developed from the 2008 (DFCS) model, (itself based on Piagetian, Vygotskian and Bowlbian principles) as well as current research which recognised that children develop at different rates and at different times and need a loving secure environment in which to thrive, the main thrust of the curriculum is not on how well this is provided but on prescribed learning outcomes and children's attainment. This contemporary view which may be seen to reflect a desire for accountability mechanisms to justify the use of public funds in the education of young children can put tremendous pressure on settings to focus on the curriculum rather than the individual child and group of children and their individual needs. From this perspective it is clear to see that there is a conflict between responding to the individualism of young children as they grow and develop and, in particular, to the needs of children with special educational, or additional learning needs, and the achievement of common early learning goals that may not be appropriate.

Understanding the development of young children, including the role of play and language in facilitating learning and emotional growth, is crucial to our thinking about what might constitute difficulties in learning or barriers to progress that are significant enough to warrant special educational, or additional, support. We would like to conclude this chapter with the words of Isaacs (1929, p. 3):

> Children need all our affection and sympathy; but they also need all our intelligence, and our patient and serious efforts to understand the ways of their mental growth. And we cannot leave this to our professional teachers, for they come upon the scene of the child's life too late in the day. By the time children go to school, some of the most important things that happen to them are in the past.

Chapter 3

Understanding, assessing and addressing difficulties in communication and interaction

Major questions addressed in this chapter are:

- What do high quality research studies tell us about young children's difficulties in communication and interaction?
- What is the relationship between such difficulties and learning?
- How can these difficulties be addressed through the learning environment, curriculum and differentiated teaching approaches?

Introduction

This chapter focuses on understanding and addressing difficulties experienced by young children in communication and interaction that are widely acknowledged as potentially creating barriers to learning and progress. The UK charity I Can that provides help and advice about speech, language and communication estimates that over one million children in the UK experience communication difficulties (www.ican.org.uk/). Such difficulties constitute the first of the four broad areas of need outlined in the *Special Educational Needs Code of Practice for Wales* (NAW, 2004, §7.52), and the *Special Educational Needs and Disability Code of Practice: 0 to 25 Years* (DfE, 2015a, §5.32) in England. In Northern Ireland (DENI, 1998, appendix), 'speech and language difficulties' are defined in a broadly similar way. The *Code* in Scotland also recognises young children's experience of 'language and communication difficulties' as potentially requiring the 'use of specialist learning and teaching approaches' (Scottish Government, 2010, §77, p. 53).

Descriptions of young children's difficulties in communication and interaction often overlap with those in cognition and learning, often, for example, when individuals have autistic traits (DfE, 2015a, §5.33). In the current chapter, we begin by outlining links between language and communication and go on to discuss receptive and expressive language, and ways to address difficulties in these areas. We include here a particular focus on pragmatic language impairment and autism to discuss the kind of difficulties in communication and interaction that may be experienced by some young children, and ways in which these might be addressed.

Communication, language and learning

Communication is vital in building and sustaining relationships, sharing experiences, expressing our thoughts and feelings and understanding those of others and in learning. Talking, for example, is an essential intellectual and social skill that forms part of how we communicate with others and make sense of the world. It is shaped by how we think and, in turn, shapes how and what we think. The young child's thought development begins through interpersonal negotiation with others, caregivers, teachers and peers at school and this is internalised into personal understanding (Vygotsky, 1962).

From the time a child first begins to understand the world s/he appears to do so by means of story. 'Any understanding we have of reality is in terms of our stories and our story-creating possibilities' (Mair, 1988, p. 128). It seems to be through story that children learn to become functioning members of the society into which they are born. There is no way to enable children to understand society

> except through the stock of stories which constitute its initial dramatic resources ... It is through hearing stories ... that children learn or mislearn both what a child and what a parent is, what the cast of characters may be in the drama into which they have been born and what the ways of the world are.
>
> (Sarbin, 1986, p. 201)

If children are deprived of stories 'you leave them unscripted, anxious stutterers in their actions as in their words' (ibid.).

There is a close link between language and communication. However, they are not synonymous. Language is 'the words (vocabulary), phrases, grammar and expressions we use and how we organise them to communicate' (NDCS, 2010, p. 8). Communication is really more 'the means by which we convey language, both to get our meaning across and to understand the meaning of others' (ibid.). Communication is crucial for social and emotional development. It involves not only language, but also 'other things like eye contact, gesture, tone of voice, facial expressions and body language' (ibid.).

Expressive and receptive language

Most children learn to communicate naturally. Language ability can be seen as both receptive (that is, comprehending what is said and/or written) or expressive (that is, putting thoughts coherently into words, verbal or written). During their first year of life babies usually acquire a lot of receptive language. By the age of one, children can often understand quite a lot of what is said. Expressing themselves verbally comes later, as we see below. In general terms, to encourage language development, as Wearmouth (2009) notes, it is important to ensure that children realise they are being spoken to, and when they are being asked a question. Family members and those in early years settings should check that they speak calmly and evenly, and their faces are clearly visible (Wearmouth, 2016a). They might use visual aids related to the topics being discussed, and explain something several different ways if they have not been understood the first time. They might also make a point of repeating what young children say in discussion or question and answer sessions.

The difficulties some young children experience in language acquisition may involve receptive or expressive language impairments.

Receptive language

Reflective activity: understanding receptive language difficulties and their effects

It is very important to have an overall understanding of a common pattern of development of receptive language, in other words comprehension of language, in order to grasp the significance of difficulties in this area, their likely consequences and ways to address them. As Allenby *et al.* (2015) note, most children:

- by 18 months, can follow simple instructions, for example 'Find your shoes', and point to familiar objects when asked;
- by 3 years of age, can understand the function of familiar objects, for example scissors, make the match between pictures and objects; and follow simple instructions involving two key words, for example 'Put teddy on the bed';
- by the age of 4, can understand the meaning of a range of prepositions, for example 'behind', 'in front of', 'under' and so on, some concepts of size, 'long/short', 'big/little', 'biggest' and some colours;
- by 5 years of age, can follow straightforward conversations and more complex instructions, and have some understanding of time, for example 'yesterday', 'today' and 'tomorrow'.

What effect on social skills and/or learning do you think the experience of difficulty in understanding language might have on a young child?

Young children who experience difficulty in following language, especially spoken language, in early years settings, may find it hard to sit still and concentrate, socialise and make friends with peers, be unable to follow stories and, later on, learn to read accurately but without understanding the meaning of text – so-called 'barking at print' (Ballard, 1915/16, p. 154, cited in Carroll *et al.*, 2017).

Strategies to address difficulties in receptive language

Any strategy to address a difficulty of any kind should take account of the individuality of the young child: age, severity of the difficulty that is experienced, the context in which the difficulty occurs, available resources and so on. In addition, as Nind (1999) comments, very often, interventions intended to support young children who experience communication difficulties make the assumption that some young children have an innate inability to learn from natural interactive processes and therefore are designed to incorporate direct training in communication skills, teacher direction and behavioural intervention. We discuss some of these below in the context of programmes intended to address pragmatic language impairment. There are, however, other non-directive interactive routes to developing communication skills such as Intensive Interaction that adopt a different approach.

Intensive Interaction

Intensive Interaction aims to facilitate the development of fundamental social and communication skills for children and young people with the most severe difficulties. It is designed to support practitioners to adopt a holistic, nurturing and problem-solving framework for interaction (Yoder, 1990). An important premise underlying Intensive Interaction is that learning to communicate cannot be broken down into sub-tasks that can be taught separately. Instead, the best approach is the holistic model of caregiver–infant interaction in which the interactions resemble the 'natural' interactions between caregivers and infants (Nind, 1999).

The practitioner or caregiver begins by trying to 'connect' with the learner and developing into 'a familiar repertoire of mutually enjoyable interactive games and playful ritualised routines based on the learner's own preferences'. The adult modifies his/her facial expressions, body language, vocal and gaze behaviours and so on to fit the rhythms of the young child's behaviour just as the primary caregiver does. The adult's behaviour resembles what infants elicit from their caregivers in deliberately responding to the learner as if his/her behaviour has 'intentional and communicative significance' (Nind, 1999, p. 97). The repertoire of playful routines provides a safe context for learning the conversational rules of turn-taking and mutual interactions (Field, 1979).

Encouraging early literacy

There is an important question for all young children about how they can take the step 'from speaking to understanding writing on a page or screen, to realise that knowledge of life and language can help them make sense of words and texts' (Gregory, 1996, p. 95). Orally told stories, rhymes, songs, prayer and routines for meeting and greeting people that all have an important role in literacy acquisition are common within many cultures long before children begin any form of formal education. Well-chosen stories told at home by family members and in early years settings or schools by the practitioner can scaffold children's learning about written texts in a way that conversation cannot. Ways in which beginning readers might be introduced to story-reading sessions include explicitly discussing the context for the story, one or more of the characters and the plot, reading the story slowly, clearly, with 'lively intonation' and without interruption, discussing the story and the themes and relating these to the children's lives (Gregory, 1996, p. 112). For younger children this may involve using picture boards, small world resources[1] and story sacks to punctuate the story and give visual, first hand tools to augment their understanding of the aural telling of the story. Sessions can draw on the child's emotions, including fear, love, sympathy, hate, and aim to tell an adventure or drama, and make use, for example, of puppets to mediate learning. Gregory (1996, p. 120) gives an example of a text, 'The Clay Flute' by Mats Rehnman, that seems complex but is popular with young children. It tells the story of a poor boy in the Arabian Desert who suffers many misfortunes but finally 'makes good'. The language is difficult but rich in imagery and emotive vocabulary (witch, horrible, grab, scream, kiss, tear, sword, heart and so on). Reasons for its popularity may include its clear development in the plot, its portrayal of the universal values of courage and kindness and the way good is seen to triumph over evil.

Expressive language

Reflective activity: effects of expressive language difficulties

In order to understand the effects of difficulties in expressive language for the individual young child, it is important to have an overall picture of a common pattern of development of spoken language. As Allenby *et al.* (2015) note:

- By 18 months of age, a child may be using up to 20 recognisable words, but often points to communicate his/her wishes.
- By 3 years of age, the child may be using 'what', 'where' and 'who' questions, a greater range of vocabulary and simple two- or three-word sentences.
- By the age of 4, the child may recite nursery rhymes, may talk about recent events and express more complex ideas with the use of adjectives, prepositions, plurals and past tenses.
- By the age of 5, speech is often grammatically correct and intelligible, the child may 'play' with language, enjoy jokes and ask the meaning of words.
- Given the complexity of language use acquired by most children by the time they go to school, what effect on social skills and/or learning do you think the experience of difficulty in verbal expression might have on a young child?

Allenby *et al.* (2015) comment on the difficulty in developing turn-taking skills and establishing friendships with peers, a sense of isolation and consequent withdrawn behaviour and the potential frustration in not being able to make needs known and/or share ideas experienced by some young children who cannot express themselves in language. In early years settings, a child's learning may be affected by inability to join in group discussions, or ask and answer questions. Early writing may also be affected to the extent that writing reflects something of speaking.

Using Alternative and Augmentative Communication (AAC)

Alternative and Augmentative Communication (AAC), that is, any kind of communication that replaces standard means of communication, for example, speech, is often used when young people experience particular difficulties in verbal communication (Research Autism, 2016). One form of AAC is the Picture Exchange Communication System (PECS). Pictures can be used to express preferences, for example, an adult might teach a child to exchange a picture of something for an item s/he wants. A picture of a biscuit might be exchanged for an actual biscuit, as we discuss below in the case of autism (see page 66). The child might be supported through PECS progressively to make whole sentences, but it may well take a long time to reach this stage of development in communication.

Objects of reference and symbol systems

Objects of reference and electronic banks of pictograms may be included in AAC to assist children with varying degrees of difficulties to communicate. Objects of reference are physical objects that can represent people, events, activities and so on. These objects can be used as a 'bridge' to more abstract forms of communication such as a sign, symbol or word. The contexts in which various objects have meaning are different for different children. It is therefore important that the same item is always used with a child to signify the same event. As Park (1997) notes, objects of reference are often chosen because of their multi-sensory properties to give the individual a clue about what is about to happen. For example, soap or a sponge may be used to signify that washing is about to take place.

Other pictorial means, for example, symbol-based language programs, have been developed over many years to also support communication. Widgit Software, for example, has produced an array of software that uses pictorial symbols to support the development of these skills. Widgit describes its Symbol Set as 'comprehensive collections of images' designed to 'support text, making the meaning clearer and easier to understand' by providing a 'visual representation of a concept'. The Symbol Set often 'follows a schematic structure, or set of design 'rules', that enables the reader to develop his/her own receptive and expressive language skills (Widgit, 2016).

Reflective activity: using symbol systems to develop communication skills

It is often claimed that AAC is a useful means of communicating for those with limited or no speech and that, in supporting the development of expressive and receptive language, it can reduce frustration levels. An example of a software program for AAC is the symbol system produced by Widgit Software. Widgit explains this symbol system as follows:

'It is important to understand that symbols are different from pictures. ... A picture conveys a lot of information at once and its focus may be unclear, while a symbol focuses on a single concept. This means that symbols can be put together to build more precise information'.

'There are different types of symbols ...'.

'Symbols are grouped in different sets. The most commonly used across the UK are Widgit Literacy Symbols (previously known as Rebus)'.

(www.widgit.com/parents/information/)

Widgit claims that symbols can help to support:

- **'Communication** – making a symbol communication book can help people make choices.
- **Independence and participation** – symbols aid understanding which can increase involvement, choice and confidence.
- **Literacy and learning** – symbol software encourage users to 'write' by selecting symbols from a predetermined set in a grid.
- **Creativity and self-expression** – writing letters and stories and expressing your own opinions.
- **Access to information** – all of us need accessible information and this should be presented in such a way that the reader can understand and use.'

(www.widgit.com/symbols/about_symbols/symbol_uses.htm)

You might like to access Widgit's website at www.widgit.com/sectors/education/special.htm and ask yourself whether, and how, you might use the symbol-based programs outlined here to support the needs of young children with communication, language or learning disabilities.

Support for acquisition of speech sounds

Some young children experience difficulty in using particular sounds in words, and their speech may be unintelligible. Before a young child can change his/her production of a sound it is very important for a specialist to establish which sounds a child can discriminate, so it is really important to make a referral to a speech and language therapist for advice and, possibly, assessment. The acquisition of phonological awareness, which is the ability to discriminate the sounds within words, is really important in contributing to the development of early literacy skills (Snowling, 2000). Many programmes are available to support such acquisition which, whilst they may differ in resourcing, broadly include activities to develop:

- awareness of rhythm and rhyme;
- beginning and ending sounds in words;
- syllabification (number of syllables in a word);
- identification and blending of letters in words.

Development of oral skills

It is clearly very important, once young children have progressed to the stage of talking, to build up oral language skills in shared, sustained conversations, by supporting them to talk about what they have been looking at, and about how what they have been looking at connects with what they already know. Young children who experience difficulty in expressing themselves need frequent opportunities for exploratory talk in every area of family life and the life of the early years setting in order to put new information and ideas into their own words and link subject matter to what they already know. Family members and adults in settings might give the child their full attention as frequently as possible when s/he is speaking, deliberately offer running commentaries on activities to encourage the child to talk, and then use feedback for the child that corrects what s/he says and is supportive rather than pressuring. As Allenby *et al.* (2015) note, it can also be helpful if adults model language for the child to imitate, and/or expand on what the child has said. Other strategies that facilitate oral language development might include talk that builds on stories they have just heard, for example, 'The Clay Flute' mentioned on page 55, problem-solving aloud, explanations of how something is made, or how and why things happen, dramatisation and role-play.

Pragmatic language impairment (formerly 'semantic pragmatic disorder')

A few young children may experience special challenges with the pragmatics of language (the use of appropriate language in social situations) and/or semantic aspects of language (the meaning of what is said). Children identified as having such a pragmatic language impairment (PLI), previously called semantic-pragmatic disorder, can experience quite serious barriers to their learning given that so much of the communication and teaching at home and at school depends on spoken and written forms of language (Adams and Lloyd, 2007; Smedley, 1990). Children who have PLI are likely to experience difficulties developing conversational skills, including turn taking and maintaining the topic of the conversation (Bishop, 2000). Some talk endlessly about their own preoccupations and are insensitive to their listeners. Some experience problems following the logic of stories or telling stories in a logical order (Norbury and Bishop, 2003); with over-literal use of language, and making and understanding inferences (Leinonen and Letts, 1997). Some children experience difficulties in understanding but are competent in using the formal structure of language (Rapin and Allen, 1983; 1998). While teachers and speech and language therapists may report that there are increasing numbers of these children, there are no accurate figures for children who experience these difficulties (Law *et al.*, 2002). Indeed, Rutter (2005) suggests that the increased numbers may relate to better identification rather than a real increase in prevalence.

Programmes to address pragmatic language impairment

Numbers of published programmes are available to address difficulties associated with PLI. Firth and Venkatesh (1999), for example, outline practical strategies for use in settings. These include activities to develop skills in following and giving instructions, saying 'yes' or 'no' in answer to factual questions, listening and responding to requests, for example, during play-shopping, asking and responding to questions related to, for example, choice of food and drink and turn-taking.

Adams and Lloyd (2007, pp. 229–30) describe a highly structured classroom intervention to address PLI, using 'modelling and individual practice; role-play; practising specific pragmatic skills in conversations; … promoting self-monitoring and coping strategies … to make both immediate and hidden meanings of language and communication explicit', as well as the pragmatics of grammatical structure:

- First, good practice 'in interacting at an appropriate social and language level with the child' was established. The complexity of the language in the classroom was modified, typically by 'having an assistant translate language into short meaningful utterances' accompanied by a visual demonstration.
- Next, the children were taught 'the vocabulary of social situations and insight' into others' emotions. Small incremental changes to routines were added and discussed before they were implemented. Children were supported to understand 'social and verbal inferences, metaphors and hidden meaning in language'.
- Finally, work on the pragmatics of language focused on 'explicit exercises and classroom support in exchange structure, turn-taking, topic management, conversational skills, building sequences, cohesion and coherence in narrative and discourse'.

Language therapy programmes

Language therapy programmes may be designed to address a whole range of difficulties, including pronouncing and/or using certain sounds in words, comprehension of language, word order and sequencing, the pragmatics of language and so on. Approaches often rely on training or direction for young children.

Reflective activity: considering effectiveness of language therapy

Gallagher and Chiat (2009) describe a direct intensive group therapy intervention focused on both comprehension and expressive language for a group of pre-school children with specific language impairment. This group made significantly greater improvements in language acquisition than carefully matched groups who received a more consultative nursery-based approach.

To enable an understanding of this kind of intervention it is useful to set out an example of the therapy activities that were used:

Therapy activities

Activity 1 Hello/Welcome routine: The children and speech and language therapist (SLT) would sing a song, which included each child's name. Each child would then have to wait for their turn to be welcomed into the group.

Activity 2 Picture Description/Information task: This activity was carried out during story time. It was split into 'listening' and 'talking':

Listening task

- The SLT would tell a story using a book with the text reduced to an appropriate level for the group. Each utterance would then be repeated four times.
- The SLT would then retell the main components of the story using visual props for each picture. These might include the use of miniature dolls and objects or laminated pictures from the story which the SLT referred to. Each utterance would be repeated four times.

Talking task

Children would take turns in retelling the 'story' using the visual props or the book. The SLT would provide the correct model as and when the child produced an incorrect target.

Activity 3 Vocabulary task: For the Intensive group, this involved a range of activities using both phonological and semantic approaches. The phonological approach used puppets in 'did I say it right games'. The semantic approach was used to teach new words through categorising and describing items according to similarities and differences in function/physical description. The Nursery-based group received only the semantic techniques.

Activity 4 Grammar task: Intensive group only. This task involved the use of puppets and miniature dolls and objects depending on the target of therapy. The puppet would provide the correct model and the child would then be asked what the puppet had said. At the end of the repetition task, the puppet produced grammatical errors as well as correct models related to the focus of the therapy, and the child was asked to identify when it was correct and repeat it.

Activity 5 Expressive information: Expressive information was targeted through a range of 'make and do' activities, again divided into listening and talking tasks. These activities were based around the group topic, e.g. if the topic was food, then these activities might be making sandwiches or fruit smoothies.

Listening task

The SLT would explain the items needed for the make and do task as well as the sequence of the tasks using Makaton symbols and short target utterances which were repeated twice.

Talking task

- The child would have to request items required for the activity and explain the sequence using the previously modelled utterances.
- The child would be given an immediate behavioural reward each time he/she successfully requested the necessary items and described the sequence of the activity.

Activity 6 Free play: Intensive group only. The children played with a range of toys based on the topic of the group. In this less structured session, the SLT modelled language to support sharing and negotiating amongst the group, and provided recasting when appropriate. The children receiving the nursery-based therapy had play opportunities outside of the group, as part of the normal nursery routine.

Activity 7 Linguistic concepts: This used multi-sensory, experiential approaches to learning.

Tasks were organised along a continuum of difficulty from active experiential learning opportunities to understanding concepts as picture representations. For example, in learning about prepositional concepts such as 'in', 'on' and 'under', first the children would have the opportunity to experience going on and under various pieces of furniture while the SLT modelled the utterance for the concept. Then the therapist used miniature objects and a box providing further modelling opportunities. Games might include 'hide and seek' of toys with the SLT modelling the concept. Finally, games would involve the use of pictures representing the concepts.

Activity 8 Closing activity: The children and the SLT would sing a song, which included each child's name. The children would wait for their turn to sing goodbye to the group.

(Adapted from Gallagher and Chiat, 2009, pp. 636–7)[2]

You might like to look back at this set of activities and ask yourself what you see that is based on direct teaching by the therapist, and what reflects more naturalist, less structured activities that are more reminiscent of everyday interactions. What do you think?

Autism

One 'condition', autism, commonly spans the areas of need noted in the *Code of Practice* (DfE, 2015a, §5.33).

Reflective activity: what do you already know about autism?

Note down what you already know about:

- How, in your experience, the general public tends to regard autistic individuals;
- What kind of assessments of difficulties associated with autism are commonly carried out in the early years;
- Approaches to teaching young children identified as experiencing aspects of autism.

Diagnoses of autism were first made in the 1940s in the USA. Grandin and Panek (2013, p. 3), in a personal account of the experience of autism, note how, when Temple Grandin, one of the authors who is a very famous autistic American academic, was born in 1947, 'the diagnosis of autism was only four years old'. Grandin comments how 'fortunate' she was to have been born prior to a time when a diagnosis of autism commonly resulted in institutionalisation. As it was, her mother was left to work out for herself how to help her child:

> Mother did heroic work. In fact she discovered on her own the standard treatment that therapists use today. … The core principle of every program – including the one that was used with me … is to engage with the kid one-on-one for hours every day, twenty to forty hours per week.
>
> (Grandin and Panek, 2013, p. 4)

It was in 1943 that Leo Kanner identified what he called 'early infantile autism' from the Greek αυτος (autos) to denote excessive focus on the self. This refers to a difficulty marked by profound 'aloneness', inability to relate to people and social situations, failure to use language competently to communicate, obsessive desire to maintain sameness, fascination for objects which are handled with skill in fine motor movements, a good rote memory, over-sensitivity to stimuli and, often, difficulties in learning, some at a severe level (Kanner, 1943).

In the following year, 1944, Hans Asperger noted traits similar in some ways to this 'early infantile autism' (Wing, 1996). Features noted by Asperger were unusual responses to some sensory experiences: auditory, visual, olfactory (smell), taste and touch, an uneven developmental profile, good rote memory, circumscribed special interests and motor co-ordination difficulties. Individuals with Asperger Syndrome tend not to experience the learning difficulties that are associated with autism, and often have measured levels of intelligence that are average or above (National Autistic Society, 2016).

Building on previous work, Wing and Gould (1979) identified a 'triad of impairments' in a broad group of 'autistic' children:

- Difficulty in social interaction and social relationships, for example, appearing indifferent to other people, difficulty in understanding unwritten social rules, recognising other's feelings, or seeking comfort from others. Grandin (1995) recalls pulling away when others tried to give her a hug because being touched overwhelmed her senses, always wanting to participate in activities with other children but not knowing how and never fitting in. In another very personal account of the experience of being autistic, Higashida (2007, pp. 47–8) describes what aloneness feels like to him:

  > 'Ah, don't worry about him. He'd rather be on his own'.
  > How many times have we heard this? I can't believe that anyone born as a human being really wants to be left on their own, not really. No, for people with autism, what we're anxious about is that we're causing trouble for the rest of you, or even getting on your nerves. *That* is why it's hard for us to stay around other people. That is why we often end up being left on our own.

- Verbal and non-verbal social communication, including difficulty in understanding the meaning of gestures, facial expressions or tone of voice. Higashida (2014, p. 43) explains why, for him, making and sustaining eye contact is so difficult during conversations:

  > True we don't look at people's eyes very much. … I've been told again and again, but I still can't do it. To me, making eye contact with someone I'm talking to feels a bit creepy, so I tend to avoid it.
  > Then, where exactly am I looking? … What we're actually looking at is the other person's voice. … we're trying to listen to the other person with all our sense organs. When we're fully focused on working out what the heck it is you're saying, our sense of sight sort of zones out.

- Social imagination, meaning inability to think and behave flexibly, restricted, obsessional or repetitive activities, difficulty in developing the skills of playing with others. Children often find it hard to understand and interpret other people's thoughts, feelings and actions, engage in imaginative play, predict what will or could happen next, understand the concept of danger and cope in new or unfamiliar situations.

In addition to this triad, obsessive repetitive behaviour patterns[3] are often a notable feature, as well as a resistance to change in routine.

More recently, however, the diagnostic manual, DSM-V, of the American Psychiatric Association (APA, 2015) has combined the first two descriptions of difficulties into one. It also adds an additional element to the third: an unusual interest in, and way of responding to, sensory stimuli in the environment. As Frederickson and Cline (2015, p. 283) note, this dyad is comprised of difficulties in:

- social communication and social interaction;
- restricted, repetitive patterns of behaviour, interests or activities including sensory difficulties.

The *Code of Practice* in England (DfE, 2015a, §6.27) concurs with this description and suggests that 'young people with an Autistic Spectrum Disorder (ASD) may have needs across all areas, including particular sensory requirements'. They 'are likely to have particular difficulties with social interaction. They may also experience difficulties with language, communication and imagination which can impact on how they relate to others' (DfE, 2015a, §6.29).

Assessment of 'autism'

Autism is a biological explanation of individual behaviour. It can be difficult, as Sheehy (2004) notes, to separate out the effects of autism from those of profound difficulties in learning, given that 80 per cent of children with autism score below 70 on norm-referenced intelligence tests (Peeters and Gilberg, 1999) and increasingly severe general learning difficulties are correlated with an increasing occurrence of autism (Jordan, 1999).

As Klin *et al.* (2000, p. 163) comment, 'There are no biological markers in the identification of autism, despite advances in neuroscience'. Grandin and Panek (2013, pp. 4–5) go on to note challenges that relate from the lack of specificity in identifying autism in the first place.

> ... autism can't be diagnosed in the laboratory ... Instead, as with many psychiatric syndromes ... autism is identified by observing and evaluating behaviors. Those observations and evaluations are subjective, and the behaviors vary from person to person. The diagnosis can be confusing, and it can be vague. It has changed over the years, and it continues to change.

Hence, a profile of symptoms and characteristics of autistic behaviour with agreed diagnostic criteria is used to identify autism in young people. The DSM criteria noted above are very influential and form the basis, for example, of the Autism Diagnostic Observation Schedule (ADOS) that is used in some LAs in the UK as a diagnostic tool. However, DSM is an American publication, and, many assessments of autism spectrum disorders in the UK are based on the *International Classification of Diseases* (ICD), published by the World Health Organisation. In the ICD-10 (WHO, 1994, F84.0), autism is described as a disorder that is 'pervasive' and 'developmental', and that is identified through 'abnormal and/or impaired development' that is evident before 3 years of age and by particular 'abnormal functioning' in social interaction, communication and 'restricted, repetitive behaviour'. Boys are affected three to four times more often than girls. Impairments 'in reciprocal social interaction' which manifest as 'an inadequate appreciation of socio-emotional cues' are always present. Impairments in communications include a 'lack of social usage of whatever language skills are present', as well as poorly developed 'make-believe and social imitative play'. During conversations, the ability to synchronise personal responses to the utterances of others is impaired as well as the ability to respond with feeling to other people's overtures. Autism is also said to be characterised by 'restricted, repetitive, and stereotyped patterns of behaviour, interests and activities' that are demonstrated by 'a tendency to impose rigidity and routine on a wide range of aspects of day-to-day functioning'. The next version of the ICD is due to be published in 2018 (www.who.int/classifications/icd/revision/en/) and may well align this more closely with the DSM-5.

Reflective activity: recognising autism spectrum disorders

The National Institute for Health and Care Excellence (NICE) (2011) has provided three 'Signs and symptoms' tables for use with pre-school, primary and secondary-aged children in Appendix 3 of its publication *Autism in under 19s: Recognition, referral and diagnosis.* These are available at www.nice.org.uk/guidance/cg128/resources.

- Access these tables yourself and compare the lists of signs and symptoms with the description of autism above.
- What use do you think early years settings, lower/infant and primary schools might make of these tables?

These tables 'are not intended to be used alone, but to help professionals recognise a pattern of impairments in reciprocal social and communication skills, together with unusual restricted and repetitive behaviours' (www.nice.org.uk/guidance/cg128/chapter/Appendix-C-Signs-and-symptoms-of-possible-autism).

- What might be negative consequences of open access to tables such as these, do you think?
- Do you feel there might be any danger of overdiagnosis of ASD if tables such as these are used in early years settings and schools? If so, why might this be the case?

In its publication, NICE (2011, p. 4) has produced scenarios to assist professionals 'to improve and assess users' knowledge of the recognition, referral and diagnosis of autism in children and young people'. It is available at www.nice.org.uk/guidance/cg128/resources/clinical-case-scenarios-183180493 . You might also choose to access this document and consider the advice given by NICE in relation to each of the young people whose experiences are described here.

Co-ordination between health agencies and other key services such as education, social care and the voluntary sector is important. NICE (2011) advises that a local autism multidisciplinary group (the autism team) should include, in its core membership, a paediatrician and/or child and adolescent psychiatrist, a speech and language therapist and a clinical and/or educational psychologist. Multi-agency staff should also work in partnership with the child or young person with autism and their family or carers. Once a concern about possible autistic tendencies has been raised, a member of the core autism team should advise on whether a referral should be made for a formal assessment.

Strategies to address autism

The Treatment and Education of Autistic and related Communication Handicapped Children programme (TEACCH) (Mesibov, Shea and Schopler, 2004) is designed to combine cultivating individual strengths and interests with structured teaching. The principles include improving skills through education and modifying the environment to accommodate individual autistic students, structured teaching rather than more informal approaches and parents collaborating with professionals as co-therapists to continue the techniques at home.

Teaching communication skills

In a recent interview (Wearmouth, 2016a, pp. 45–6), Martha, the mother of an 8 year old autistic child, N, described how she and her husband taught N to communicate with them at home, using PECS (see above) and other strategies. The hardest thing for the parents was how long every aspect of development in his ability to communicate took. They started with teaching him the purpose of communication. Up till then he had not seen the purpose of it because his mother had done everything for him. To teach him they used the technique of object exchange: at first his mother stuck a picture of a chocolate biscuit to a fridge magnet, put his hand on to the magnet, removed it from the fridge and put it into her own hand saying, 'Chocolate biscuit, please'. Then she gave him the biscuit, saying, 'Chocolate biscuit,' to make the link between the picture and the sound symbols of the words. Finally she helped him to put the magnet back on the fridge as an end to that routine. Now there was strong motivation for N to want to communicate and he quickly learned to do it for himself. Also, a 'stop' sign was put on the fridge to symbolise 'no more'.

Signing in order to communicate became important at this point. Mother and child together learned Makaton signing from the CBBC programme 'Something special' which has an actor signing all the way through. They found Makaton simple and fun to use together. The mother encouraged the boy to connect words to signs by quite deliberately giving him the verbal equivalent every time she used one. 'Every time you sign, you also say at the same time, and he makes the connection'. Signing was also used at a special pre-school group to teach him to transition between tasks – when to stop an activity and so on.

At this point the speech therapist advised that he might become very anxious if activities were sprung on him without any warning. Next, therefore, came pictures to forewarn him what was about to happen, for example, pictures of a car and the local supermarket to show that they were about to go shopping. A picture of a timer to indicate 'time to go' proved to be of no use, probably because the concept of time was too complex.

Following this N's mother made line drawings on the pictures to make the link between pictures of the real thing and symbols to represent them. For example, a line drawing of a red door represented the supermarket. The line drawings made the instigation of simple communication, through picture exchange (PECS, see above), possible for him. This was always around requests for food and drink.

Signing continued, accompanied by a running commentary from his mother on what was happening around N. To do this, she spoke in very short, punctuated sentences.

Subsequently, the use of PECS made scheduling possible. 'There is so much safety in schedules for an autistic child because one thing leads to the next'. After a while words can be written underneath the drawings to encourage literacy. N's mother described the family's use of scheduling as follows:

'We regularly use scheduling with picture cards at home. The cards have pictures of what we do during the day, places we visit and tasks to be completed. At the beginning of the day, we choose pictures that represent what will happen that day. We stick the cards on a Velcro strip, and as we complete activities through the day we unstick each card and 'post' it in a 'completed' box. The benefit is that my son can see the whole day's happenings and can predict what will happen next. I have found that using schedules has reduced my son's stress, and built his confidence and, over time, has increased his flexibility. 'If the schedule needs to change, it can be discussed and my son can see that the rest of the schedule remains unaltered, which can be reassuring to him'.

It is essential that an autistic child knows that s/he can communicate with others, so other members of the family and friends learned to sign too.

When he went to school at the age of nearly 5, N spoke three words: 'hippo', 'purple' and 'ten'. A very sensitive TA supported him through his first year by deliberately setting out to understand him as a person and how to communicate with him. There were times when he ran into problems, however. His schedule for going to the toilet included washing his hands and turning off the tap, but one day the tap was stuck in the 'on' position. He would not leave the washroom because he could not complete the activity as listed on his schedule.

By the end of Year One his vocabulary had increased considerably. The target on his IEP was to learn how to ask for help so he was given a card that said: 'Help me'.

Now N is about to move to a middle school, so the concern for his parents is how to liaise effectively with the SENDCo and other staff, and hope that they are all prepared to get to know, communicate with and understand their son.

Addressing autistic tendencies in classrooms

In early years settings and in school classrooms, to take account of the challenges facing autistic young children, broadly practitioners might consider addressing needs of children in a number of ways (Wearmouth, 2016a, p. 45):

- paying close attention to clarity and order, reduce extraneous and unnecessary material in order that children know where their attention needs to be directed, and maintain a predictable physical environment with very predictable and regular routines, ensuring that everything is kept in the same place.
- teaching children agreed signals to be quiet or to call for attention.
- providing specific low-arousal work areas free from visual distractions. Headphones might be made available to reduce sound.
- providing a visual timetable with clear symbols to represent the various activities for the day, and a simple visual timer with, for example, an arrow that is moved across a simple timeline to show how much time has passed and how much is left.

In order to develop greater understanding of personal emotions children might be taught in a very deliberate, overt and structured way:

- to name their feelings and relate these to their own experiences, predict how they are likely to feel at particular times and in particular circumstances and recognise the signs of extreme emotions such as anger. A visual gauge showing graduated degrees of anger in different shades of colour can often be helpful here.
- to identify and name others' feelings and link these to possible causes, and identify appropriate responses to others' emotions. … Teachers might use art, drama and social stories to identify the different kinds of emotions and/or explore their physical aspects and/or talk through situations that need to be resolved.

Above all, it is really important to get to know the young child really well and to understand his/her individuality, strengths, weaknesses, likes, dislikes and so on. Vanessa, for example, the SENDCo in a lower school, exemplifies just how important this is (Wearmouth, 2016a, pp. 198–205). She had taken advice from a number of professionals about how to provide appropriately for a young child, 'Ray', who had been identified as autistic prior to entry to her school.

> Ray's speech and language report provided a summary of his communication and language delay and offered advice to support his development. Although these recommendations appeared straightforward, in practice we found them difficult to implement … . I found myself asking questions such as; what does a language programme look like? What methods could be used for alternative communication?

Vanessa and the support staff started looking at visual supports that might be useful for Ray:

> Staff took photographs of places and everyday objects Ray would use, e.g. toilet, playground. The plan was to show Ray the photograph, e.g. his lunch box and say 'lunchtime' and take Ray to the hall to collect his lunchbox.

However, lack of confidence and conflicting advice from external specialists led to some confusion in how best to provide for Ray:

> The specialist advisor thought the photographs were too distracting and he would benefit from simple pictures. Ray's speech and language therapist thought he would be better shown the photographs and the objects. None of us had any previous experience working with a pupil with such limited communication and the professionals were offering different advice; this caused some confusion and at the same time staff were frustrated since it took a great deal of effort just to gain Ray's attention to the photograph and hear the spoken word because he would avoid most adult attempts to communicate unless he had initiated it.

After a while, much uncertainty among the teaching and support staff and little progress in Ray's acquisition of communication skills, Vanessa realised

> … we had all been placing too much emphasis on developing Ray's speech and language and the mode of communication (photographs, pictures or objects) and not

addressing the fundamental issue of learning what communication was before he could learn to use a system of communication.

Vanessa quotes from the work of Jordan (2001, p. 52) at this point:

> Language and communication are so closely bound together in normal development that it does not often occur ... that speech alone is not the answer ... the speaking child with autism may still not be able to communicate, to express needs, or to explain what the matter is when s/he is upset. Speech in fact may become a barrier to communication in some cases, with the child talking incessantly, leaving no space for communication.
>
> (Jordan, 2001, p. 52)

Vanessa notes that 'staff needed a great deal of support understanding and accepting Ray may never use speech and it was agreed developing his communication and using alternative methods would be a priority'. For herself, she

> ... came to understand that the early stage of communication is attention. ... To help Ray begin to understand the purpose of communication by making requests, we needed something highly motivating. This proved a challenge owing to his limited interests, so we finally opted for food, something his parents suggested.

Choice of which visual support to use was paramount here. With guidance from his speech and language therapist:

> we decided against an object representing a cake since he was likely to put it in his mouth or throw it on the floor. We considered a photograph but decided a simple drawing was the best option. The cake was cut up into small pieces and placed in sight but out of reach. Ray was then taught that when he tapped the drawing he was given some cake.

Both parents and staff were shown how to encourage Ray to communicate by tapping a picture, and tapping a drawing subsequently became an important stage in Ray's understanding of what communication was all about. As Vanessa says of her own developing understanding of the needs of autistic children: 'Jordan explained that it is communication that is the main problem in autism, not necessarily speech and language; this changed the direction of my work'.

> Children with autism will need to be taught communicative functions and what communication is about. The dimensions of communication should be tackled one step at a time. There are specific problems in language and communication in autism but these are best dealt with, not by trying to suppress them, but by understanding their function for the child and helping him or her develop towards meaningful communication.
>
> (Jordan, 2001, p.72)

Summary

Acquiring receptive and expressive language and being able to communicate with others in the context in which a young child lives and is educated is crucial to his/her learning and social and emotional growth and development. Difficulties in communication and interaction are not immediately visible, however, in the very early days of a child's life in the same way as, for example, physical disabilities. Pragmatic language impairment, autism and other areas of difficulty in this area of a child's development become obvious later, sometimes at home in interaction with parents and siblings, but often when a young child enters an early years setting. Given the importance to future life chances of this area of development, it is really important for those in early years settings and schools to get to know their young children, their strengths, interests and any areas of difficulty really well in order to respond to their learning needs in discussion with their families.

Notes

1 Examples of 'small world' resources are small cars, dolls' house-type figures or Duplo/mobile figures, small plastic/wooden animals for jungle/farm/seaworld-type play.
2 Example of therapy activities reproduced with kind permission of the first author.
3 Such behaviour patterns should not be confused with schematic behaviours that are typical and not necessarily an indicator of autism.

Chapter 4

Understanding, assessing and addressing difficulties in cognition and learning

Major questions addressed in this chapter are:

- What understandings of the learning process can enable us to address difficulties in cognition and learning in a principled way?
- What kinds of challenges are experienced by young children identified as having moderate and/or more profound learning difficulties?
- What do we know about Down's syndrome, and what kinds of support can be effective in addressing difficulties in cognition and learning that may be experienced?
- How can we understand and address difficulties associated with dyslexia?

Introduction

The chapter will focus on the second of the four broad areas of need outlined in the *Code of Practice* in both England (DfE, 2015a) and Wales (NAW, 2004): cognition and learning. Here we begin by looking particularly at the kinds of challenges faced by young children identified as experiencing 'moderate' and more profound difficulties in learning, and exemplify the discussion with difficulties associated with Down's syndrome. We go on to look at what is often called a 'specific learning difficulty', a term that is used in the *Codes of Practice* (DENI, 1998; NAW, 2004; DfE, 2015a) to relate to a particular area of learning and not to overall attainment and cognitive ability terminology. We discuss one example of a specific learning difficulty: dyslexia.

Understanding cognition and difficulties in cognition

The Latin root of the word 'cognition' is 'cognoscere', which means 'to get to know', or 'to recognise'. In general terms, the frame of reference within which 'cognition' is used in the *Codes of Practice* (DENI, 1998; NAW, 2004; DfE, 2015a) relates largely to information-processing associated with problem-solving, language, perception and memory and the development of concepts. The cognitive difficulties experienced by some young children clearly extend to the area of communication and interaction discussed elsewhere. It is obvious, for example, that language acquisition and use are integral to thinking, learning, problem-solving and communication (Wearmouth, 2016b).

Understanding children's modes of learning

Children may experience difficulty at any point in their development. An example of a common feature that can be readily identified in children who experience cognitive difficulties is weakness in understanding and remembering that a symbol can represent something else, for example, something concrete or an action (Grauberg, 2002). There are some very useful frames of reference within which to think about what this means about the level of learning at which a young child is operating, the difficulty s/he might be experiencing and how teachers and others might support young children to make progress.

Understanding learning and difficulties in learning

As we noted in Chapter 2, it is crucial to understand the learning process during which difficulties in learning may occur so that we can think about ways to address such difficulties in a principled way. We discussed the work of three leading theorists: Jean Piaget, Lev Vygotsky and Jerome Bruner.

- Jean Piaget, you may recall, concluded that there were four universal stages of learning: sensorimotor (0–2 years), preoperational (2–7 years), concrete operational (7–11 years) and formal operational (11+ years). As we pointed out in Chapter 2, this staged model of learning has been critiqued. It is now widely believed that sensory motor representations are not replaced by symbolic ones but are gradually augmented by symbolic ones acquired through action, language and so on. However, Piaget's work is useful in pointing out that a young child will not develop the ability to reason in the abstract until later on in his/her development.
- The distinctiveness of Vygotsky's (1978) work lay in the importance he placed on the social context in which learners construct new knowledge and understanding. Crucial to the process are 'mediators' to mediate learning during interactions between the child and the environment. An important concept in explaining learning is the zone of proximal development (ZPD): effectively, the next steps that the child can take if a more informed/expert other 'scaffolds' new learning.
- A related way to conceptualise young children's learning is through Bruner's (1966) three modes of representation of reality: enactive, iconic and symbolic, that move from the concrete 'learn by doing' to the abstract.

Understanding moderate difficulties in cognition and learning

> ### Reflective activity: stages of learning and modes of representation
>
> Please re-read the summaries above and in Chapter 2, pp. 38–42 on Piaget's stages of learning, Vygotsky's (1978) work and Bruner's (1966) model of three modes of representation of reality. Then note down your responses to the following questions:
>
> - To what extent do you feel these models are useful frameworks within which to think about young people's developing conceptual understanding of the world?

- How might you begin to conceptualise a plan for addressing cognitive difficulties based on the work of one or all of these educators?
- In your experience, what kind of strategies can teachers and others incorporate into their teaching to facilitate access to the learning of new concepts in ways that address these difficulties? For example, you might consider that some children require much more time to acquire concepts through experience of using and manipulating concrete objects or of discussing ideas with peers.

All young children need the experience of doing before they understand more symbolic, and then more abstract, concepts, some for a longer period of time than others. In the early years, learning to use number symbols is likely to occur simultaneously with acquiring the alphabetic principle and sound-symbol correspondence in literacy acquisition (Rogers 2007, p. 2). However, learners' ability to understand symbolic representation depends on understanding of the first-hand experience to which the symbolic representation refers. Pictorial symbols or icons are clearly different from abstract symbols (Piaget, 1969; Piaget and Inhelder, 2016; Bruner, 1966). It can require a lot of concrete activities in a variety of different contexts before a child with cognitive difficulties understands the concept of 'numberness' (Grauberg, 2002).

Strategies to address moderate learning difficulties in learning

As we discussed above, one of the ideas that has been developed from a sociocultural view is that of 'scaffolding' to support learning (Wood, Bruner and Ross (1976). The nature of the scaffolding can be very important when young children experience difficulties. To be successful, the interaction must be collaborative between the child and the more knowledgeable other and operate within the child's zone of proximal development. The scaffolder must access the child's current level of understanding and then work at slightly beyond that level, drawing the child into new areas of learning. The scaffold should be withdrawn in stages as the child becomes more competent. In schools, the final goal is for the child to become autonomous, secure enough in the knowledge required to complete the task.

To ensure that all young children understand what is said, as Wearmouth (2009) notes, it is important to ensure that they realise they are being spoken to, and when they are being asked a question. Teachers should check that they speak calmly and evenly, and their faces are clearly visible. They might use visual aids related to the topics being discussed, and explain something several different ways if they have not been understood the first time.

Difficulties commonly experienced in mathematics learning

Much teaching in the area of mathematics takes place in the context of a symbolic representation of number and computation, that is, through written text and pictures (Rogers 2007, p. 2). Activities involving reading and writing numbers tell us something about children's ability to read and write numbers, but do not necessarily tell us anything about children's conceptual understanding of 'numberness'. Young children's ability to understand mathematical symbols depends on the first-hand experience to which the symbolic representation refers, for example, in the case of younger learners, handling and counting of everyday items.

Many children appear to adopt mathematical symbols without understanding their underpinning concepts. As Rogers (2007, p. 13) notes, a weak conceptual framework for understanding number in the early years on which to begin formal mathematics teaching makes it difficult to engage children's interest and to correct later:

> It is also well documented that such difficulties soon become compounded, resulting in distress and further delay (Adult Literacy and Basic Skills Unit, 1992). Attention needs to be paid to the negative effects of incomprehension of a prominent part of the mathematics curriculum in which young children are involved on a daily basis. It may be that such incomprehension prompts the early lack of confidence in mathematics that characterises further failure and poor problem-solving during the later school years. They can often learn to count up and down 'in ones' and can take part in counting games and activities. However, understanding that a number, for example, five, is not just the last number in the series 15 (the ordinal principle), but also means the whole set of five (the principle of cardinality) is another matter.

Very great care must be taken in working out ways to support children's understanding by making clear links from one small step to the next. Early years settings and primary schools in particular have a lot of equipment that can be used to play games in adding, subtracting and balancing. Bearing in mind Bruner's three modes of representation, for some children it might be important to use concrete aids to establish number learning, for example, Cuisenaire rods, Numicon and/or an abacus, for much longer than for other children. A major question is how to move from the act of adding, taking away or balancing to competent use of the abstract symbols. The context in which this takes place really matters. One way to do this might be to spend time thinking about ways in which children will move into and through the iconic mode of representation and to encourage children to devise their own symbols for the actions first so that the icon visibly represents their own understandings (Wearmouth, 2017). Hughes (1986), for example, describes the substantial knowledge about number which children acquire prior to entering formal schooling, and contrasts this with the difficulties experienced as a result of formal written symbolism of mathematics. He argues that children need to be encouraged to bridge between informal and formal understanding of number, to avoid difficulties experienced later on as a result of formal written symbolism of mathematics introduced at too early a period in the child's development of conceptual understandings.

Understanding numberness

Numberness:

> … means the concept of 'twoness', 'threeness', 'nness'. Through his [sic] experience with many different materials we want him to see what is common to all (the fact that there are, for instance, 'two' of each) and we want him to learn to ignore what is irrelevant (e.g. size, colour, feel).

> (Grauberg, 2002, p. 12)

It will take a lot of concrete activities in a variety of different contexts before a child with cognitive difficulties understands this.

Teaching number in the early years through the use of number sequences, for example, from nursery rhymes to number lines, seems to be common in the UK (Grauberg, 2002). In some other countries, for example, Japan, the preference is for teaching the rudiments of numberness through recognition of small quantities rather than counting. Recognising, for example, four, as a quantity, involves one operation of matching a sound symbol or visual symbol to an amount. This seems, logically, easier than recognising four from a number sequence. This latter involves remembering that four comes after three and before five, and simultaneously counting up to the total amount.

Time

Time is a complex concept for children to develop. It includes points in time, duration and sequence of events, frequency of events and intervals between them (Piaget, 1969). There is no constant point of reference in relation to many indicators of time. 'Late' can refer to a point in time in the morning, if the child should have arrived earlier, or to a point at night when that child could be early or on time. Our sense of the passage of time often seems to distort depending on the context and/or activity. For example, the few days before a birthday often seem to young children to pass much more slowly than most other days (Wearmouth, 2017).

Bruner's enactive, iconic and symbolic modes of representation can offer a framework for conceptualising activities for young children who experience difficulties in the acquisition of time-related concepts. Using a timer of some sort or concentrating on the sounds emitted on striking a percussion instrument might help in the initial stages to enact the representation of time passing. Family members or teachers might help young children to act out a regular sequence of events in their own lives and then represent the sequence in pictorial form (Bruner's iconic mode of representation). These days the concept of a visual timetable for use in schools with young children who experience cognitive difficulties, and, in fact, for all young children, is quite common (Selikowitz, 2008).

Memory problems

Within the area of moderate learning difficulties, very poor memory is a problem for a number of young children. Some young children experience problems absorbing and recalling information or responding to and carrying out instructions within a busy classroom situation. There are a number of possible reasons for this. For example, children may not have grasped the information clearly in the first place. They may not have linked new information to previous knowledge sufficiently, or they may not have distinguished new knowledge from what is already known, so that the new information interferes with the old.

There is a further issue here. As Goswami (2015, p. 14) notes, the ability to 'categorise exemplars as similar is an important *cognitive process*'. Some children may experience difficulty in this area of cognition, however, finding it problematic to generalise within categories. They do not, therefore, see discriminating differences. If similar concepts are introduced together, for example, donkeys and ponies, and the child is told that the donkey is the one with the big ears, it may be that the child is forever afterwards confused about which is which because there is insufficient discriminating detail. Babies' brains form a generalised representation, or a prototype, of what they see, and divide the world into objects and categories in what Rosch (1978) terms a relational way. There are co-occurrences that lead the brain to recognise natural categories. As prototypes form the basis for conceptual development, where a young child has perceptual impairment this will necessarily affect conceptual development.

Young children have to learn sequences of certain items relating to particular areas that are important for everyday living: letters of the alphabet, months of the year, days of the week and numbers and so on. There are many young people who, even in secondary schools, cannot recite either the alphabet or the months of the year in the correct order. Difficulties in this area, however, can be improved with training. Practitioners and/or families might try increasing the span of items that are to be remembered and the length of time between presenting the sequence and asking for recall. It is important to encourage the child to repeat the instruction before carrying it out and use his/her own voice to aid his/her memory. The child should be able to see, hear, say and, if possible, touch the materials to be learned. This reinforces the input stimuli and helps to consolidate the information for use, meaning and transfer to other areas. Teachers can keep verbal instructions clear and concise and ensure young children are attending before teachers start to speak. It can help to preface instructions with a warning (for example, 'Peter, in a moment I am going to ask you') to ensure that the child is ready to listen. They might also encourage children to repeat back key points as well as to talk through tasks in their own voice to help to direct their motor movements, and try supplementing auditory verbal material with visual cues and practical demonstrations (Wearmouth, 2009).

Profound and multiple learning disabilities

For very many years there was a general assumption that children with multiple and profound difficulties were ineducable. However, since the 1970 Education Act, the right of all children to an appropriate education, irrespective of the degree of difficulty in learning, has been acknowledged. Some children with profound and multiple learning disabilities may have profound autism or Down's syndrome. Others may have Rett syndrome, Tuberous Sclerosis or another disorder.

- Rett syndrome, so named after an Austrian doctor, Andreas Rett, who first described it in 1966 (www.rettuk.org/what-is-rett-syndrome), is a genetic disorder caused by a change in a gene on the X chromosome that affects brain development in around one in 12,000 girls. It often results in severe cognitive and physical disabilities, for example, severe problems with communication and language, memory, hand use, mobility, co-ordination and other brain functions.
- Tuberous sclerosis causes benign tumours to develop in many parts of the body. Nearly 50 per cent of young children will have a learning disability, for example poor memory and/or attention, poor planning and organisational ability, slower learning than peers and, sometimes, difficulty in communicating.

One common factor for everyone is that they experience great difficulty communicating. Mencap (undated, p. 4) notes how many people with profound and multiple learning disabilities 'rely on facial expressions, vocal sounds, body language and behaviour to communicate'. Some people may only 'use a small range of formal communication, such as speech, symbols or signs'. Another factor is that learning is likely to be very slow. 'Short-term memory may well be very limited and children may need frequent repetition of the same concepts in the same situations' (ibid.). Some may not reach the stage where they can communicate intentionally. Many may find it hard to understand what others are trying to communicate to them.

Strategies to address profound difficulties in learning

Reflective activities: ways to address barriers to learning arising from profound difficulties in learning

It is very important that those people who support young children with profound and multiple learning disabilities 'spend time getting to know their means of communication and finding effective ways to interact with them' (Mencap, undated). You might like to look at some of the discussion in Chapter 3 on difficulties in communication and interaction on ways to support the development of communication through, for example, Alternative and Augmentative Communication (AAC) including PECS, and the use of symbols such as Widgit Literacy Symbols available at www.widgit.com/parents/information/ .

- How might you use these systems to support communication skills among students whose profound difficulties in this area create barriers to their learning?

Down's syndrome

Down's syndrome is often associated with some impairment of cognitive ability. Young children with Down's syndrome tend to experience difficulties ranging from mild to moderate in learning, although some have more severe or profound difficulties. The average age IQ is around 50 (Dykens and Kasari, 1997). There is no 'cure' for Down's syndrome, but learning and other difficulties associated with it can be addressed if appropriate help is offered and other people behave in an inclusive way. Above all, it is important to stress that children with Down's syndrome are individuals and vary in their abilities and achievements and the barriers they experience to their learning.

A 'syndrome' is a combination of factors that regularly occur together. Down's syndrome is a congenital condition – one present at birth – first described by an English doctor, John Langdon Down, in 1866. Down's syndrome occurs because each of the body's cells contain an extra copy of chromosome 21. This means it can be identified in a foetus through amniocentesis during pregnancy or in a baby at birth. In the UK, around one baby in every thousand, around 775 per year (www.nhs.uk/conditions/downs-syndrome/pages/introduction.aspx), is born with Down's syndrome, although, statistically, it is much more common with older mothers. At maternal age 20, the probability is one in 1,450 and at age 45 it is one in 35 (Morris *et al.*, 2003). There is also data to suggest that paternal age, especially beyond 42, is associated with a greater incidence of a child being born with Down's syndrome (Fisch *et al.*, 2003).

Gower College Swansea
Library
Coleg Gŵyr Abertawe
Llyrfgell

The medical consequences of the extra genetic material are highly variable; the function of any organ system or bodily process may be affected. Young children with Down's are at higher risk of congenital heart defects, for example (Selikowitz, 2008), where the incidence is up to 50 per cent (Freeman *et al.*, 1998). Eye disorders are common. Almost half have strabismus, where the eyes do not move in tandem (Yurdakul *et al.*, 2006). In the past, there was also a high incidence of hearing loss among young children with Down's syndrome, but, in recent years, with more systematic diagnosis and treatment of ear disease such as 'glue ear' (see page 110 below) almost all children have normal hearing levels.

Commonly, young children with Down's syndrome have a speech delay (Bird and Thomas, 2002), and it is common for receptive language skills to surpass expressive. Overall cognitive development is quite variable which underlines the importance of highlighting individuality during assessment of young children individually (Selikowitz, 2008). Fine motor skills often develop more slowly than gross motor skills with consequent delay to cognitive development. Development of gross motor skills is variable. Some children will begin walking at around 2 years of age, while others not until age 4. Some may benefit from physiotherapy, and/or participation in other specially adapted programmes of physical education that promote development of these skills.

One parent's strategies for addressing difficulties associated with Down's syndrome

Down's syndrome cannot be cured, but the learning and other difficulties associated with it can be addressed if appropriate help is offered and other people accept and include. Above all, it is important to stress that children with Down's syndrome are individuals and vary in their abilities and achievements as well as the barriers they experience to their learning.

A number of accounts of parenting children who experience difficulties of various kinds have been published at different times. Hebden (1985), for example, described how she first realised that her daughter had Down's syndrome at a time, 1961, when children were called 'mongols', and their experience of difficulties 'handicaps'. She says (Hebden, 1985, pp. 18–19)

> [Cathy's] first birthday came and passed. One day I was … with Cathy in her push-chair, when I met an old friend whom I had not seen for years.
>
> After exchanging greetings … she glanced down at Cathy.
>
> 'And this is your latest, is it?' Her expression altered slightly, then she said in a bright but casual manner: 'Oh, she's a little mongol, bless her!'
>
> I stared at her, shock like an icy hand, clutching at my heart.
>
> 'No – no – she's not!' I heard myself stammering.
>
> 'Oh, but she is, love. I've been working with them for years and there's no mistaking –' She evidently read and understood the expression on my face. 'Oh, Lord! Hadn't they told you? I'm so sorry –'
>
> I mumbled something unintelligible, turned and stumbled out of the store into the harsh, unsympathetic brightness of the sunlight outside. It took me only five minutes to reach home, running all the way.

Hebden (1985, p. 50) reports that, in the beginning, her husband:

> did not want to consider the possibility of Cathy being handicapped and therefore studiously avoided all discussion of the subject. I could not understand his attitude at all, but I was later to find out that this was a typical reaction on the part of the father.

She reflects, however, that, with the advent of early counselling and support for new parents, the fathers are as much in evidence as the mothers at parent meetings.

In the early 1960s, there seemed to be little attempt by professionals to focus on the positives of what a child with Down's syndrome might achieve.

> The so-called experts seemed to concentrate solely on stressing the difficulties to parents, pointing out what the child could not, and never would, do.
>
> (Hebden, 1985, p. 66)

The author therefore realised that (1985, p. 66)

> The only thing to do ... was to work out a system of my own. ... Without realising that my child was mentally handicapped I had managed to carry out all the basic training that I had given my other children. ...

She describes how she began:

> By letting her grip my fingers while I carefully raised and lowered her, I had finally taught her to sit up on her own. These exercises were interspersed with gentle massage and a certain amount of stimulation by moving her limbs rhythmically while I sang to her. Of course, once she could sit up on her own a whole range of new experiences opened up to her, she ... was able to reach out and grasp the toys and other articles I placed nearby. These she could examine at her leisure by touch, taste and sight and even by hearing.

Eventually, at the age of 23

> Cathy Hebden became a national heroine. Born with Down's Syndrome and written off as ineducable by the professionals who assessed her in childhood, she nevertheless became the first person with this handicap to win the Duke of Edinburgh's Gold Award, competing against people with 'normal' levels of ability.

That Cathy achieved this

> is largely due to the intelligence and determination of her mother. ... Joan Hebden ... proceeded to treat her in exactly the same way as her previous three children. ... Certainly Cathy took longer to reach each stage of development, but with patience and persistence she got there in the end.
>
> (Hebden, 1985, back cover)

Dyslexia

Dyslexia among learners in educational contexts is known as 'developmental dyslexia', as opposed to dyslexia that is acquired as a result of brain injury. It is a psychological explanation of difficulties in learning in which the information-processing system of dyslexic individuals is seen as different from that of non-dyslexics. Being dyslexic does not necessarily mean that a young child will not learn to read, but they will complete literacy tasks slower than their peers and are very likely to experience difficulty with spelling. We are increasingly aware of the significance of the learning environment in exacerbating or minimising the effect of a young child's dyslexia. School curricula are so focused on the acquisition and application of literacy skills that dyslexic difficulties may well create barriers in other areas of the curriculum. They are very likely to be fatigued because they have to work much harder than others to achieve a competent level of literacy (Wearmouth, 2004). Besides, the more skilled readers read the more skilful they become, and the more the gap grows between competent, practised readers and those who struggle and read less, the so-called 'Matthew effect' (Stanovich, 1986).

Neuroimaging studies examining brain anatomy and function of people with and without dyslexia have yielded useful information about dyslexia. For example, functional magnetic resonance imaging (FMRI) is widely used to study the brain's role in reading and its components (phonology, orthography and semantics). FMRI assumes that activity in the brain where neurons are 'firing' is associated with an increase of blood flow to that specific part of the brain. From this signal, researchers infer the location and amount of activity that is associated with a task, such as reading single words that the research participants are performing in the scanner. It seems that reading is supported by activation in a network of regions in the left hemisphere of the brain, most clearly the language centres (Price, 2012), but that there may be activation of other centres as well. This is hardly surprising given that reading involves multiple processes.

Some of the brain regions known to be involved in dyslexia are also altered by learning to read, as demonstrated by comparisons of adults who were illiterate but then learned to read (Carreiras *et al.*, 2009), which is a very important consideration in thinking about whether or not dyslexic learners in the early years are destined never to be able to acquire literacy to a competent level.

Impact on performance

The difference in the information processing system of dyslexic children may have an impact on a number of areas of performance. Some researchers define dyslexia only in relation to difficulty in acquiring literacy as reflected by its derivation from Classical Greek: δυσ (dys), meaning 'bad' or 'difficult', and λεξις (lexis), meaning 'word' or 'speech'. A recurring focus in the study of dyslexia has been on phonological skills: the ability to recognise and apply speech sounds as they are used in words, especially as they are used in reading and writing (Snowling, 2000). Difficulties in encoding the phonological features of words (that is, the sound system of a language) are core to the difficulties experienced by dyslexic children:

> Dyslexia is a specific form of language impairment that affects the way in which the brain encodes the phonological features of spoken words. The core deficit is in phonological processing ... Dyslexia specifically affects the development of reading and spelling skills.

> (Snowling, 2000, pp. 213–214)

The British Psychological Society (BPS) working party adopted this view of dyslexia as related solely to literacy:

> Dyslexia is evident when accurate and fluent reading and or spelling develops very incompletely or with great difficulty. This focuses on literacy learning at the 'word level' and implies that the problem is severe and persistent despite appropriate learning opportunities. It provides the basis for a staged process of assessment through teaching.
> (British Psychological Society, 1999, p. 18)

Discussion of dyslexia may also include difficulties associated with mathematics, music and rhythm and organisational and sequencing and there is continuing debate about whether they are part of a dyslexic profile or personal to the individual. It may also include a wider range of aspects of information-processing: difficulties in co-ordination, personal organisation, balance, patterning, directionality (right/left confusion), sequencing, rhythm, orientation, memory and so on.

Effect at pre-school and primary levels

Riddick, Wolfe and Lumsdon (2002, pp. 12–13) describe various areas in which dyslexia affects young children's performance. At the pre-school level there may be a delay in spoken language, including difficulty in learning nursery rhymes and verbal sequencing, for example, days of the week and letters of the alphabet. There may also be poor gross motor co-ordination, for example, in learning to ride a bicycle or swim, poor fine motor skills, for example, in copying shapes and letters, and poor short term memory, for example, remembering a sequence of instructions and/or names.

At the primary age, a dyslexic child is likely to experience difficulties in reading, writing, spelling and number work. The child may be unable to identify rhythm and alliteration, or read single words accurately. S/he may reverse some words, for example, 'pot' and 'top', miss out whole lines and read some sections of text twice without realising it and have better understanding of text than word accuracy. Reading age for fluency and accuracy is likely to be below chronological age. A child may spell the same word different ways in the same text, spell incorrectly words learnt for spelling tests, make several attempts to spell words with frequent crossings out, spell phonetically but incorrectly, use what look like bizarre spellings, for example, 'bidar' for 'because', leave out syllables, for example, 'onge' for 'orange', or part of a letter blend especially when there is a blend of three letters, for example, 'sred' for 'shred', reverse letters, especially 'b' and 'd', 'p' and 'q'. S/he may experience difficulty copying from the board, produce work that is chaotic or very untidy, begin writing anywhere on the page, confuse upper and lower case letters, produce very little output and what there is may be unintelligible even to the child.

If such difficulties persist over time, despite systematic, appropriate teaching, especially if the child is distressed, a teacher or family member might begin to reflect on the possibility of dyslexic tendencies.

Identifying dyslexic tendencies and difficulties in literacy acquisition

The Rose Review on identifying and teaching dyslexic children (Rose, 2009, p. 30) identifies dyslexia as a learning difficulty associated with 'difficulties in phonological awareness, verbal memory and verbal processing speed' that 'affects the skills involved in accurate and fluent word reading and spelling', but also acknowledges a wider range of information-processing difficulties in various 'aspects of language, motor co-ordination, mental calculation, concentration and personal organisation'. However, these aspects alone are not markers of dyslexia. A 'good indication' is the extent to which 'the individual responds or has responded to well-founded intervention'. In other words, as the BPS (1999) implies also, if a child experiences difficulties but has not received good teaching, then it cannot be assumed that s/he is dyslexic.

There are both formal and more informal ways of identifying dyslexic tendencies and difficulties in literacy acquisition more generally.

Formal diagnostic criteria

The International Classification of Diseases, tenth revision, that tends to be used in Europe (WHO, 2016), describes 'Specific developmental disorders of scholastic skills' (F81) under which it classifies a 'specific reading disorder' as:

> The main feature is a specific and significant impairment in the development of reading skills that is not solely accounted for by mental age, visual acuity problems, or inadequate schooling. Reading comprehension skill, reading word recognition, oral reading skill, and performance of tasks requiring reading may all be affected. Spelling difficulties are frequently associated with specific reading disorder and often remain into adolescence even after some progress in reading has been made. Specific developmental disorders of reading are commonly preceded by a history of disorders in speech or language development. Associated emotional and behavioural disturbances are common during the school age period. (F81.0)

A 'specific spelling disorder' is classified as:

> The main feature is a specific and significant impairment in the development of spelling skills in the absence of a history of specific reading disorder, which is not solely accounted for by low mental age, visual acuity problems, or inadequate schooling. The ability to spell orally and to write out words correctly are both affected. (F81.1)

Norm-referenced testing

A number of norm-referenced test instruments that include tests of reading accuracy, comprehension, spelling and handwriting have been developed to identify indicators characteristic of dyslexia. Norm-referenced test results are designed to compare a child's score with scores of a whole population. However, in the early years in particular, these instruments cannot identify dyslexia with certainty in part because to be dyslexic implies experiencing difficulties in literacy that are intractable over a long period of time. As a result, they claim to identify tendencies and potential likely to require focused support.

Early Years Foundation Stage Profile assessment

In England, difficulties in literacy acquisition might also be identified and learning plans designed to address needs in relation to the *Early Years Foundation Stage Profile* (STA, 2016) assessment that has now been extended until at least 2017. This assessment defines literacy development as:

> encouraging children to read and write, both through listening to others reading, and being encouraged to begin to read and write themselves. Children must be given access to a wide range of reading materials – for example books, poems, and other materials to ignite their interest.
>
> (2016, p. 25)

A child's level of reading acquisition can be profiled against the following statement (Early Learning Goal 09):

> Reading: Children read and understand simple sentences. They use phonic knowledge to decode regular words and read them aloud accurately. They also read some common irregular words. They demonstrate an understanding when talking with others about what they have read.

Writing should be profiled as follows (Early Learning Goal 10):

> Writing: Children use their phonic knowledge to write words in ways which match their spoken sounds. They also write some irregular common words. They write simple sentences which can be read by themselves and others. Some words are spelt correctly and others are phonetically plausible.

Reflective activity: implications of profiling young children's literacy development

Have another look at the statements above for reading and writing in the *EYFS* profile assessment. Note down your responses to the following:

- How appropriate do you feel the levels expected in the profile are for the Reception-aged child in general?
- To what extent do you feel it is appropriate to expect very young children in one year group all to be at the same level regardless of age differences when the ages of children in Reception can be almost 12 months apart, that is, 25 per cent of their life experiences?
- In your experience, might there be any concern that practitioners and teachers will feel the need to drill and directly teach the skills over longer periods of time during the day than is necessary so that goals drive the literacy curriculum?
- What do you consider might be the advantages and disadvantages of such profiles for young children who experience difficulties in learning and/or literacy acquisition?

Early years phonics screening check

The introduction, in England, in 2012 of the early years phonics screening check at age 6 is a further early test of literacy skills (DfE, 2016a). This check is intended to assess children's phonological knowledge through the accuracy of reading of twenty real and twenty non-words. The rationale underpinning this is that children will be forced to work out the sound of the non-words phonologically. One criticism of this test, however, is that competent readers who understand the purpose of reading for meaning will try to read the non-words as if they are real and, hence, may mispronounce them and thus confound the test results.

Identification through noticing

Observation is a very important aspect of identifying any particular cause for concern in children's learning in the early years. Such observations can provide information about how a child behaves, but not usually the reason for this. As will be further discussed in Chapter 8, observations may be informal and unstructured, or structured and systematic.

Pavey (2016) comments that, informally, a teacher might 'start to wonder about' possible difficulties a young child experiences in literacy development if s/he displays any or all of the following:

- lack of interest in printed texts or books;
- reluctance to engage in, or slowness in completing, literacy-based activities such as retrieving or finding words;
- poor memory for nursery rhymes and word games;
- difficulty in recognising rhyme or repeating simple rhythmic patterns;
- confusion in word choices.

Persistence and severity over time may suggest possible dyslexia.

Purposeful listening to a child's reading provides a useful opportunity to assess and monitor the acquisition of reading. Alternatively, an observer may well choose to use some kind of observation schedule that records aspects of the learning environment, including the teacher's teaching approach, availability and nature of the texts in use, classroom displays of the outcomes of literacy-based activities that may affect the child's literacy learning and so on. 'Time sampling' may be used to record an activity or behaviour at pre-specified times, or 'event sampling' may be chosen to record how often a particular behaviour occurs.

Ways to address dyslexic-type difficulties

Pavey (2016) offers a number of approaches to teaching literacy in the early years that are appropriate for dyslexic children, for example:

- Using a multi-sensory approach that includes combining visual and auditory techniques and motor movement, for example, looking, listening, reading, writing and saying words simultaneously or in quick succession and using a range of tactile stimuli. Children might write letters or words with their fingers in sand or on coarse-grained paper, in large letters or in three-dimensional shapes, saying the sounds as they do so. Or they might tap out the rhythm or sequence of sounds in sentences;
- Giving instructions in a restricted number of small steps, with a visual representation of each if necessary;
- Including games and practice in reading and spelling through the numerous software programs that are available and are designed to create a sense of fun as well

as learning. Two well-known computer programs are Wordshark (/www.wordshark. co.uk/wordshark.aspx) that incorporates games for reading and spelling with an integral reward system, and Successmaker (www.pearsonschoolsandfecolleges.co.uk/ Primary/Mathematics/AllMathematicsresources/Successmaker/SuccessMaker.aspx) that includes literacy, language and mathematics activities. Both are designed for children from aged 5, are commonly used for those children who experience difficulties and contain assessment records;

- Using rhymes, songs and games as a way to encourage remembering important facts or sequences;
- Using mnemonics to support memory;
- Using larger font sizes for text on a light-coloured, but not white, background;
- Finding creative ways to enable young children to show what they can do, rather than relying largely on the written form;
- Using visual representations and keeping these close to written text.

Where there is left-right confusion, it is the experience of one of the current authors that one side should be taught and repeated over and over before there is any attempt to teach the other side. If both are taught together there is a danger that children will forever be confused about which is which. Use of mnemonic can reinforce memory for the first side that is taught.

As Stansfield (2014) notes, there are similarities between the learning attributes of very young children and those older children with dyslexia. These include 'difficulties of short-term memory, distractibility, letter or number reversals, sequencing issues, difficulties around language and both gross and fine motor skills' (Pavey, 2016, p. 18). The difference is that young children with dyslexia will experience these difficulties over a longer period of time. This suggests that literacy activities designed to build concepts for younger children may need to be provided for longer and designed to be developmentally appropriate. Pavey describes 'putting in a step' when a young child struggles to learn a letter or sound. Effectively, this is precision teaching. It means identifying the child's current level of skill, knowledge and/or understanding, having a clear view of what the learning target is and working out very small steps in between them that the child can achieve in sequence. For many children with dyslexic-type difficulties, adopting a multi-sensory approach to teaching and learning can be very powerful.

Reflective activity: feasibility and usefulness of multi-sensory approaches for young dyslexic children

Pavey (2016, p. 20) offers an example of a multi-sensory approach to teaching sounds and letters:

'... a child who is struggling to remember a letter shape or a sound might remember it better by drawing it, modelling it in clay or some other material, scribing it in the playground by writing with a 'squirty' bottle, matching it to a physical movement, handling it, or drawing or modelling a picture or object to remind themselves of it ... a child who is experiencing possible dyslexia may need a lot of help of this kind, over a long time, and perhaps involving several small steps, plus recall and rehearsal'.

Young children who experience dyslexic-type difficulties are likely to need this kind of approach for much longer than peers.

- How do you think practitioners in early years settings might integrate this approach for individuals into activities that all young children can access?
- How might practitioners involve family members in supporting their children in this way?

Simple games, using plastic or wooden letters, or cards with target sounds or words on them, that can be home-made or published, can be used to reinforce letters, sounds or whole words.

A number of educators, for example, Pavey (2016) and Reid (2017), note how important it can be for children with dyslexic-type difficulties to continue building foundational skills to support literacy learning past the point where formal teaching of literacy has begun. Activities might include a focus on:

- precision in listening, through identifying voices and sounds, counting and repeating beats and rhythms and repeating songs and rhymes;
- the articulation of speech sounds, through, for example, exaggerating the opening of mouths for fun in singing, talking and reciting;
- developing a sense of rhythm through clapping syllables in words in, for example, games where one group might clap one pattern whilst, simultaneously, another group claps a different pattern;
- remembering new words or the sequence of story narratives through drawing, painting and modelling in a discrete area of the classroom where required resources are available;
- using new words in expressive language through retelling stories, seeing who can use a new word during the school day and so on;
- visual discrimination through shape-matching and sorting activities whilst the child verbalises the way in which s/he is setting about finding the solution;
- sequencing and organisation, through using construction toys, setting out the order of toys by shape, colour, size and so on, making storyboards of familiar activities in arranging the elements in the logical sequence, for example, feeding a pet;
- fine motor skills, for example, making a game of tying shoe laces supported by think-alouds to add to the multi-sensory aspect of the activity;
- memory, through developing personally meaningful mnemonics, techniques to enable individuals to enable memorisation of something. Objects or letters that look similar should not be taught together, otherwise there is the probability that they will forever be confused. Instead, one should be taught first.

Many of these strategies are effective practice in early years but may need to be used for a longer period with some dyslexic children.

Summary

The way in which 'cognition' is generally understood in the area of SEND relates largely to information-processing associated with problem-solving, language, perception and memory and the development of concepts. Difficulties in cognition experienced by some young children clearly overlap with those in the area of communication and interaction discussed on p. 71 of this chapter. Dyslexia, for example, is commonly understood as a psychological explanation of learning difficulties in which individuals' information-processing systems are implicated, but it also clearly affects communication.

With regard to moderate and profound cognitive difficulties that young children may experience, it is very useful to have a grasp of the learning process so that we can take a principled approach to thinking about, and planning how to, address learning needs. Young children who experience difficulties in cognition are very likely to need much more time than peers without such difficulty to absorb and understand new concepts, with representation through concrete objects, using an enactive mode to learn by doing. It can be effective to devise approaches that understand this need.

Chapter 5

Understanding and addressing social, emotional and mental health needs

Major questions addressed in this chapter are:

- What kind of understandings of young children's behaviour are helpful in thinking about how positively to address social, emotional or mental health difficulties?
- What are some of the interventions and programmes that are effective in meeting young children's needs in these areas?

Introduction

The third broad area of need outlined in the *Code of Practice* in England is now described as 'social, emotional and mental health' (DfE, 2015a, §5.32). This has been amended from the description 'behaviour, social and emotional development' in the previous *Code* (DfES, 2001, §7.52). In relation to children in the early years, as to other young people, the new *Code* advises:

> Children … may experience a wide range of social and emotional difficulties which manifest themselves in many ways. These may include becoming withdrawn or isolated, as well as displaying challenging, disruptive or disturbing behaviour. These behaviours may reflect underlying mental health difficulties such as anxiety or depression, self-harming, substance misuse, eating disorders or physical symptoms that are medically unexplained. Other children … may have disorders such as attention deficit disorder, attention deficit hyperactive disorder or attachment disorder.
>
> (DfE, 2015a, §6.32)

Similar kinds of behaviours are outlined in the *Code* in Wales:

> Children and young people who demonstrate features of emotional and behavioural difficulties, who are withdrawn or isolated, disruptive and disturbing, hyperactive and lack concentration; those with immature social skills; and those presenting challenging behaviours arising from other complex special needs.
>
> (NAW, 2004, §7:60)

In this chapter we begin by reviewing a range of frameworks within which behaviour seen as problematic in settings and schools is commonly understood. We go on to discuss a number of interventions and programmes designed to address social, emotional and mental health needs.

Giving meaning to behaviour

The way we understand, and give meaning to, young children's behaviour linked to 'social and emotional difficulties' and/or 'mental health difficulties' is really important. Over time, since the advent of compulsory primary education in the nineteenth century, a number of different descriptors have been used to describe children whose behaviour is seen as worrying. Some descriptors imply that there is a universally accepted position on what behaviours are normal or acceptable and what are not, for example, delinquent, maladaptive and anti-social. Still others imply more about the way in which specific behaviours affect other people than they do about the behaviours themselves, for example, 'challenging, disruptive or disturbing' behaviour (DfE, 2015a, §6.32). The change of category from 'behaviour, social and emotional development' in the previous *Code* (DfES, 2001, §7.52) to 'social, emotional and mental health' in the current *Code* in England is a case in point. In adopting the 'health' view, it appears to locate the problem within the young child, in other words to assume the deficit or 'medical' model of a difficulty that can be treated like a disease (Wearmouth, 2009), instead of acknowledging very clearly that behaviour may also be the result of external factors such as the context in which it occurs, including peers and adults. The point here really is that the way in which causes of behaviour are understood matters because it can have a strong effect on the way families and practitioners in early years settings and schools deal with young children. As Poulou and Norwich (2002, p. 125) concluded from a review of international studies, the more teachers, and, one might add, families, think problematic behaviour stems from problems within the child him/herself, 'the more they experience feelings of "stress", "offence" and even "helplessness", especially for conduct and mixed behaviour difficulties'. Following a similar line of thinking, Bennathan (2000, p. 5) comments in relation to a previous category 'emotional and behavioural difficulties' that was introduced by Warnock (DES, 1978):

> … children with EBD should not be seen as a race apart. Understanding the processes that make a few children incontrovertibly 'EBD' helps to a greater awareness of the potential hazards for many more of the children in our schools. It can lead to an increased awareness of the emotional needs of all children, an understanding which ought to be part of the professional competence of all teachers.

The example of 'maladjustment'

One of the problems with categorising young children's behaviour is that descriptors developed within a particular national context at a particular time period become pervasive and 'sticky' and it may be difficult to think outside current discourses. The history of the rise and demise of the term 'maladjusted' within special education illustrates this point. The origins of the term 'maladjusted' can be traced back to the 1913 Mental Deficiency Act. This Act 'created a category of moral imbeciles or defectives, and children who displayed emotionally disturbed or disruptive behaviour [that] came to be associated with both mental defect and moral defect (Galloway *et al.*, 1994, p. 110). In 1945, the formal category of 'maladjusted' was enshrined in government regulations as a category of child requiring special educational treatment. Subsequently, all local education authorities had a responsibility to establish special educational treatment in special or ordinary schools for 'maladjusted' children, even though what constitutes 'maladjustment' was not clearly defined. The Underwood Committee was set up in 1950 to enquire into 'maladjusted' students' medical, educational and social problems. An overall definition of what constitutes 'maladjustment' proved difficult. The subsequent report (Underwood, 1955, chapter IV, para 96) listed six 'disorders' indicative of 'maladjustment' and identified as requiring professional help from psychologists, child guidance clinics or doctors: 'nervous', 'habit', 'behaviour', 'organic', 'psychotic' and 'educational and vocational difficulties'. The 'common point to emerge … is that it is a ragbag term describing any kind of behaviour that teachers and parents find disturbing' (Galloway and Goodwin, 1987, p. 32). However, invent the category, create the student (Wearmouth, 2016b). From nil in 1945, by 1960, there were 1,742 students classified as maladjusted and by 1975, there were 13,000 'maladjusted' students (Furlong, 1985).

'Maladjustment' is thus a vague term. Nevertheless, there is a major problem in that once a category has been 'invented' it tends to float around waiting to 'gobble up' victims (Mehan, 1996). 'Jack', for example, was a participant in a series of interviews with adult male inmates in one of HM prisons (Wearmouth, 1999). He related how he was born into an unsettled family and taken into care at an early age as a result of his parents' divorce.

> Social Services were involved in his life from an early stage. When he started infant school he was deemed to be out of control because he used to run around, disrupt classrooms, upset the dustbins in the school yard and climb on to the roof. He was quickly referred to an educational psychologist for an assessment of his behaviour.
>
> (Wearmouth, 2016b, p. 139)

The psychologist identified him as 'maladjusted' and social services and the local education authority decided to send him away to a boarding school for 'maladjusted' pupils at 6 years of age. These days Jack would not be identified as 'maladjusted' because the category is no longer in use, but 'thus began his career in special schools, firstly through his primary years and then through secondary' (ibid.).

Current frameworks for understanding behaviour

Currently, there exists a number of different frameworks within which the behaviour of young children who display features of 'social, emotional and mental health difficulties' may be understood. For example, difficulty in interacting with peers may be interpreted in various ways. Some young children may simply not have learnt what kind of behaviour is generally seen as appropriate in social contexts in families, early years settings or schools. Some may not have developed the strong bonds with caregivers that are often seen as prerequisites to later confident socialising with peers and adults. They may be anxious as a result of disruptions, stresses and/or bereavement in their own families. Factors, for example, bereavement, can cause intolerable stress with a huge impact on the children in the family. In an interview (Wearmouth, 2016a, pp. 167–8), an inmate of one of HM prisons related the following experience from his early childhood:

> … when I was seven years old, my mum was killed in a car crash and this seemed to devastate our family you know. My dad turned to drink and I had a sister, a year old sister and up until then it was kind of a normal happy life really, you know. I remember before then I was just a normal child, you know …. Fairly soon my dad met another woman and we moved in with her. She had two kids, and we kind of moved in with the kids and everything but he wasn't very happy at all – always drank pints … She didn't like me very much this lady and I was relegated really … She would compare us, me and the oldest son who was going to grow up to be a lady killer, but I was an ugly bastard. It was quite cruel stuff … We … lived in her house but occasionally they would argue and fight and he would, you know … real physical violence, and she would throw my dad out! So, he would take me and my sister down to the local police station.

Some young children may be frustrated and depressed if they experience dyslexic-type difficulties because they cannot engage in literacy-related activities in the same way as peers, or may be disorganised and jumbled in their day-to-day living. They may experience difficulty in social interactions or with isolation associated with autism or with long-term medical conditions, or with a sensory impairment that precludes seeing and hearing the world around them in the same way as peers.

Behaviourist understandings

Behavioural methodologies hold that all behaviour is learned. It can be unlearned, therefore, through intervening in the environment and teaching behaviour that is more socially appropriate. Where the problem is located determines the location of the solution. Discourses which locate behaviour difficulties as an individual attribute can ignore contextual factors that influence behaviour: family, early years settings and schools (Wearmouth, Glynn and Berryman, 2005).

Understanding the principles underlying behavioural approaches is particularly important in the area of special educational needs in settings and schools because of the dominance of these approaches in underpinning interventions over a long period of time (Wearmouth, 2016a, b). Behavioural researchers strive to find ways of talking about behaviour that focus on what is observed, not on identifying 'inner', subconscious, causes of behaviour. There are two different ways of looking at this:

- First, research over a long period of time (Glynn, 1982) suggests that elements of a setting may exert powerful control over behaviour. It may be that something about a particular learning environment, for example, the physical properties or the presence or behaviour of an adult, has provoked good, or alternatively poor, behaviour and that the young people have come to associate good, or poor behaviour, with that setting. In his interview Jack described how the lack of structure and disorganisation in the secondary special school for maladjusted pupils to which he was transferred led very predictably to frustration, rage and very uncontrolled behaviour:

  > The school was total crap. It was rubbish. It was totally unorganised. There was no foresight in the school at all. There was no purpose. I wasn't studying towards

exams, I was going over the same things again. The things they tried to teach me, I'd already done it. ... I was laughing in their face because I knew how far they could push, how far they can go. I've been in children's homes and in boarding schools, so I know exactly how far they can go with you. When they overstepped the mark I was the first one to step in there and say: 'You can't do that!'

(Wearmouth, 2016b: 147)

In behaviourist terms we would consider that the setting has created 'antecedent conditions' for that good, or poor, behaviour to occur. If a parent, carer or practitioner can work out what these antecedent conditions are, s/he can modify (mis)behaviour through intervening in that environment and altering the setting in which the behaviour occurs.

- Second, particular behaviour can be learned if it is rewarded and thus reinforced, especially if this is done in a consistent, predictable way. Many behaviourist principles were derived from work with laboratory animals. In a famous sequence of trial-and-error learning tasks related to the effective use of rewards, rats learned to press levers in order to find food (Skinner, 1938). Pressing the lever resulted in a reward, finding food. Learning involved the formation of an action-response association in the rats' memory. If the reward of food was removed, the rats' behaviour would gradually cease through 'extinction'. Translating this interpretation into human terms, young children can learn how to behave appropriately in response to positive reinforcement (rewards). When young children behave badly, a parent, carer or teacher might work out whatever it is that seems to be reinforcing (rewarding) this behaviour and remove the reward(s). Whenever they behave more appropriately, s/he might reward them in a way that recognises the greater acceptability of the new behaviour.

The opposite of positive reinforcement is negative reinforcement. From this view, families and practitioners can encourage compliance at home and in settings and classrooms by making home, setting or classroom rules and the consequences for unacceptable behaviour very clear. Children may learn appropriate behaviour through avoiding punishment.

Applying behaviourist principles to teach socially acceptable behaviour

There is a lot of evidence to demonstrate that approaches derived from behavioural methodologies can be effective in establishing positive behaviour and reducing incidents of disruption or challenging behaviour. When behavioural principles are applied at home, in early years settings, classrooms and schools, the reinforcing conditions or consequences of behaviour as well as the physical and social context in which the behaviour occurs can be systematically modified in order to improve children's behaviour.

Use of applied behaviour analysis to address individual challenging behaviours

The field of applied behaviour analysis employs strategies based on behavioural principles such as positive reinforcement, negative reinforcement, response cost, extinction, generalisation and discrimination. We illustrate the process with reference to an early paper of an educator working from behaviourist principles (Merrett, 1985). Whilst this work may appear dated, given that it was written 30 years ago, since that time a number of well-known educators, some very recently, have followed a very similar line, for example, Rogers (2013) and Watkins and Wagner (2000).

Behavioural methodology is a scientifically based technology. Therefore, and as we note in Chapter 8, the first requirement is a clear definition of the target behaviour which is of concern. For instance, if a child is thought to be 'hyperactive,' an objective, non-evaluative description of behaviours such as 'out of seat' is needed. Once the behaviour has been defined, systematic observational sampling across times of day, situations, nature of activity, person in charge and so on is required. Such observations need to be taken over a period of about 5 days to establish the baseline level of responding. Subsequently, the evidence from the observations is analysed to identify antecedents, behaviour and consequences:

A – the antecedent event(s), that is, whatever starts off or prompts;

B – the behaviour, which is followed in turn by;

C – the consequence(s).

… If it is possible to identify the setting or the prompt then it may be possible to change the behaviour by changing one or the other of these. Alternatively, identification of the consequences, whether positively reinforcing or aversive, which are controlling the behaviour also allows us to intervene with a good chance of success. … The reasoning is very direct. Teachers aim to change their pupil's behaviour. Behaviours are changed chiefly by changing the consequences. Therefore, teachers change their pupil's behaviours by changing the consequences of classroom behaviour. … When a consequence of a behaviour is shown to be maintaining that behaviour at a high level then that consequence is, by definition, and regardless of its nature, reinforcing it positively. … If that positive reinforcement is removed then the rate of occurrence of the behaviour will be reduced. It will eventually become extinguished.

(Merrett, 1985, p. 8)

Establishing positive antecedent conditions

Antecedent conditions, in other words the physical properties, such as space, arrangement of furniture, availability of toys and resources, including siblings or peers, adults at home and in classrooms, playgrounds and other areas, may exert a very powerful control over children's behaviour. Parents, carers and practitioners are in a very good position to make changes in the learning environment to bring about improvement in behaviour where required.

Young children look towards adults for a sense of security and order, an opportunity to participate in activities at home and in early years settings and in the classroom. Establishing the feeling of safety, being able to learn without disruption and being respected and treated fairly is essential as the basis for instituting clear rules and routines (Rogers, 2013). From this perspective, it is obvious why the behaviour of Jack, mentioned above, was so lacking in control while he was very young. He had no one setting and maintaining boundaries for him. Parents, carers and teachers who are able to control children most effectively are those who can command respect and, often but not always, those whom children like. In early years settings and schools, these teachers know how to get the best out of young children (DES, 1989; DfES, 2006).

Ways to reinforce young children's positive behaviour

In Rogers' (2013) view, a child's background is no excuse for poor behaviour because appropriate behaviour can be taught. The way in which parents, carers and teachers reward behaviour, sometimes inadvertently, by their own actions can be a very strong reinforcer of good, or poor, behaviour. Adults therefore need to know that changing children's behaviour using behaviourist approaches depends on consistency in their own behaviour around and towards young children. As Berryman and Glynn (2001) comment, behaviour learnt most readily has consistent positive consequences: social attention, praise, recognition, access to favourite activities and so on.

Procedures or strategies to maximise children's learning of new behaviours and/or skills can include 'shaping' or successive approximations either through forward chaining or backward chaining, which break complex tasks down into compound steps, and ensures that each step is reinforced in a particular sequence. To be effective in teaching a new behaviour, positive reinforcement must be applied contingently, immediately, consistently and abundantly. Reinforcers can be tangible and social reinforcers, for example, smiles, praise and social attention, and also access to enjoyable social interaction or shared activities with adults or peers.

It may well be possible to address a young child's inappropriate and/or disruptive or even aggressive behaviour by defining another behaviour that is incompatible with the undesirable behaviour, modelling this and reinforcing it with positive consequences. For example, in the author's local community, some primary schools were experiencing problems of aggressive, bullying and violent behaviour at break times. After some deliberation, the teachers took the decision to organise group games at lunchtime when the problem was at its worst. This helped to solve the problem. Whilst the pupils were involved in the games – and were enjoying themselves and learning how to socialise with peers in doing so – they could not at the same time engage in anti-social behaviour. Similarly, the use of Play Pods, large metal containers filled with a mixture of junk materials (such things as cable rolls, bread trays, rope, thick cardboard tubes and old tyres) termed 'loose parts' by Nicholson (1971), can encourage cooperative, creative play across a range of ages of children playing together. Play Pods offer opportunities for highly inclusive play for children of all ages and capacities. As Armitage (2009) demonstrated, using Play Pods can encourage improved behaviour of children at lunchtimes, with both adults and children sharing the enjoyment at these times, too.

Use of structured teaching to address behaviour relating to autism

A behaviourist understanding that inappropriate behaviour can be unlearnt and more appropriate behaviour learnt is an underpinning assumption of some of the more popular interventions used to address behavioural concerns associated with particular disabilities, for example, autism. One glance at the DSM-5 diagnostic criteria for an assessment of autism spectrum disorder that includes difficulties in social communication and social interaction, and persistent repetitive behaviour that inhibits socialising with peers and adults indicates how disabling these difficulties can be for a young child's social and emotional development. These criteria read as follows:

Autism Spectrum Disorder 299.00 (F84.0) (DSM-5)

A.   Persistent deficits in social communication and social interaction across multiple contexts, as manifested by the following, currently or by history …:

1.   Deficits in social-emotional reciprocity, ranging, for example, from abnormal social approach and failure of normal back-and-forth conversation;

to reduced sharing of interests, emotions or affect; to failure to initiate or respond to social interactions.

2. Deficits in nonverbal communicative behaviours used for social interaction, ranging, for example, from poorly integrated verbal and nonverbal communication; to abnormalities in eye contact and body language or deficits in understanding and use of gestures; to a total lack of facial expressions and nonverbal communication.

3. Deficits in developing, maintaining and understanding relationships, ranging, for example, from difficulties adjusting behaviour to suit various social contexts; to difficulties in sharing imaginative play or in making friends; to absence of interest in peers.

B. Restricted, repetitive patterns of behaviour, interests or activities, as manifested by at least two of the following, currently or by history (examples are illustrative, not exhaustive; see text):

1. Stereotyped or repetitive motor movements, use of objects, or speech (e.g., simple motor stereotypes, lining up toys or flipping objects, echolalia, idiosyncratic phrases).

2. Insistence on sameness, inflexible adherence to routines, or ritualized patterns or verbal nonverbal behaviour (e.g., extreme distress at small changes, difficulties with transitions, rigid thinking patterns, greeting rituals, need to take same route or eat food every day).

3. Highly restricted, fixated interests that are abnormal in intensity or focus (e.g., strong attachment to or preoccupation with unusual objects, excessively circumscribed or perseverative interest).

4. Hyper- or hyporeactivity to sensory input or unusual interests in sensory aspects of the environment (e.g., apparent indifference to pain/temperature, adverse response to specific sounds or textures, excessive smelling or touching of objects, visual fascination with lights or movement).

C. Symptoms must be present in the early developmental period (but may not become fully manifest until social demands exceed limited capacities, or may be masked by learned strategies in later life).
(www.autismspeaks.org/what-autism/diagnosis/dsm-5-diagnostic-criteria)

Children with 'marked' or 'severe' deficits in 'verbal and nonverbal social communication skills; social impairments apparent even with supports in place'; 'limited' or 'very limited initiation of social interactions; and reduced or abnormal responses to social overtures from others may be identified as autistic. For example, a person … whose interaction is limited to narrow special interests, and who has markedly odd nonverbal communication' is understood to need 'substantial', or 'very substantial' support to address these difficulties.

TEACCH programme

The primary aim of the TEACCH programme is to help prepare children with autism to live or work more effectively at home, at school and in the community. In this programme there is a special emphasis 'on helping people with autism and their families live together more effectively by reducing or removing "autistic behaviours"'(www.autism.org.uk/about/strategies/teacch.aspx).

The TEACCH approach was developed in the early 1970s by Eric Schopler (Schopler *et al.*, 1980; Schopler, 1997). It includes a focus on the individuality of the person with autism, 'the culture of autism' and the development of a programme around individual skills, interests and needs (Mesibov, 2015). The focus on individuality implies assessment that requires understanding children with autism as they are, and then building programmes around each child's skill levels to help them develop as far as they can go. Important, also, to any TEACCH programme is developing communication skills and the opportunity to pursue social and leisure interests.

References to 'the culture of autism' suggests that children with autism are part of a distinctive group with common characteristics that are different from peers. This implies not assuming a model of normal behaviour for every child where they are all expected to conform, whether that suits them or not. In his personal account of the experience of autism, Higashida (2014, p.16) emphasises the importance of not assuming that there is one 'normal' model of behaviour:

> … even a straightforward activity like shopping can be really challenging if I'm tackling it on my own. During my miserable, helpless, frustrating days, I've started imagining what it would be like if everyone was autistic. If autism was regarded simply as a personality type, things would be so much easier and happier for us than they are now. For sure there are bad times when we cause a lot of hassle for other people, but what we really want is to be able to look towards a brighter future.

Structured teaching is an important priority 'because of the TEACCH research and experience that structure fits the "culture of autism" more effectively than any other techniques we have observed' (Mesibov, 2015). This approach bears a close resemblance to a behaviourist understanding of learned behaviour. It advocates a clearly structured physical environment, development of schedules, expectations that are made clear and explicit, use of visual materials to represent, for example, timetables and precision teaching that breaks new skills and more appropriate behaviours into a clear hierarchy of development with specific targets and goals to measure progress. As we note elsewhere in the current publication, the Portage Programme that is offered in many areas in the UK has adopted the principles of precision teaching derived from behaviourist understandings of learning as a framework within which to conceptualise small, step-by-step interventions for young children to be carried out at home.

Young children who experience barriers to learning associated with other 'conditions' may also benefit from a similarly structured approach that builds on strengths and pays attention to the individual. As Bentley *et al.* (2016, p. 36) note, for example, children with Down's syndrome may also behave inappropriately at times, just like their peers, and may benefit from being taught how to behave and interact in a socially acceptable way. 'Increasing independence alleviates behavioural issues, so approaches such as TEACCH may benefit some pupils [with Down's syndrome]'.

Taking account of cultural values and preferences

From a behaviourist view, the specific behaviours identified as appropriate for reward or punishment are just as important as the choice of reinforcer. This is an area where cultural values, preferences and practices may be crucial in encouraging young children's behaviour. For example, some cultures value children's avoidance of eye contact with teachers or other authority figures as a means of showing respect. However, many adults of European descent may regard children's avoidance of eye contact as showing disrespect. Some cultural groups value individual achievement in a competitive context and families and teachers from these cultures may choose to reinforce individual high achievement. However, some cultures may value children's behaviours more highly that contribute to the well-being and achievement of the group.

Where practitioners are from different cultural groups from their children, they may 'mis-cue' in their application of behaviour management strategies. Gee (2000) illustrates this point vividly with an example of a small African-American girl who tells a story at the class 'sharing time'. The story was full of rhythm, pattern and repetition and had the other children's appreciation. The child was basing her story on an oral discourse which was valued in her community, namely that a story should be a good performance, an entertainment. The teacher, however, was looking for a different (unarticulated) discourse, that of being informative, linear and to the point, and did not appreciate the child's own poetic or entertainment discourse. This child was eventually sent to the school psychologist for telling tall tales.

We might make two very important points here, in relation to understanding cultural differences, and also the importance of fantasy play to children's learning and development:

- Clearly a considerable level of cultural knowledge and competence is required of practitioners intending to implement behaviourist approaches with students from cultural backgrounds different from their own;
- We noted in Chapter 2 that engaging in fantasy play occurs in all cultures and should be understood as helping young children understand the real world, take risks without endangering themselves and develop their emotional lives.

Implementing behavioural management strategies while ignoring issues of culture and play that are significant to young children will seriously limit their effectiveness.

Attachment theory

Although consistency in the use of behavioural approaches may be effective in changing young children's behaviour, they are often criticised also for failing to take adequate account of the emotions. As Hanko (1994) comments:

> … for children with problems, emotional factors affect learning, especially if we see only their provocative or withdrawn facade which usually hides children in constant misery, loneliness, self-loathing and fear.
>
> (Hanko, 1994, p. 166)

In Chapter 2, we discussed how attachment theory (Bowlby, 1952) is an example of a psychological theory of human development that takes account of the relationship between the emotions and behaviour and how it has been influential in some instances over educational provision for young children whose behaviour in settings and schools is challenging and anti-social. The scientific study of early childhood is now well established.

It is accepted that babies quickly attach themselves emotionally to their adult carers and progress through well-recognised stages of development towards maturity. Moving successfully to the next stage depends on needs having been adequately met at the earlier stage. If this is not the case, then:

> Unless there is skilful intervention they will persist in inappropriate attachment behaviour, whether over-anxious, or avoidant and aggressive, or will become quite incapable of warm attachment and therefore indifferent to human relationships (Harris-Hendriks and Figueroa, 1995).
>
> (Bennathan, 2000, p. 11)

Greenhalgh (1994) draws on attachment theory to argue that feelings affect the capacity to learn. The capacity for learning, that is the individual construction of the meaning of reality gained through experiences of operating in the world, depends on emotional growth. Relationships and sense of place in the wider world depend on emotional maturity (Salmon, 1998). The capacity for effective learning, Greenhalgh claims, depends on the development of:

- emotional safety and trust in others (Winnicott, 1984; Hirschorn, 1998) which has an essential implication for teacher and learner relationships;
- internal confidence or strength to perceive oneself as a separate person (Winnicott, 1984; Hirschorn, 1998) which has an implication for teachers to use transitional objects or strategies to enable learners to move from feelings of incompetence to competence, dependence to independence;
- a sense of inner security gained from attachment to a significant figure enabling some detached exploration of the world (Bowlby, 1988) in which a secure feeling of attachment to a teacher is necessary for autonomous exploration of the world and to feel that independent exploration is respected and encouraged.

Nurture groups

Attachment theory has influenced education in the early years through the development of 'nurture groups' in some nursery settings and infant schools. The underlying assumption of the nurture group is that children who have fared badly though the learning processes of early childhood need extra support and appropriate experiences before they can interact and learn in a normal school setting. The emphasis within nurture groups is 'on growth not on pathology' (Bennathan, 2000, p. 11). Participation in nurture groups is understood as facilitated social interaction and development and not as a permanent withdrawal from mainstream classroom settings. Nurture groups are intended to accept and work with children who present major challenges to regular class teachers and other students. The critical challenge for nurture groups is to ensure that their role remains a short term developmental one and that children will be included in regular classrooms after a relatively short time.

There is a strong argument that nurture groups, when organised and run as originally intended, allow for children with serious social behaviour developmental difficulties to be included in mainstream schooling (Bennathan, 2000; DfE, 2016b). Boxall (2002) argues that learning, personality and behaviour difficulties, which are more likely in the young children of families experiencing disadvantage and deprivation, are the result of inadequate early care and support from parents who struggle with poverty, damaged relationships and harsh and stressful living conditions. The nurture group attempts to create the features of adequate parenting within school. Opportunities are provided to develop trust, security, positive mood and identity through attachment to a reliable, attentive and caring adult and to develop autonomy through the provision of secure, controlled and graduated experiences in a familiar environment.

Some features in nurture groups are also considered effective early years practice generally: easy physical contact between adult and child; warmth and intimacy and a family atmosphere; good-humoured acceptance of the children and their behaviour; familiar and reassuring routines; a focus on tidying up and putting away; the provision of food in structured contexts; opportunities to play and the appropriate participation of the adults; adults talking about and encouraging reflection by children on trouble-provoking situations and their own feelings and opportunities for children to develop increasing autonomy. These opportunities incorporate visits outside the nurture group, participation in games, visits to regular classrooms leading to children's eventual return to a full-time class.

Early childhood nurture groups (Bennathan and Boxall, 2000) were first established in the 1970s in the Inner London Education Authority (ILEA) as a response to a perceived rise in the numbers of young children arriving at school from backgrounds of social deprivation. Bennathan and Boxall (2000, p. 15) describe 'extremely harsh social conditions' that they felt gave rise to the difficulties experienced by some of the children included in the nurture groups:

> There was the loss of extended family support; the loss of safe play space; poor housing conditions; the necessity for mothers to work long hours, often at the hardest and worst paid jobs; and a serious lack of good child–care facilities. Not surprisingly, many children came into school showing the effects of this stress.

One was based in an infant school and one in a junior school.

> Nurture groups were special classes of some 12 children in primary schools run by a teacher and a helper. They were for children already in the school who were showing signs of severely deprived early childhoods, unable to learn because of extreme withdrawal or disruptiveness. For some children, 'everything that could go wrong had gone wrong', and it seemed that the only thing to do with them was to start again. This meant recreating in school the total experience of a normally developing child from babyhood onwards. The routine of the nurture group day was planned to provide a predictable, reliable structure in which the children would come to feel safe and cared for, so that they began to trust the adults, to explore and to learn. The structure combined the nurturing of an adequate family with the control required to manage in a group, taking turns, waiting, making choices, carrying tasks through to completion and clearing away. The children then began to make sense of their experiences, to be able to ask questions, to discuss, to feel some control over their environment and to internalise some control over their behaviour.
>
> … the nurture groups were an integral part of the school, the children maintaining daily contact with their base class, so that the support and understanding of all the school staff was needed. This meant that whole-school preparation was needed before a group could be set up, which in itself proved to be a valuable exercise in spreading an understanding of the developmental processes underlying good educational progress

and in creating a positive school ethos. The groups were quickly so successful that by 1978 the Warnock Committee could report:

> 'Among compensatory measures which may be taken we have been impressed by the 'nurture groups' which have been started in a number of primary schools in London for children approaching or over the age of five who are socially and emotionally affected by severe deprivation in early childhood. We believe that children under school age who are suffering from the same effects of severe deprivation could also benefit from this specific, intensive kind of help'. (DES, 1978, 5.30)
>
> (Bennathan and Boxall, 2012, pp. 8–9)

Nurture groups operate on the assumption that, as the children's emotional needs are met consistently rather than responded to as they may have been in the regular classroom, children will develop greater trust, self-confidence and personal self-organisation and will be more ready for formal learning.

Although in the London area in the 1970s and 1980s there was considerable support for the establishment of nurture groups in mainstream infant schools, in some quarters this approach was heavily criticised as discriminatory against particular groups of children. This criticism coincided with the dismantlement of the Inner London Education Authority (ILEA) where the initiative had begun, and in many schools nurture groups were discontinued.

Cooper, Arnold and Boyd (2001) claim that children who demonstrate emotional and behavioural difficulties often experience emotions and demonstrate behaviours more appropriate to younger children. The nurture group aims to provide the experience of positive relationships in a secure environment through a trusting relationship with the teacher developing age-appropriate personal, emotional and social skills through membership of a small group within the mainstream school. The emphasis is on supporting social, emotional and cognitive development.

Entry to the group, progress within the group and departure from the group was determined by diagnosis and evaluation. The *Boxall Profile* (Bennathan and Boxall, 2000) is an observational tool based on attachment theory and developed to identify children's developmental needs and the levels of skills they possess to access learning. In 1984, a Diagnostic Developmental Profile was standardised for children aged 3–8 years to support work in nurture groups, but has recently been developed for use in secondary schools. The preliminary findings of Couture *et al.*'s (2011) study highlight the concurrent validity between the Boxall Profile and the *Goodman's Strengths and Difficulties Questionnaire* (Couture *et al.*, 2011).

Nurture groups have spread to many LAs in the UK and Library Boards in Northern Ireland. Recently the DfE document *Mental health and behaviour in schools* (2016b, p. 40) has acknowledged the potential effectiveness of 'well-established nurture groups to address emerging social, emotional and behavioural difficulties'. In the so-called 'classic model', (Cooper and Lovey, 1999) children remain on the register of their normal primary school class and attend that class one half day per week. For the rest of the week, they attend a nurture group of about ten or twelve students at the primary school and have a teacher and a learning support assistant.

Encourage social communication to address loneliness and emotional upset

Not all young children who experience difficulties in social communication are either autistic or experience lack of attachment to primary caregivers, of course. We have already discussed some of the strategies that might be used to support the acquisition of receptive and expressive language skills in Chapter 3 on difficulties in communication and interaction.

For a young child, an inability to understand and/or express oneself in the same way as others can lead to feelings of isolation, loneliness and marginalisation from the peer group as well as frustration and, consequently, withdrawn and/or challenging, attention-seeking behaviour and/or non-compliance and non-engagement in group activities. Some settings and schools adopt deliberate strategies to support children, sometimes from quite a young age, to overcome these feelings, be able to join in informal and formal activities with peers more positively as a result of developing the interpersonal and communication skills they need in a social context. An example of one of these strategies is 'Circle Time' (Mosley, 1996).

Using 'Circle Time'

Circle Time has been used for the past 20 years in many places to give children the opportunity to share feelings and ideas, and to talk about matters that are important to them. In many traditional communities the circle is a symbol of 'unity, healing and power'. Using circles for members of a group to exchange views is 'ancient' and can be found in the traditions of groups as diverse 'as the North American Indians and Anglo–Saxon monks' (Tew, 1998, p. 20). As used in schools, 'Circle Time' refers to a meeting, following the traditional protocols of involving all participants in discussion where all are bound by strict rules for both teachers and children:

> No one may put anyone down
> No one may use any name negatively (creating 'safety' for all individuals including teachers and parents)
> When they speak, everyone must listen
> Everyone has a turn and a chance to speak
> All views are taken seriously
> Members of the class team suggest ways of solving problems and
> Individuals can accept the help or politely refuse it.
>
> (Mosley, 1996, p. 36)

Looking at this list, it is obvious that Circle Time can enable children with difficulties in both receptive and expressive language to develop skills in turn-taking, attentive listening, interacting with others in a controlled way, speaking intelligibly and thinking about what peers have said (Allenby et al., 2015).

The activity has to be carefully controlled by the adult. No child is made to speak. Sometimes an object is passed to the speaker to signify what is 'holding the floor'. Children should not be excluded from the group for previous inappropriate behaviour. Mosley (1996, p. 36) notes the skills needed by the adult in charge for a 'Circle Time' programme to run effectively:

> The ability to listen well;
> The ability to be honest sometimes about your own feelings and thoughts;
> The ability to use good eye contact and show emotional warmth and empathy;

The ability to recap what pupils have said and reflect it back to them to show you have understood;

The ability to notice and thank pupils for the skills focused on in Circle Time: i.e. thinking, looking, listening, speaking and concentrating.

'Circle Time' is probably best known for its use with younger children. To be most effective for supporting speaking and listening, as well as enabling the development of the language of emotions and feelings, skills of turn taking, positive attitudes towards the viewpoints of others and self-regulation, it is important to remember to keep sessions with the youngest children short in terms of length spent on the carpet and small in relation to the numbers of children within the group. Small, easily managed groups give plenty of opportunity for young children to take an active part and to express their ideas, maintain focus and interest, as well as provide a sense of security.

The model developed by Mosley follows a given structure:

- warm up and fun;
- a round where all children have the opportunity to speak;
- 'open forum' where individual issues and problems can be raised;
- negotiation of group action plan to address the issues raised, if necessary;
- celebration of success;
- closure, ending on fun.

The rules must be followed strictly. If a student breaks a rule, a visual warning is given. If this persists, time away from the circle follows.

Circle Time can thus give young children with language and communication difficulties the opportunity to practise the skills they need to thrive and make progress in a social context and observe those skills being modelled by peers.

Taking account of emotions associated with long term neurological or medical conditions

Young children may undergo similar emotional upset, including feelings of isolation, loneliness and marginalisation from the peer group, frustration and, consequently, withdrawn and/or attention-seeking behaviour if they experience long-term neurological or medical conditions. For example, as Coulter *et al.* (2015) note, they may be resentful, angry or embarrassed at some of their symptoms. They may be bullied or teased, dislike the treatment that may be needed to control the condition, find it difficult to maintain friendships and/or be afraid that the condition might deteriorate.

Tourette syndrome

If we take the example of Tourette syndrome, across the world the prevalence among school children 'range from 1 to 10 per 1000, with a rate of 6 per 1000 replicated in several countries' (Piacenti *et al.*, 2010, p. 1929). Tourette syndrome (TS) is a neurological disorder characterised by motor and vocal tics: repetitive, stereotyped, involuntary movements and vocalisations. Motor tics are, as NINDS (2005) outlines, commonly, sudden, brief, repetitive movements that may include eye blinking and other vision irregularities, facial grimacing, shoulder shrugging and head or shoulder jerking, or, more dramatically, touching objects, hopping, jumping, bending, twisting or motor movements that result in self-harm such as punching oneself in the face. Tics tend to start in early childhood, between the ages of 4 and 6 years (Bloch and Leckman, 2009). Vocalisations often include repetitive throat-clearing, sniffing or grunting sounds – or, at the extreme, 'coprolalia' (uttering swear words) or 'echolalia' (repeating the words or phrases of others). These may all cause extreme embarrassment, both to the young child and peers.

Medication can be prescribed for young people whose tics are severe enough to interfere with their functioning. The most effective appear to be antipsychotics. However, as Piacenti et al. (2010, p. 1930) comment, these 'rarely eliminate tics and are often associated with unacceptable sedation, weight gain, cognitive dulling, and motor adverse effects', such as tremors. In recent years, particular interventions based on a behaviourist approach have been developed that seem, from small controlled trials, to be effective in reducing tic severity (NINDS, 2005). Rather than drugs, behavioural interventions that constrain tics, such as 'habit-reversal therapy', should be offered to children (Bloch and Leckman, 2009). Children with Tourette syndrome often report that tics are preceded by an urge or sensation in the affected muscles, commonly called a 'premonitory urge' that builds up to the point where it is expressed. Excitement, anxiety or particular physical experiences can trigger or worsen tics. 'Habit-reversal training' acknowledges that tics have a neurological basis and takes into account the child's context as well as the internal experience of premonitory urges. Piacenti et al. (2010, p. 1930) describe the main components of habit reversal as tic-awareness and 'competing-response training'. This means training the child, when s/he is old enough, to become aware of the early signs that a tic is about to occur. Competing-response training involves deliberately engaging in a behaviour that is not physically compatible with the tic as soon as the premonitory urge is felt. In this way tics are not suppressed. Instead, the child is taught to initiate an alternative socially acceptable behaviour that replaces the tic. For vocal tics, the most commonly competing response that is taught is slow rhythmic breathing from the diaphragm. With practice, children learn to complete the competing response without stopping their routine activities.

Advice to parents from NHS Choices (www.nhs.uk/Conditions/Tourette-syndrome/Pages/Symptoms.aspx) reads:

> If your child has Tourette's syndrome, their tics will probably tend to follow a set pattern. They may be worse during periods of:
>
> * stress
> * anxiety
> * tiredness
> * illness
> * nervous excitement
> * relaxation after a busy day.
>
> On the other hand, the tics are often reduced when they're doing an enjoyable activity involving a high level of concentration, such as reading an interesting book or playing competitive sports.
>
> You may find your child is able to control their tics when they're in situations where they would be particularly noticeable, such as in a school classroom. However, controlling tics can be difficult and tiring over prolonged periods of time.

Many children with Tourette's syndrome often experience a sudden 'release' of tics after trying to suppress them – for example, after returning home from school.

All children with Tourette syndrome, as with any other kind of special educational need or disability, benefit from a home or learning environment in settings and schools that are supportive and flexible enough to accommodate their individual learning needs. Children with Tourette's often cope well in mainstream classrooms. Peers can often be sensitive to needs and can be a support, emotionally. It is important to encourage children with Tourette's to develop strong interests and good friends who will help them to develop confidence and self-respect. If well controlled and led, Circle Time may well provide a good opportunity for children to explore and discuss issues arising from the experience of Tourette's, so that all the children, as well as adults who participate, may become sensitised and develop greater awareness, understanding and receptivity.

Including young children with sensory impairments

Children with a hearing loss that is not treated may experience increasing outbursts of anger and frustration, embarrassment and depression as they struggle to hear and understand peers and adults (Blairmires et al., 2016, p. 26). This is even more reason why early detection and treatment is important as, with appropriate support, children with hearing impairments 'can develop speech and language skills at the same rate as their normal hearing peers' (Blairmires et al., 2016).

As Blairmires et al. (2016, p. 24) comment, 'Using deaf role models can help deaf pupils to understand any feelings of isolation [and] resolve wellbeing issues'. In terms of the development of interpersonal skills needed in social environments from the earliest years, role models can help children to 'develop strategies for becoming an independent and confident communicator in unfamiliar or difficult situations'. One way of relieving feelings both of isolation and frustration is to enable deaf children to be educated alongside hearing-impaired peers. In addition, deaf awareness training for hearing peers is really important, and should also be continuing so that, for example, sympathetic others will not mock a deaf child's pronunciation.

In terms of visual impairment, young children may find difficulty interacting and making friends with peers because they find it problematic to observe and understand gestures and facial expressions, with consequent damage to personal self-confidence. Visually impaired children can be supported to acquire the skills they need in a social context and, hence, feel less isolated and more confident if, from the early years, they are encouraged to socialise in a variety of contexts, for example, in baby and toddler groups, being encouraged to listen and share with others, playing with siblings and other family members and, later, in settings and schools, joining in games and songs.

Addressing emotional aspects of dyslexia

We have already noted how difficulties associated with dyslexia can affect a whole range of areas of young children's learning and development. Sometimes, repeated failure to acquire or recall sound or letter knowledge, or repeat simple rhythmic sequences in the same way as peers, or slow processing of literacy-based tasks, or inability to find pleasure in singing or remembering nursery rhymes or in taking part in simple word games with family and/or peers in early years settings may result in feelings of frustration and anxiety, or in reluctance to engage in literacy-based activities, or in obviously withdrawn behaviour. By 2 years of age young children generally have a sense of themselves ('me'), and by 5 years old they usually recognise themselves, not only from their own viewpoint but also by recognising how others see them. 'Academic self-concept', that is, how children see themselves in terms of academic matters, may be influenced by the comments and views of their families and caregivers, or by the quality of relationships with practitioners in early years settings and schools (Verschueren, Doumen and Buyse, 2012). Riddick (1996, p. 32) notes that among clinicians and educationalists there is general agreement about the 'devastating effects' that serious difficulties in literacy development can have on young children and their families. She has a particular interest in children's experience of dyslexia, and in her (1996) study of the personal experiences of 22 children, aged from 8 years and identified as 'dyslexic', and their families, children often reflected on feelings of disaffection and of dread of 'visible public indicators' of their difficulties in literacy, such as reading aloud and always being the last to finish work (Riddick, 1996, p. 124). She identifies key qualities of the 'best' teachers as a propensity to offer praise and encouragement linked with understanding of the difficulties experienced by the child. The 'best' teachers (Riddick, 1996, p. 133):

- encourage and praise;
- help pupils, adapt work and explain clearly;
- understand pupils and do not attempt to humiliate them;
- do not shout;
- have a sense of humour;
- know if children are dyslexic;
- treat all children as if they are intelligent.

The worst teachers, on the other hand:

- are cross, impatient and shout;
- criticise and humiliate pupils;
- are not helpful, and are negative about pupils' efforts;
- ignore some pupils and show they consider some pupils 'useless';
- do not understand the problems faced by pupils with difficulties in literacy and are insensitive;
- blame pupils for their problems and call them 'lazy';
- put red lines through pupils' work.

As Pavey (2016) comments, success is often associated with confidence. It is therefore very important that, for young learners who experience difficulty in activities associated with literacy acquisition,

> … a range of opportunities is needed which will both promote success in literacy learning and put a 'safety net' under young learners at possible risk of dyslexia. We need to help children who might be dyslexic to move from a position of uncertainty, doubt or resistance to one of resilience and perseverance. … Younger learners are only just starting their journey to literacy and we can aim to minimise the

development of poor confidence and lack of self-esteem through sensitive, careful and focused teaching.

(Pavey, 2016, pp. 37–8)

For many families and carers worried about their child's progress, it may be very helpful if a child is identified as dyslexic. Families may have noticed differences between those children who experience specific difficulties and their siblings. It may help them to understand the difficulties experienced by their child and think about ways to support his/her learning. For a child, it may also be reassuring to know that the difficulties they experience are attributable to something outside their own intelligence. However, early screening for dyslexia only identifies the possibility of diagnosis. Educators in the early years are perhaps more concerned about how to address the particular difficulties they have identified (Pavey, 2016, p. 38) before they become entrenched, rather than agreeing on a specific label.

In her (2010) work, Riddick comments that some of the mothers who reported that their children experienced particular dyslexic-type difficulties noted that once their offspring had experienced formal literacy learning in school they became anxious, depressed, withdrawn and resistant to literacy-related activities. Aside from support to develop specific skills associated with dyslexic-type difficulties, it is obvious that young dyslexic children also need good friends who will understand, listen and talk about mutual interests, and not mock them when they cannot read, spell or organise themselves, or when they are clumsy. Here, too, Circle Time, or well controlled similar activities, can provide the opportunities for expressing worries and upsets in a safe environment.

Supporting young children through bereavement

The death of a parent, carer or sibling will necessarily have long term emotional effects on a young child and, potentially also, a sense of well-being, safety and security. It may result in changes in the child's behaviour, for example, regression to an earlier phase and over-dependence on an adult. Under the age of 5, children often do not understand the permanency of death and may ask questions about when their sibling, parent or carer is coming back. They may seem to show little reaction to the news although they will be able to recognise the loss of someone close to them.

The Somerset Educational Psychology Service (undated) has published a pamphlet for teachers and others in early years settings and schools that offers particularly useful advice about ways to support young children who have experienced bereavement: *Supporting Young Children through Bereavement and Loss. Information and Advice for Staff in Early Years Settings.*[1] It suggests that bereaved children, just like any other, need to know who will be caring for them so that they feel safe. Regular routines should be maintained as far as possible. A familiar adult should let them know what has happened, using words that they can understand, a little at a time. Young children may repeat the same questions over and over, and they will need time to do this. They may react to their grief with very powerful feelings that may frighten them and they will need to know that this is normal and that they are not responsible for the death. It is important to help young children to understand the situation by, for example, looking at pictures of the person who has died, talking about him/her and involving them in rituals, for example, the funeral, associated with the death.

Children's grief can also affect the adults working with them. It is important to acknowledge this possibility and be aware of where to look for personal support systems.

Summary

As we noted from the work of Bennathan (2000), it is really not helpful to see young children whose behaviour is associated with social, emotional and mental health needs as qualitatively different from their peers. Understanding the processes and contexts that may influence young children's behaviour and emotional development can help to a greater awareness of how sensitively to plan for addressing needs in this area – 'an understanding which ought to be part of the professional competence' of all of us, whether parents and families, teachers or professionals (Bennathan, 2000, p. 5).

Note

1 This is available online at www.somerset.gov.uk/EasySiteWeb/GatewayLink.aspx?alId=52787

Chapter 6

Understanding and addressing sensory and/or physical difficulties

Major questions addressed in this chapter are:

- What is the relationship between sensory difficulties and learning needs?
- How can we address barriers to learning effectively in relation to these needs?
- What is the relationship between physical difficulties and learning needs?
- What are some of the ways in which we can meet these needs effectively?

Introduction

This chapter focuses on sensory and physical difficulties in the early years, learning needs that may result and potential ways to address these. As Miller and Ockleford (2005) aptly comment, young children are individuals. Across all areas of special educational needs and disabilities in settings and schools, a whole range of information is needed to ensure that support to address the difficulties they experience is appropriate. However much is known about their sensory or physical difficulties, they all have their own personal strengths and needs, interests, experiences, family backgrounds and so on that, together with their own views and the views of their families, must all be taken into account when drawing up any intervention plan. As the National Deaf Children's Society has commented, for example, in relation to hearing impairments:

> The 'best' communication approach for any child and family is the one which works for them, both fitting in with the family's culture and values and most importantly, allowing the child to develop good self-esteem, a positive self-image, successful relationships ... in all aspects of her life.
>
> (NDCS, 2010, p. 50)

In this chapter, there is a particular focus on hearing and visual impairments and physical and motor difficulties to illustrate:

- what research studies tell us about the relationship between sensory and/or physical difficulties and needs and young people's learning and future life chances;
- ways that the barriers to learning experienced by young children with difficulties can be addressed in early years settings and elsewhere.

Sensory difficulties and needs

The greatest challenge for a young child with a sensory impairment is, most commonly, communication (Spencer and Marschark, 2010). A child who can hear and see will usually reach out and explore his/her surroundings naturally. A child with a sensory impairment will not necessarily do this and may need encouragement to explore and interact with others. For a deaf child, for example, normal progress in language may be hard and necessitate intensive education and support throughout the child's life. Visual impairment may well delay development and learning in the early years as a result of slower speed of working, reduced environmental and spatial awareness and the constraints on social interaction that occur as a result of difficulty in facial expression. Children with more severe visual impairment may have difficulty recognising body language and seeing facial expressions, moving around the home, watching television, interacting with their peers and, when older, experience reading difficulties. Slow progress in relation to peers may well affect self-confidence. Early intervention in the child's life is therefore clearly very important.

Hearing impairments

There are many reasons why a child can be born deaf or become deaf early in life. Around half the deaf children born in the UK every year are deaf for a genetic reason. Deafness can also be caused by complications during pregnancy. Infections, for example, Rubella and Herpes, can cause a child to be born deaf. Premature babies are often more liable to infections that can cause deafness. Severe jaundice or a lack of oxygen at some point can also cause deafness. Infections such as meningitis, measles and mumps, a head injury or exposure to loud noises can damage the hearing system (World Health Organisation, 2016). Few children are totally deaf, however.

The ear and how it works

The ear has two main functions: it receives and converts sound into signals that the brain then interprets, and it helps us to balance.

There are three parts to the hearing system, all of which must work well to allow us to hear sound clearly: the outer, middle and inner ear. Impaired hearing occurs when one or more parts of the system is not working effectively.

- The outer ear, the pinna, catches sound waves and directs them down the ear canal to the eardrum.
- Sound waves cause vibrations on the eardrum. Three tiny bones, the hammer, anvil and stirrup, pass these vibrations across the middle ear. As they do so, these bones increase the strength of the vibrations on which they travel into an organ called the cochlea in the inner ear.
- The cochlea contains fluid and is filled with thousands of tiny hair-like sound-sensitive cells. As the vibrations enter the cochlea they cause the fluid and sound-sensitive cells to move, and this movement creates a small electrical charge. The auditory nerve carries this signal to the brain which interprets them as sound.

Balance

In the inner ear are three semicircular canals, tubes and filled with liquid and movement-sensitive hair cells. When we move, the fluid moves and creates signals that are sent to the brain.

Different types and causes of deafness

Deafness can be of different types. Deafness can be:

- Conductive, when sound cannot pass efficiently through the outer and middle ear to the cochlea and auditory nerve. The most common type in children is caused by 'glue ear' (NDCS, 2010), a build-up of fluid in the middle ear which affects about one in five children at any time. For most children, the glue ear clears up by itself. A few need surgery to insert 'grommets' into the eardrums, tiny plastic tubes that allow air to circulate in the middle ear and help to prevent the build-up of fluid.
- Sensori-neural, which is permanent and occurs when there is a fault in the inner ear or auditory (hearing) nerve.

Assessment of hearing

A decibel (dB) is a measure of sound pressure level. Normal voice measures 60 dB at a distance of one metre, a raised voice measures 70 dB at one metre and shouting measures 80 dB at one metre. The severity of a hearing impairment is measured in decibels of hearing loss and is ranked according to the additional intensity above a nominal threshold that a sound must be before being detected by an individual. There is a variety of tests that can be used to find out how much hearing a child has. The tests used will depend on the child's age and stage of development. 'One to two babies in every 1,000 are born with a permanent hearing loss in one or both ears' (National Health Service, 2015). It is possible to test the hearing of all children from birth onwards. Since 2006, babies have been screened to test their hearing within a few days of their birth. Babies 'begin to develop language and communication from their earliest months', so early screening means that 'much can be done to positively support and encourage that development ... when early identification of deafness is combined with effective early intervention, with parents and professionals working together, language outcomes for deaf children can be similar to those for hearing children' (NDCS, 2015a, p. 6).

Two screening tests are carried out soon after birth. The first tests for Oto-Acoustic Emissions. It involves putting an earpiece in the baby's ear with a microphone and speaker that emits a clicking sound. A properly functioning cochlea will produce a response that the earpiece picks up. The second tests Auditory Brainstem Response, that is, that sound received by the cochlea is transmitted as a signal through the auditory nerve to the brain. Headphones are placed on the baby's head, and three sensors on the ears. If following the screening tests the decision is taken that hearing aids will be needed, the audiologists will inform a range of services, including, possibly, Education and Speech Therapy, so that ongoing advice and support can be given to the family. Pre-school teachers of the deaf may offer the family advice about options relating to modes of communication. This may include the offer of tuition in signed communication, the management of hearing aids or cochlear implants, where used at home and in early years settings. They may also provide support to the family, including liaison with other professionals that may include social services, speech and language therapists, Children's Centres and audiology clinics.

For children of school age, hearing is usually measured with behavioural tests using pure tones. The sounds come through headphones and each time a child hears a sound they respond by moving an object, pressing a button or saying 'yes'.

Quantification of hearing loss

Hearing sensitivity varies according to the frequency of sounds. To take this into account, hearing sensitivity can be measured for a range of frequencies and plotted on an audiogram. Hearing sensitivity is indicated by the quietest sound that an animal can detect, called the hearing threshold, in other words, the quietest sound to which the person responds. The test is carried out for sounds of different frequencies.

Four categories of hearing impairment are generally used: mild, moderate, severe and profound. As noted by NHS (2015) (www.nhs.uk):

- With 'mild deafness: 20–40 dB', a child could hear a baby crying but may be unable to hear whispered conversation. Mild deafness can sometimes make hearing speech difficult, particularly in noisy situations.
- With 'moderate deafness: 41–70 dB', a child could hear a dog barking but not a baby crying. A young person may have difficulty following speech without using a hearing aid.
- With 'severe deafness: 71–90 dB', a child would hear drums being played but not a dog barking. S/he would usually need to lip-read or use sign language, even with the use of a hearing aid.
- With 'profound deafness: >90 dB', a child might hear a large lorry but not drums being played. Children who are profoundly deaf can often benefit from a cochlear implant. 'With cochlear implants or hearing aids the child may require additional communication support (for example, through sign language or cued speech) to access speech, especially within background noise or within a group conversation' (NDCS, 2015b, p. 65). Other forms of communication include lip reading and sign language.

Deaf children with the same level of deafness may experience sounds differently. About 20 per cent of primary age children suffer from conductive hearing loss caused by middle-ear problems; this reduces to 2 per cent by secondary age.

Effects of hearing impairment

A major problem with late identification of deafness is the effect on language development (Goldberg and Richberg, 2004; Moeller *et al.*, 2007). A delay in identification can mean a delay in establishing effective communication with the child which, in turn, can have a long-term impact on his/her social and educational development. The consequences on development of undetected hearing impairment may be long lasting (Yoshinaga-Itano, 2003).

In the early years, a child's brain is still developing and putting the right building blocks in place for future development. If the child's brain is not exposed to lots of communication and language, this can have a knock-on effect on other areas of development later in life, such as memory skills, ability to organise thoughts, solve problems and social development.

(NDCS, 2015b, p. 7)

Children who do not hear clearly or whose hearing varies may be late to start talking, have difficulties with speech sounds or fail to develop good listening skills.

> Babies and young children therefore require early and consistent auditory stimulation so that they have the best opportunity to develop their hearing pathways. … Hearing aids and cochlear implants should be offered as early as possible so that babies and young children have the opportunity to access sound and develop hearing pathways.
>
> (NDCS, 2015b, p. 8)

Young children whose hearing impairments are not identified early so that appropriate support and help may be provided may also have poor memory and language-processing skills, poor basic vocabularies as a result, experience reading and spelling problems, difficulty with sentence structure and comprehension and achieve lower attainments in reading and mathematics. Children with a conductive hearing loss have a higher tendency to behaviour problems, poor motivation and attention, shyness and withdrawal (Spencer and Marschark, 2010). The most vulnerable are those whose conductive deafness started in early infancy and persisted undiagnosed for long periods.

Supporting the acquisition of communication and language skills at home and in early years settings and schools

One of the most important considerations in supporting young children to acquire communication and language skills is that, from birth, all of them, including those with a hearing impairment, need a rich communication and language environment, where there is a lot of interaction between children and adults. When children are very young, gestures, facial expressions and body language constitute a significant part of communication and help to provide visual access to language, which is especially important for children with a hearing impairment. The National Deaf Children's Society offers the following advice to families in this regard:

> It's important to make sure that you face your child as much as possible and maintain eye contact to get their attention. This will allow your baby to see your face clearly as they begin to watch faces and lips during communication. You should also try to make sure that your face is in the light. For example, try and avoid having your back to a window. This will help your child to see your face and gestures.
>
> (NDCS, 2015a, p. 10)

It is important to acknowledge, at home and in early years settings and schools, that deaf children may well need more time to communicate than hearing children. This includes extra time to take part in a conversation, for example. It is essential not to turn the child's head to face other speakers, but to give the child that time so that s/he realises it is his/her chance to speak.

There are a number of different methods of communicating that are available to deaf children, their families, carers, teachers and others in early years settings and schools. The three major 'types' of approach are Auditory-Oral (or 'Oral/Aural'), Sign-Bilingual or Total Communication.

> Generally the evidence for any one method working better than another for deaf children as a whole is unclear, and all the approaches can point to some evidence which shows successful outcomes for children.
>
> (NDCS, 2015b, p. 45)

The aim of Auditory-Oral approaches is that deaf children should learn to use whatever residual hearing they may have to develop good listening and speaking skills which will enable them to communicate and mix with hearing people as part of the wider hearing community (Beattie, 2006). These approaches emphasise the use of amplification such as hearing aids, cochlear implants and radio aids to maximise the use of the child's 'residual' hearing (Spencer and Marschark, 2006). The most widely used of these approaches is the Natural Aural Approach. Here no sign language is used and children are not encouraged to rely on lip-reading (Lewis, 1996).

Sign Bilingualism in the UK uses British Sign Language (BSL) (or Irish Sign Language in Ireland) and whatever is the spoken language of the home (Moores, 2008). It assumes that a visual language is essential for deaf children to have full access to language learning, education, information and the world around them, and to develop a strong positive deaf identity. Use of BSL can make a connection with Deaf culture and the Deaf community as well as the hearing world (Burman, Nunes and Evans, 2006). BSL has its own linguistic rules that are different from English, so it cannot be used at the same time as spoken language. It developed as a visual medium and uses body language, head position, facial expressions and gesture as well as the hands. Finger-spelling is used to represent words such as names which have no signs.

Total Communication is based on the principle that deaf children can learn to communicate effectively by using whatever combination of means works best: sign, speech and hearing, finger-spelling, gesture, facial expression, lip-reading and cued speech. Signed/ Signs Supported English (SSE) uses signs taken from BSL, together with finger-spelling (Moores, 2001) and is used in the word order of English to supplement what is spoken. Signed English, similarly, uses signs taken from BSL together with some specially developed 'markers' made with the hands, and finger-spelling, to give an exact representation of the word order and the grammar of English. It is mainly used to support the teaching of reading and writing. In finger-spelling, each letter of the alphabet is indicated by using the fingers and palm of the hand (Padden and Gunsals, 2003). Lip-reading is the process of reading words from the lip patterns of the person speaking (Spencer and Marschark, 2010). It is never enough on its own because many speech sounds are not visible on the lips, and lip patterns vary from individual to individual. Also, eating whilst talking or a lack of clarity around the face caused by, for example, beards or moustaches that obscure the mouth can make lip-reading difficult. Cued Speech is a sound-based system that accompanies natural speech and uses eight hand shapes in four different positions (cues) to represent the sounds of English visually (Hage and Leybaert, 2006). Some spoken sounds: 'p', 'm' and 'b', all look the same on the lips, so cannot be fully lip-read; some sounds, for example, 'd', 'k' and 'g' cannot be seen on the lips. The association between the sounds and letters of spoken English is intended to help develop literacy skills as well as spoken language, so hand shapes are 'cued' near to the mouth to make clear the sounds of English which look the same when lip-read.

Reflective activity: using Total Communication at home, in early years settings and at school

It is often useful if siblings and the rest of the family, peers and teachers and schools in early years settings learn to use Total Communication with students who experience hearing impairments of a severe nature.

How, in practice, might this be arranged in settings, schools and for the family?

Minimising barriers through assistive devices

For educational purposes, young children with hearing impairments will probably require hearing aids, adaptations to their environment and/or particular teaching strategies in order to access the curriculum. 'Hearing aids and cochlear implants should be offered as early as possible so that babies and young children have the opportunity to access sound and develop hearing pathways' (NDCS, 2016, p. 8).

Deaf children often use assistive listening devices to assist them to hear what a speaker is saying, particularly in noisy listening conditions. Personal FM systems (often known as radio aids) can be very useful at school or at home. 'They can help reduce effects of background noise in, for example, a school classroom, and help a child to concentrate on one person's voice, often their teacher' (NDCS, 2008, p. 31). Radio aids have a transmitter with a microphone and a receiver. The person talking wears the transmitter and the sounds are transmitted by radio waves to the receiver. The deaf child wears the receiver which picks up the signal from the transmitter and converts it back to sound. The child's hearing aids or implants amplify the sound so that the child can hear what is said. Either teachers of the deaf, or audiologists, will usually assess whether a radio aid would be useful and appropriate for a young child. Criteria used for making this decision may well include the child's age, hearing, listening and language levels, ability to use a hearing aid independently, the child's emotional development, family views, the environmental acoustics and appropriateness of using hearing aids within the context.

Soundfield systems, that some LAs provide for use at home and for use in classrooms, are designed for similar reasons as radio aids. Here, a microphone worn by the family member(s) or teacher is linked to an amplifier by either an FM radio transmitter or an infra-red transmitter, and speaker(s) can walk around a room with no need for wires. The room is fitted with loudspeakers. The soundfield system amplifies speakers' voices to produce a clear level of sound above background noises (NDCS, 2008). Most children with hearing aids or cochlear implants will still need radio aids in rooms with a soundfield system.

Sound waves reverberate and increase the amount of background noise in rooms with hard surfaces (Moeller *et al.*, 2007). Soundfield systems and the acoustic treatment of rooms at home or teaching spaces in early years settings and schools can improve the listening environment for all students. For example, a good listening environment at home might mean keeping background noise low by turning off the television or noisy electrical appliances during conversations, using soft furnishings: carpets, rugs and so on, to absorb sound and reduce echo and keeping within the young child's field of vision when communicating.

It is important for family members and practitioners to think carefully about the clarity of their spoken language (Wilkins and Ertmer, 2002). Using natural speech patterns is more effective in communicating with deaf children than exaggerating lip movements or shouting. For teaching purposes, practitioners should highlight key terms and concepts and place themselves in a position appropriate for children to lip read or benefit from a hearing aid where the maximum range is often two metres. To acquire spoken and written English, children may also need the additional support of visual and written forms of language, as well as lip-reading or multi-sensory clues (Harris and Moreno, 2006).

In some places there is a serious difference of opinion between those who believe that deaf children can be taught to speak using auditory-oral approaches, that is, assisted by hearing aids, cochlear implants, radio aids and so on, and be integrated into mainstream society, and those who believe they should be taught through sign language. What suits the child best may depend on the degree of hearing loss, the extent of the delay in language acquisition and, of course, what the child him/herself and the family feel about his/her situation. Which approach is the most effective for any individual child, family and setting

> is the one which works for them, both fitting in with the family's culture and values and most importantly, allowing the child to develop good self-esteem, a positive self-image, successful relationships, and to achieve her potential in all aspects of her life.
>
> (NDCS, 2015a, p. 50)

In 1908, regulations by the Board of Education in England and Wales laid down that teachers in schools for the blind and deaf must obtain, within 2 years of their appointment, an approved qualification. The 1908 regulations have broadly continued to the present day. These days many children with sensory impairments are in mainstream settings and schools. It is essential, therefore, that non-specialist as well as specialist practitioners and teachers understand how to include them most sensitively and effectively.

Key to successful inclusion is the ethos of the setting or school in which young hearing-impaired children are placed. The Royal National Institute for the Deaf (RNID) (2004) strongly promotes the message that effective pedagogy for children who experience hearing difficulties is effective pedagogy for a whole range of other children also. They state that 'Reviewing and adapting teaching styles, presentation methods, listening conditions and differentiation of the curriculum to address the needs of deaf pupils will also improve the learning conditions for many other pupils in the school' (RNID, 2004, p. 8).

Blairmires et al. (2016) offer some very clear practical advice about enabling children with hearing impairments to participate in settings and classrooms. Their suggestions for teachers and others include:

- standing still, facing the child and speaking clearly in complete sentences;
- using visual aids, and writing new words and important points on the board;
- in group discussion, indicating who is speaking, ensuring only one child speaks at a time, and repeating other children's questions and answers;
- speaking without covering the face;

- seating the child away from extraneous noise at the front of the class and slightly to one side so that s/he can follow other children's responses, or arranging circular seating in classrooms;
- ensuring that adult assistants do not obstruct children's view;
- ensuring that the light falls on the teacher's face to enable lip-reading where appropriate;
- enabling the opportunity to mix with a hearing-impaired peer group where possible, to avoid a sense of isolation.

Visual Impairment

Visual impairment (VI) is a general term that indicates a continuum of sight loss (Mason, 2001).VI is estimated to affect around 25,000 children between the ages of 0–16 years in the UK (Tate *et al.*, 2005), and 15,000 people between the ages of 17–25 years.At least 4 in every 10,000 children born in the UK are diagnosed as severely visually impaired or blind by their first birthday (Miller and Ockleford, 2005).VI might be the result of a number of genetic or hereditary illnesses, including congenital optic nerve and retinal disorders, damage to the eye before, during or sometime after birth, or damage to the visual cortex or to other areas of the brain concerned with information processing. Fifty per cent of blind and partially sighted children also have additional disabilities and this includes 30 per cent with severe or profound and multiple learning difficulties.

It has been estimated that around 3 per cent of blind and partially sighted pupils, aged 5 to 16, use Braille as their sole or main format for reading and writing (Morris and Smith, 2008).

Total blindness is extremely rare. The vision of each eye is recorded separately, as well as both eyes together. It can be difficult to accurately assess vision in very young children, so it can be very helpful to have an idea of 'normal' milestones for the development of a child's vision.A young child can, usually:

- At birth: focus on objects 8–10 inches away, but not be able to use both eyes together;
- At 3 months: visually follow moving objects and look around with eyes beginning to work together. 'By twelve weeks the child should be able to move his eyes in a range of 180 degrees to a moving finger held 20 to 25 cms away from his face' (Dixit, 2006, p. 112);
- At 6 months: turn his/her head to see objects and pick up toys that s/he has dropped;
- At 12 months: point and gesture, judge longer distances, show an interest in pictures, place shapes in frames and follow a rapidly moving toy held in front of him/her without moving his/her head;
- At 18 months: recognise familiar objects, be interested in exploring and scribble with crayons or pens;
- By 2.5 to 3 years old: be able to point to a flying bird, moving car or train and so on.

In the early years, looking at a young child's eyes can offer a lot of information about how s/he sees the world:

- The child may not look at a speaker when s/he speaks;
- The eyes may look unusual, squint or seem sensitive to light;
- The child may rub the eyes, or have an excessive amount of tears;

- S/he may tilt the head to look at something;
- S/he may be excessively clumsy, bump into things and/or have poor balance;
- When looking at something, the eyes should be still, and not drift.

Referral to an ophthalmologist or orthoptist if there is a concern about a young child's vision will be able to give some indication of the degree of possible visual impairment.

Eye tests are offered routinely to newborn babies and children to identify any problems early on in their development. Within 72 hours after birth, parents are offered a physical examination of their baby by a health professional, for example, a doctor, midwife, nurse or health visitor. This professional looks into the baby's eyes with an ophthalmoscope to check their appearance and movement. Further checks may be carried out when the child is between 6 to 8 weeks old, between that point and compulsory school age and on entry to school.

For young children, a test of vision may be carried out using objects, pictures or symbols. When the child can recognise or match letters, his/her vision is tested using charts with rows of letters and numbers of decreasing sizes. These charts are called Snellen or LogMAR charts. The most well-known chart used to test sharpness of sight is the Snellen eye chart, originally devised by a Dutch ophthalmologist, Dr. Hermann Snellen, in 1862. This has a series of letters or letters and numbers, with the largest at the top. As the child reads down the chart, the letters gradually become smaller. Other versions can be used for children who cannot read the alphabet.

In the Snellen fraction 20/20, the top number represents the test distance, 20 feet. The lower number represents the distance at which the average eye can see the letters on a particular line of the eye chart. So, 20/20 means that the eye being tested can read a certain size letter when it is 20 feet away. If a person sees 20/40, at 20 feet from the chart s/he can read letters that a person with 20/20 vision could read from 40 feet away. Originally, Snellen worked in feet but later (in 1875) he changed from using feet to metres (from 20/20 to 6/6 respectively). Currently, the 20-foot distance continues to be used in the USA, but 6 metres is used in the UK.

More recently, the LogMAR chart has been introduced to test eyesight, described by the Royal College of Ophthalmologists (2015) as 'more accurate than other acuity charts' and, therefore, now quite commonly used in eye clinics. A comparison between Snellen and LogMAR charts is available at www.rcophth.ac.uk/wp-content/uploads/2015/11/LogMAR-vs-Snellen.pdf.

Measures of visual acuity such as Snellen and LogMAR relate to the recognition of letters or symbols with high contrast, but tell us nothing about the quality of vision, for example, seeing larger objects and objects with poor contrast, or whether vision is more or less efficient when using both eyes together (Strouse Watt, 2003).

A clinical assessment of vision usually focuses on four aspects: distance, near, field and colour vision (Mason, 2001). However, children with the same eye condition may have very different strengths and needs from each other, with different interests, background experiences and so on, as well as differing degrees of useful vision (Miller and Ockleford, 2005). A whole range of information is therefore needed to ensure that support for a young child is appropriate (Miller and Ockleford, 2005). This includes the views of the child and the parents/family, medical and school records as well as the clinical assessment of vision.

Many people who are classed as blind have some 'functional' vision, and it is important to teach the child how to make best use of this (Davis, 2003). Where a distinction is necessary for any reason, the term blind is used to refer to pupils who rely on tactile methods in their learning, for example, Braille or Tactile diagrams, and the term low vision is used with reference to children and young people who are taught through methods which rely on sight (Mason *et al.*, 1997).

Addressing difficulties

Sensory stimulation is very important for brain development from birth. 'As the child with VI has little incidental motivation to use his vision, there may be a tendency for him [*sic*] to withdraw into passivity or self-stimulation within his own body, e.g. eye-poking, hand-flapping' (Blairmires *et al.*, 2016, p. 57). Family members, carers, teachers and others should therefore use touch or noise to communicate, for example, pleasure and approval. Young children will benefit from personal undivided attention, tuning in to what is important to the child at the time, exploring objects together and giving a running commentary on what is going on, introducing low vision aids and the use of ICT where appropriate.

Including children with a visual impairment

In early years settings, rooms should be well lit with signposting that includes Braille, symbols and/or large print, passageways should be clear of hazards that may trip a child. An initial orientation may well assist movement around the learning spaces. Contrasting coloured walls and floors, and edges of steps highlighted with paint or coloured strips can be very important also. In terms of learning materials, tactile materials with a variety of textures and smells can be used to differentiate and modify pictures, books, models, toys, games and mathematics equipment, depending on the developmental needs of the young child, and the learning environment.

As a result of their visual difficulties, children may well have less opportunity to explore their environment and learn through observing and copying the actions of others (Douglas and McLinden, 2005). Both academic progress and children's social skills may be influenced by this. Children may therefore need teaching of literacy development through specialist codes such as Braille or Moon or through print/modified print Braille, and/or specialist teaching of mobility, tactile and keyboard skills, as well as social and life skills generally. Moon is a tactile code based on the shapes of letters in the alphabet, and developed by William Moon in 1847. It is important to consider whether and when to withdraw the child from the mainstream classroom for specialist or additional teaching so that the child does not become socially isolated and the mainstream practitioner or teacher maintains full responsibility for him/her.

Davis (2003) notes that visually impaired children may become very tired as a result of the amount of concentration required to complete tasks, and/or need more time to complete tasks. Special consideration of the learning environment, in particular the classroom, may well be necessary, for example, where to site quiet or noisy areas, Braille and/or tactile/large print signs, bulky equipment such as CCTV, a Brailler and computers, as well as classroom lighting (Mason, 2001).

Braille is the alphabet and numbers, designed to be read by fingers rather than eyes through a series of raised dots on a page (see Figure 6.1). The RNIB (www.rnib.org.uk/search/site/louis%20braille) notes that a blind French schoolboy, Louis Braille, devised the code more than 200 years ago. This code is based on six dots arranged in two columns of

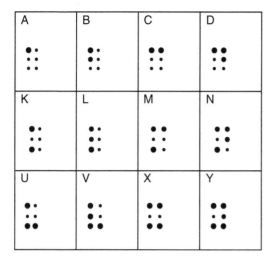

Figure 6.1 Sample from Braille alphabet

three. Different types of Braille codes use combinations of these dots, 63 in all, to represent letters of the alphabet, numbers, punctuation marks and common letter groups.

There are two grades of Braille: uncontracted (previously Grade 1) and contracted (previously Grade 2). Uncontracted includes a letter for letter and number for number translation from print. Contracted has special signs for common words and letter combinations. This usually increases the speed of reading. Particular subject areas, for example, music, mathematics, science and foreign languages, have their own specialist codes. In recent years, Unified English Braille has been developed by the International Council on English Braille (ICEB), to bring together several existing Braille codes, including codes for mathematics, sciences and literary material. This was adopted in the UK in October 2011.

For beginning readers, some reading schemes have been adapted to include uncontracted or contracted Braille on interleaved clear plastic sheets, so that the pictures and print story can be seen underneath. This enables shared reading between sighted and blind readers at home and in settings and schools.

Multi-sensory impairment

Multi-sensory impairment means difficulty with both vision and hearing. Children with multi-sensory impairment may be born with it or acquire it later as a result of illness or injury. Very few children are totally blind and deaf. In the past, Rubella (German measles) during pregnancy was a main cause of deaf-blindness. However, as a result of vaccination against Rubella usually before girls reach the age of puberty, it is now uncommon. Premature birth and/or severe infections during early childhood may also cause deaf-blindness.

The reduced and possibly distorted visual and auditory information that pupils with multi-sensory impairment receive means that they have limited and a possibly confused experience of the world (Aitken, 2000). Some children become skilled at using touch as a means of learning about the world and a means of communicating. Others may become skilled in using the sense of smell. Others may sense movement around them from differences in air pressure. Taylor (2007, p. 205) notes the difficulties experienced by many of these children in communicating:

> These include: a reduced and confused experience of the world, becoming passive and isolated, and the tendency to be echolalic or repeating the last word said to them, all of which limit their ability to make choices. Aitken and Millar (2002) also highlight the effects of hearing impairment on individuals' communication, including isolation from information and from other people. A physical impairment in association with communication difficulties will also present additional challenges. The child with MSI has all these difficulties compounded.

For those children whose visual and vocal ability is severely affected, many assistive devices are available to enable students to communicate: electronic language boards, voice synthesizers and voice recognition software.

Multi-sensory teaching

Multi-sensory teaching is the simultaneous use of visual, auditory and kinesthetic-tactile senses to enhance memory and learning. Links are consistently made between the visual (what we see), auditory (what we hear) and kinesthetic-tactile (what we feel) pathways in learning to read and spell.

The use of such an approach for children whose senses are compromised or greatly reduced could be effective if careful planning takes account of their individual sensory needs. Using a multi-sensory teaching approach means helping a child to learn through more than one of the senses. One possible approach is to involve the use of more of the child's senses, especially the use of touch and movement (kinetic). This will give the child's brain tactile and kinetic memories to hang on to, as well as the visual and auditory ones, and links to typical human development.

Helen Keller

Helen Keller is probably the best known deaf-blind child in history. A childhood illness had left her both blind and deaf. Subsequently, she became a very difficult child, showing her frustration with violent outbursts, screaming and temper tantrums. At 6 years of age, her family found a teacher who was partially sighted and had been educated in an institution for visually impaired children. When she arrived, she started teaching Helen to finger spell. At first Helen could not understand what Anne, the teacher was trying to communicate to her. The breakthrough came when Anne pumped water over one of Helen's hands and spelled out the word 'water' in the other. This made the connection between the word and its meaning. Helen made rapid progress after that. Anne taught her to read, firstly with raised letters and later with Braille, and to write with both ordinary and Braille typewriters.

(Adapted from Wearmouth, 2016b, p. 177)

Difficulties in motor movement

Movement is critically important in all aspects of learning. Motor skills are movements and actions of the muscles. Gross motor skills are required for movement and co-ordination of the arms, legs and other large body parts. They are needed for walking, running, crawling, swimming and so on. Fine motor skills are needed for smaller movements in the wrists, hands, fingers, feet and toes: picking up objects between the thumb and finger, using scissors and other tools, writing and so on. Gross and fine motor skills work together to provide co-ordination.

The developmental sequence for acquiring gross motor skills is hierarchical, developing from the head down to the feet, and from the midline of the body to the fingers. It is important for those in early years settings to be aware of this. Control of the head, shoulders and hips is needed before a child can balance while standing. This kind of control and balance is, in turn, required for so-called 'bilateral co-ordination', the ability to co-ordinate both sides of the body at the same time in a controlled way so that a child can hop, run, jump, climb, skip and so on. Co-ordination of eye, hand and foot are required for, for example, throwing, catching and kicking balls. Coulter *et al.* (2015) provide a very useful overview of the usual progression in gross motor skills.

Macintyre (2014) lists a number of competences of which families and practitioners in early years should be aware. All these competencies are needed for day to day living, and, generally, they develop naturally and become automatic:

- Bodily strength, that develops from head to toe, and from the centre of the body to the outside. Babies need to sit up to see the world around them, and might need support to do so;
- Balance, which is key to every action. Static balance is essential to maintain security in stillness. Dynamic balance is essential in motor movement;
- Co-ordination enables a child to perform different actions simultaneously. Hand-eye co-ordination, for example, enables a child to see, stretch out and pick up a toy and foot-eye co-ordination to kick a ball;
- A sense of speed, so that the child does not move so fast that s/he loses control of his/her body;
- Bodily and spatial awareness, so that the child knows where his/her bodily parts are in relation to each other, and where they function in space.

Many nursery-age children who have additional learning needs/learning differences will have delay and difficulty in achieving the basic movement patterns and without special support they struggle with the demands that accrue when greater independence is expected.

(Macintyre, 2014, p. 71)

Crawling is a particularly important skill in child development. By 20 weeks of age, most babies can roll over from their back to their front and by 28 weeks, most can push up on their arms to see the world around them. By 44 weeks, most babies can move forward on hands and knees, using a cross-lateral pattern. Crawling in this way develops strength in the arms, legs and neck, encourages a sense of balance, hand-eye and whole body co-ordination and visual acuity with the eyes following one hand, then the other.

Gower College Swansea
Library
Coleg Gŵyr Abertawe
Llyrfgell

Fine motor skills are the collective skills and activities that involve using the hands and fingers. Fine motor skills typically develop in a reasonably consistent and predictable pattern in the early years of childhood (Exner, 2005). The process begins when a 2- to 3-month-old baby first bats at a toy, then, by 6 months of age, progresses to grasping, releasing and transferring objects between their hands (Coulter *et al.*, 2015). They then progress to using fingers to manipulate and explore things, pick up small objects using a pincer grasp, stack blocks, self-feed and dress. By 5 years of age, the majority of children can copy squares, triangles, spontaneously write a few letters, draw a recognisable house and person and thread a large needle. As time goes by, during the early childhood years, children learn to use tools such as scissors, markers, crayons, pencils and glue.

Dyspraxia

According to the charity, the Dyspraxia Foundation, dyspraxia can be defined as 'a common disorder affecting fine and/or gross motor coordination in children and adults' (https://dyspraxiafoundation.org.uk/about-dyspraxia/-). Young children with dyspraxia experience difficulty in activities requiring balance, co-ordination and control: δυσ (dys) bad or difficult; πραξίς (praxis) action. One of the earliest signs is that a baby is 'floppy' and has poor muscle tone. Often, dyspraxic children miss out on the crawling stage and, therefore, all the skills that develop with it. Many of the activities of day-to-day living that require gross and fine motor co-ordination, for example, using a knife and fork, tying shoe laces, writing neatly and, sometimes, speaking clearly, are difficult. All young children are different, and families, practitioners and others in early years settings should carry out careful observation to identify the effects of dyspraxia.

As Macintyre (2014) comments, the experience of motor co-ordination difficulties may result in problems in both gross- and fine-motor skills in the early years of education. Among these are:

- clumsy movements, bumping into objects and easily losing balance;
- difficulty climbing on play equipment, jumping up with two feet and jumping from too great a height;
- difficulty pedalling tricycles and throwing and catching large balls;
- uncertainty in hand dominance;
- inability to use scissors and grip pencils properly;
- poor sitting position;
- difficulty taking off a coat and undressing generally;
- inability to use toilet facilities without help;
- difficulty learning sequences.

Serious physical, as well as sensory, impairments may be identified at the Newborn and Infant Physical Examination (NIPE) carried out within 3 days of the child's birth. In addition to the hearing and vision tests outlined above, the baby is examined to ensure there are no problems with the hips, heart and (for boys) genitals (National Health Service, 2015). Once a child's difficulties have been identified, either at the newborn stage or later on in the early years, there is likely to be a referral to health professionals, including physiotherapists, occupational therapists and speech and language therapists, and a plan put into place to address the difficulties. Plans should clearly take account of the outcomes of the assessment of difficulties, specify ways to address these and include clear targets in which the child and family should be involved. Advice from the health professionals may well be incorporated into the plans.

Muscular dystrophy

An estimated 8,000 to 10,000 people in the UK have a form of muscular dystrophy (Pohlschmidt and Meadowcroft, 2010), a group of genetic muscle diseases caused by the degeneration of muscle cells associated with progressive weakness and wasting of muscles. Most involve a defect in a protein that plays a vital role in muscle cell function or repair. This can include the heart. The severity of the condition is very variable. Symptoms can be obvious at birth or shortly afterwards. Sometimes the symptoms are very mild and are seen much later, during adulthood.

To take one example, in Duchenne muscular dystrophy, a problem in the genes results in a defect in dystrophin, which is an important protein in muscle fibres. It usually affects only boys, with around one boy in 35,000 being born with this condition. In about half of all cases the mother carries the gene but is usually not affected by it herself. Each son of a carrier has a 50 per cent chance of being affected and each daughter a 50 per cent chance of being a carrier. Most boys with this condition develop the first signs of difficulty in walking at the age of 1 to 3 years and are usually unable to run or jump like their peers. By about 8 to 11 years, boys become unable to walk. By their late teens or early twenties, the muscle-wasting is severe enough to shorten life expectancy.

Addressing physical difficulties

Regular supervision from a clinic is very important to manage particular physical conditions as effectively as possible.

> These children will need specialised equipment to aid their mobility, to support their posture and to protect and restore their body shape, muscle tone and quality of life. It is vital that children with physical needs have access to appropriate forms of therapy, for example physiotherapy and hydrotherapy, and that their carers receive training to enable them to manage their physical needs confidently on a day-to-day basis.
>
> (Mencap, undated, p. 5)

Michael, for example, a young boy with Duchenne muscular dystrophy who was featured in an Open University video programme (Open University, 2000), was a pupil in a mainstream primary school and participated in lessons in the same way as peers. A full-time learning support assistant was appointed to take care of his personal hygiene needs in school and to help him move around. As his muscles weakened, at his request she held up his hand in the classroom when he wanted to answer a question. There was a very close collaborative working relationship between her and Michael's family. Various members of outside agencies were involved in his health, well-being and academic progress. He was monitored very carefully by a physiotherapist for signs of increasing problems with his mobility, and had regular physiotherapy in school time to alleviate as far as possible the development of contractures, that is the shortening of his muscles. A member of the LA learning support team visited the school regularly to check whether he had appropriate equipment to meet his needs, for example, a laptop with peripherals that enabled him to connect to the computer easily as well as appropriate software to access the primary curriculum.

Summary

For a child with a sensory impairment the greatest challenge is communication. A young child with a visual difficulty may need help and encouragement to explore his/her physical environment and interact with others. Normal progress in language and cognitive development may be problematic for a child with a hearing impairment, so intensive support may be needed for a young child. Early assessment of learning needs and appropriate intervention is therefore clearly very important. Whatever means of communication are developed with young children, it should enable them to acquire cognitive and other skills.

Gross and fine motor movements have critically important contributions to make to all aspects of a young child's learning. As with all other areas of difficulty, individual strengths, needs, interests, experiences and family backgrounds must all be taken into account when devising intervention plans if they are to be effective and appropriate to the young child and the context in which s/he lives and is developing.

Chapter 7

Family perspectives

Major questions addressed in this chapter are:

- What are the legal entitlements of the families of young children in decision-making about SEND provision?
- What issues are involved in partnership work with families and carers of young children with SEND?
- What kind of practical initiatives can be effective in enabling positive working relationships between professionals and the home?
- What are some of the experiences of families and carers of what can happen in practice?

Introduction

In terms of day-to-day living, there is nothing 'set in stone' about the terms 'special educational needs and disability' or 'additional learning' or 'support' needs. Family and school contexts are very different. Parents and carers may have very different wishes and priorities for their young children that may or may not include similar objectives to those of an early years setting or school. Just to give one example, settings and schools are accountable for the measured achievement of their pupils which, most recently in England, enables comparison through school league tables that is open to public scrutiny, including during inspections. Necessarily, therefore, the increased focus on schools' accountability for quantified summaries of pupils' achievements and the need to meet targets set for all means that young children's needs in settings and schools may be seen in relation to what they require to reach these targets. In educational contexts, the terms 'SEND' and 'additional learning or support needs' are constructions that some might think of as an administrative convenience which is useful for identifying differences against the expected or 'normal' progression in schools. Once these differences have been identified then, in pursuance of equity, decisions can be taken about what additional resources might be needed to support young children to make formally acceptable progress. For the family, of course, things may look very different. Most parents or carers are likely to want the very best for their child, as they see it. This may or may not include identification as different from peers and meeting targets or goals set by the setting or school. Home-school relationships can be very sensitive, especially when both sides see themselves as trying their very hardest for a child but the child is not thriving. It is often not easy to see a situation through another's eyes, especially if the element of respectful discussion or exchange of important information is lacking.

In this chapter we first consider:

- what we mean by the various terms associated with the concept of home-school partnership;
- issues related to home-school relationships as they relate to young children with special educational, or additional support, needs more from an entitlement and rights perspective;
- the background to current policies on families' rights in decision-making about SEND provision for young people in schools and colleges;
- legal requirements in relation to partnership work with families and carers and some of the challenges in meeting these. Here we include examples of effective practical initiatives designed to enable more positive working relationships between schools and families and, thus, to meet families' legal entitlements to have their views taken into account.

We then turn to the experiences of families themselves. Personal accounts of what can happen in practice are included, both in a positive and less than positive sense. We have taken these from a number of sources, in particular interviews with families/carers, siblings and other family members that were carried out for the current publication. A number of personal narratives were gathered by the current authors through semi structured interviews of a range of family members about their experiences of having a child with special educational, or additional support, needs and/or disabilities. We examine their stories relating the joys and challenges of life with them, of gaining diagnoses, of contact with schools and other service providers and what they have learned along the way. Additionally, we explore the views of a range of professionals and how they conceive of relationships with families.

Definition of terms

A number of different, but related, terms are often used in a rather ill-defined way to describe the relationship between settings or schools and parents/carers, for example, parental 'engagement' and 'partnership' (Hallgarten, 2000). Parental engagement implies actual engagement in the child's learning process (Harris et al., 2010) that research has shown can have a significantly positive impact on achievement and well-being (Desforges and Abouchaar, 2003; Campbell, 2011; Shah, 2001; Wearmouth and Berryman, 2011). Parent partnership involves a 'full sharing of knowledge, skills and experiences' between families and the setting or school and, ideally, 'must be equal' (Jones, 2004, p. 39). It seems logical, therefore, that settings and schools might aim to encourage parental/family engagement and partnership in order that the information families have as experts about their children combined with the information teachers have about learning and the curriculum may work together in the interests of all young people. We refer here, particularly, to young children with SEND, who need additional support to overcome their barriers to learning (DfE, 2015a).

Changes in the focus on parental rights and entitlements

Parents and carers have not always had a statutory entitlement over decision-making in their children's education in state-funded educational institutions. For a long time after education for (almost) all children became compulsory, families had obligations rather than entitlements. In the 1870 Act (p. 471), School Boards were empowered, with the approval of the Education Department, to make byelaws that *required*:

(1) … the parents of children of such age, not less than 5 years nor more than 13 years, as may be fixed by the byelaws, to cause such children (unless there is some reasonable excuse) to attend school.

In the context of special education, an Education Act in England in 1921 mandated that the parents of blind, deaf, mentally and physically defective and epileptic children were required to see that their child attended a suitable special school from the age of 5, in the case of blind or deaf children, or aged 7 for other children, until the age of 16.

Much more recently, however, parental engagement in children's education has been a key issue in education policy in the UK with discussion of this in, for example, the Plowden Report (CACE, 1967), the Taylor Report (DES, 1977), the Warnock Report (DES, 1978) and the 1981 Education Act. Plowden (1967, p. 41) comments, for example:

Heads and class teachers should make themselves accessible for informal exchanges, so that, as one parent said, parents know their children's teachers at least as well as they know the milkman. They will then feel confident in entrusting their children to them.

Warnock (§4.51) notes:

as we have consistently stressed in this and other contexts, parents must be consulted and their views given full weight in the assessment of their children's needs; and this is especially true where decisions can touch deep-seated sensitivities.

Portage

An example of a service that was designed from the beginning to take the family context very clearly into account in supporting families of pre-school children identified as experiencing disabilities from a very young age is Portage (www.portage.org.uk/). The first Portage service in the UK was established in Winchester in 1976, interestingly 6 years after the 1970 Handicapped Children Act gave all children the right to an education, including those deemed ineducable as a result of identified multiple and profound difficulties in learning. Key underpinning principles were agreed for the delivery of the new service. For example, it would

- be home based and respond to the child's day to day learning environment;
- draw on the family's knowledge of the child and the way s/he responded to his/her personal world;
- recognise the experience of success as important to the learning process, beginning with establishing achievable starting points for sharing and planning small attainable steps in what the child would do next;
- work in partnership with other professionals to individualise key developmental targets and strategies so that they fit the distinctiveness of each child and family;
- use precision teaching and behavioural principles to encourage positive change in the learning and development of the child.

Currently, there are over 120 registered Portage services in England and Wales. The organisation 'Achieving for Children' outlines how the Portage service operates in Kingston and Richmond where children may receive help from this service if their special educational needs are identified at an early age. Portage is described as 'a home teaching service for pre-school children whose learning and development is significantly delayed'. This may also include children with autism and/or social communication difficulties. Portage home visitors collaborate with other professionals involved in the child's care, health and education 'to plan activities that are best suited to the child and their whole family'. Every one or two weeks a trained Portage home visitor visits the home and works 'alongside parents and carers to provide structured activities that will stimulate their child's development and support early learning'. Activities are designed to be learnt in small steps 'and practised and recorded at home, as learning is often easier for the child in familiar surroundings' (www.afclocaloffer.org.uk/pages/home/social-care/portage-service). Support from the Portage services continues until the child is 3 years old. When the child enters pre-school or nursery provision, the Portage home visitor liaises with the key staff in offering support during the transition into the new early years setting.

Parental rights and entitlements: the current situation

There is a formal acceptance now that parents and carers have the right to know about decisions taken in schools in relation to their offspring, and that they themselves are, potentially, an important source of additional support in addressing difficulties in learning and/or behaviour experienced by young children. Crozier and Reay (2005, p. 155) suggest it is the 'centre piece' in 'twenty first century' education policy-making.

Entitlement in law is not always synonymous with experience in practice, however. In 2009, the Lamb Enquiry into special educational needs and parental confidence in the system concluded that 'failure to comply with statutory obligations speaks of an underlying culture where parents and carers of children with SEN can too readily be seen as the problem and as a result parents lose confidence in schools and professionals'. Lamb went on to say: 'As the system stands it often creates "warrior parents" at odds with the school and feeling they have to fight for what should be their children's by right; conflict in place of trust' (Lamb, 2009, 1.1). The recommendations in this report suggested a new framework for the provision of SEN and disability information that 'puts the relationship between parent and school back at the heart of the process' and 'trades adherence to a 'laundry list' of rules for clear principles to guide that relationship' (Lamb, 2009, 1.4). Clearly, these recommendations informed the terms of the Children and Families Act (2014) in England.

The right of parents and/or carers to be consulted at every stage of decision-making about their children is enshrined in law across the UK (Special Educational Needs and Disability (Northern Ireland) Order, 2005; Children and Families Act, 2014 in England; 1996 Education Act, Part 1V in Wales; Education (Additional Support for Learning) (Scotland) Acts, 2004 and 2009). Section 19 of Part 3 of the Children and Families Act 2014, for example, requires that the views, wishes and feelings of children and their parents, and their participation, must be central to every decision the LA makes in regard to assessing a young child's SEND and how to support him/her.

A number of guides for parents and carers have been issued to support families to understand their entitlements, for example, *The Parents' guide to additional support for learning* (Enquire, 2014) published by the Scottish government, and the *Special Educational Needs and Disability (SEND) – A guide for parents and carers* (DfE, 2014a) in England. Parents' and families' entitlements are described in these *Guides*. For example, the *Guide* in England (DfE, 2014a, p. 11) makes very clear the basic principles that parents and families 'need to keep in mind' when thinking about the special needs of their child:

> All children with special educational needs (SEN) or disabilities should have their needs met, whether they are in early years settings … in school or in college.

It advises parents and families that they:

> … should have a real say in decisions that affect their children, should have access to impartial information, advice and support and know how to challenge decisions they disagree with.

As one of the professionals that were interviewed by the current authors said of her work as a member of an LA early years advisory team that it should be:

> … very, very much about keeping the family at the very heart of what you do and actually working from what they want, rather than getting tied up in what professionals want of families. I think in early years we actually do it really, really well, you know, guiding and supporting a family without taking away from them or leaving them feeling that they're being done unto. It makes my toes curl actually when I hear quite often family experiences, especially when children go into school they feel done unto, or being put upon, that it's somebody else's agenda. The only agenda that we should be working to is the family's agenda.

Regular assessments of the progress of all children should take place, with gathering of information that should include discussion early on with both child and parents/carers so that all can be clear about the child's areas of strength and difficulty, any concerns the parent/carer(s) might have, the outcomes agreed for the child and the next steps.

Parents and families are advised (DfE, 2014a, pp. 8–9):

> If you think your child has SEN, you should talk to your child's early education setting, school, college or other provider. They will discuss any concerns you have, tell you what they think and explain to you what will happen next.

Early years settings and schools would therefore be well advised to be prepared to answer questions such as the following that the *Guide* suggests (2014a, p. 9):

> Questions you might want to ask:
>
> - Why do you think my child has SEN or a disability?
> - How do you know that my child doesn't have SEN or a disability?
> - What happens now?

If a young child is identified as having SEND, settings and schools are exhorted to put 'SEN provision', in place through a graduated approach in the form of a four part assess → plan → do → review cycle. SENDCos will need to be prepared for the implications of family's expectations of their active involvement in the process as the *Guide* (2014d, p. 9) advises:

> You may be contacted – for example in schools, this will be by your child's teacher or SENCO – if your early years setting, school or college think your child needs SEN support. Or you can approach your child's school or other setting if you think your child might have SEN. You will be involved and your views will be needed throughout the process, and you will be kept up to date with the progress made.

If the child still does not make the progress that is expected, the school or parents should consider requesting an Education, Health and Care needs assessment and provide evidence of the action taken by the school as part of its SEND support. It is expected that both parents and students will be actively involved in requesting, creating and assessing the effectiveness of the individual plan (DfE, 2014a, p. 22):

> … sometimes a child … needs a more intensive level of specialist help that cannot be met from the resources available to schools and other settings to provide SEN support. In these circumstances, you or your child's school or other setting could consider asking your local authority for an Education, Health and Care (EHC) needs assessment for your child.

Families' personal perspectives

Each family has its own way of functioning and interacting with the different members within it and with professionals outside. It is like a system, almost like a piece of machinery: shift one part and other connecting parts move as a result. For parents, the birth of a child with some kind of difficulty or disability will change their whole life and can be for many 'a chronic sorrow that continues through a lifetime' (Strohm, 2002, p. 66). Personalities can change. For example, many parents report feelings of worthlessness, failure and incompetence when responding to their changed circumstances. An altered internal working model (Bowlby, 1988) of how they see themselves will inevitably affect the ways in which to relate to the immediate family and to the outside world. For many parents, the idea of a 'typical' grief curve of shock, anger, denial, assimilation and accommodation leading to a resolution and a capacity to 'move on' and rebuild is not, as Robinson (2003) notes, as clear-cut and neat as it would appear – and perhaps this is true of *any* individual's experience of grief. Nicholas, a father of a child with Down's syndrome (Meyer, 1995, p. 14) notes that 'the peak of joy at the birth of my fine new son and the death of my expectations' led to 'powerful emotional oscillation between positive and negative emotions' which persist throughout. He later goes on to discuss the 'grip of a psychological python that inexorably squeezes time, energy, creative and financial resources' (1995, p. 21) out of both parents and the family unit as a whole. Matthew, another parent in the same study, talks of how to this day he fully struggles with the idea of letting go of his son's 'normal ghost'. One of the professionals interviewed by the authors of this book commented:

> It might be a child is presenting in a particular way, perhaps with autistic spectrum disorder traits, but working with a mum who, perhaps, is in denial that there is anything wrong at all takes considerable time and experience and you can only work at the parent's pace.

The emotional reaction is not the same for all parents, of course. Some speak of unexpected joy. For example, mothers in Janet Read's study of twelve West Midland mothers (Read, 2000) reported that their lives had been enriched in unanticipated ways. Jacqui Jackson, mother to seven children, four of whom have a range of special needs, advises that:

> It is imperative that as parents we encompass it, learn all we can about it and then move onto new horizons. We are now on a different journey to the one originally planned and it is only natural to ponder over what might have been … Sometimes it is heartbreaking and I have to say I would often love to wave a magic wand and make things easier. The secret however is not to wallow in 'what ifs' but to take a step back, smile at their differences and carry on fighting for understanding and their rights. One thing that works for me if I find myself choking back tears and making comparisons between my boys and 'typically developing' children of the same age is to do a mental stock take of all their endearing ways, their differences and their strengths – believe me, on reflection you will be amazed at how many positives you will find.
>
> (Jackson, 2004, pp. 225–6)

Parents may be very deeply affected by the way in which they discovered their child's special needs, the length of time this took and the manner in which the news was delivered. In a very moving account that is related largely through drawings accompanied by personal asides, the author of *Hole in the Heart: Bringing up Beth* (Beaumont, 2016) describes how medical professionals tried to avoid telling her and her husband that their new baby had Down's syndrome for several days. After the news was broken she recalls a nurse saying: 'I can organise a social worker to come and we can talk about adoption' (2016, p. 40). In the next few days, everything the family was told about their new child was negative. Another nurse commented, for example: 'She won't learn to read, but she might manage to understand the symbol for men and women on public toilets. She might have a spot of ENT trouble … You know! Sore throats, runny noses, bit of deafness. That kind of thing. You will be comforted to know that your daughter is likely to die before you' (2016, pp. 46–7). Commenting on how the family was told about the baby, a consultant cardiologist subsequently commented (back cover): 'It has made me embarrassed …'.

Professionals' optimism combined with realism about the future seems to be an obvious, much more productive and supportive, approach. One parent at interview recollected:

> We did have an assessment by a paediatrician who came to our house, and spent a lot of time playing with our son. He said, 'He'll do, he'll earn his own keep when he's adult. It mightn't be in the kind of profession you would have hoped for a son but he'll keep himself' and actually that was quite a crumb of comfort I've hung onto.

This conflicts sharply with the opinion of the GP in relation to the same young child who said 'some very dismissive things like "Oh, he's got learning disabilities and he's not going to be much good", something very negative'. For this parent, fortunately 'that was the only real negative that springs to mind'.

Beaumont's narrative moves from Beth's babyhood through her toddler years, with illustrations of friends' and family's reactions to her, some very positive, 'normal' or accepting, others shockingly negative. When asked by a friend some months after her birth how she felt about the baby, the author replied: 'It took a while, but once her character emerged, I fell in love with her. I stopped only seeing the Down's bit of her and started to see her for herself' (2016, p. 105).

Issues in early intervention

The parents interviewed by the current authors were largely in agreement with those in previous studies (Read, 2000; Meyer, 1995, 1997; Moore, 2004) regarding the immense relief felt at obtaining a diagnosis after time spent not knowing, not being sure, professionals not being sure (often for very good reason) or helpful.

> Is it harder to not know what the problem is with your child for 11 years than to know from the start? I don't know. What I would say is that it is hard to **not** know what the problem is and therefore how to act in their best interests. That makes it sound like diagnosis is the golden prize – it's not, of course, but at the time that's how it felt, because a diagnosis could lead to a statement and could lead to unlocking support **and** at least potentially offered some clarity. At least, that's how it seemed, **and** it would help to gather together the specialists who could help – or so I thought.
>
> (Parent)

Several parents noted the length of time it took for a child whose disabilities were not immediately obvious to gain an accurate diagnosis:

> When you don't **know** what the problem is, it's up to the individual parent/family to keep seeking possible solutions, and I felt we got pushed around a lot and the processes of finding out were so **slow**. We seemed to drift from the age of about 3 up until about 11 with some concerns, growing concerns about what were the issues for our son and how best he could be supported in school. So from then he got a statement of special educational needs, but all over about an eight year period I suppose of coming and going and various professionals but nobody really being too sure.
>
> (Parent)

It can be very difficult for professionals to give a diagnosis with certainty and for them to offer the follow up advice that is so critical. For example, when considering Asperger Syndrome (AS), there is no single presenting pattern, and many markers of the wide range of possible presenting symptoms might not easily be apparent in the early years for some children, hence the reason why so many people with AS go undiagnosed for a long time, as the personal testimony of Daniel Tammet (2006) attests. A mother reflected on the difficulty in identifying whether her son had a real need or not:

> It was his mobility that caused me some concern. He was crawling perhaps at about 9 or 10 months, that was normal spectrum but he wasn't starting to walk at about 16 or 17 months which seemed late so I asked somebody for advice, perhaps the health visitor, I can't remember how it happened, but whoever it was said they were more concerned that he wasn't vocalising at that age and sent him for further tests. So that was the first inkling I had. Looking back, and also comparing with my grandchildren, he didn't actually make the funny little noises babies make pre-speech so that was probably the first sign. But we were told that boys are slower at speaking ... My

in-laws in particular were quite dismissive. I remember my own mother … would say things like, 'He should be walking by now, he should be talking by now'. But my in-laws were more kind of, 'You're imagining, he's only slow' and this persisted into his adulthood that my mother-in-law particularly would say, 'If you didn't say he had learning disability, nobody would know. He doesn't need any extra help'.

One professional interviewed by the current authors stated:

I think the biggest, I suppose, challenge for working with children is … identifying what is a lifelong disability and what is perhaps, for example, children having attachment difficulties or just difficulties being separated from parents; children who have maybe come from a slightly deprived home environment who are just finding it hard initially and, with support, will be fine in the long run, but they are behind their peers for a short period of time … .

I think that just initial getting to know children in a holistic way and finding out what are their particular needs is the most important thing to do with children in the early years.

Some professionals too may not voice a need to 'push for' a label. This might be for many reasons. Perhaps these professionals feel that the label stigmatises the child or stereotypes them or takes away from the child's uniqueness. They may want to spare the parents' feelings, although parents are going to need to be in full possession of what the diagnosis is, entails and means for now and the future at some point. In some ways, this could be perceived as a short-term gain in exchange for longer term concerns as parents develop greater understanding.

Some parents might be concerned that professionals' reluctance to assign a firm label that identifies more of a range of challenging features, might reduce LAs' responsibility to allocate financial resources to their child's care and education in a national context of LAs' dwindling resources.

Reflective activity: effects of labelling

Luke Jackson, a young person with AS, is adamant that there should be no delay in giving the label and, in ways appropriate to that child's understanding, of informing them as well (Jackson, 2002). The child who goes without the label is significantly at risk of going without the right kind of help.

Labels stereotype … but also identify …

Labels devalue … but can also promote …

We would like you to reflect on what these ideas mean.

- Can you think of some examples?
- How do you think labels might help parents emotionally or practically?
- How might labels support practitioners in their work with children?
- How might they be counteractive or counter-productive in providing support?

Today, a child would be more likely to have parents' concerns registered formally.

> When a child is aged between two and three, early years practitioners **must** review progress and provide parents with a short written summary of their child's development, focusing in particular on communication and language, physical development and personal, social and emotional development.
>
> (DfE, 2015a, §5.23)

The aim of this progress check is to enable earlier identification of development needs so that additional support can be put in place where needed. However, the issue still exists of how easy early identification is when children all develop at different rates and in different ways. Parents, practitioners and SENDCos interviewed by the current authors all made similar comments, for example, 'I'm aware that there's a huge range of developmental normality for a child, and that many children have perhaps just lacked the opportunity to learn certain things' (SENDCo).

There is a tricky balancing act to be achieved between intervening early so that support is galvanised in a timely fashion and the watching and waiting approach, perhaps more often deployed in situations where children's needs are not immediately identified as associated with a particular 'syndrome'. Parents in Paige-Smith and Rix's (2006) study, which focused on children with Down's syndrome and parents' experiences of early intervention, noted instances of when parents felt that intervention was imposed on them. They cited Bridle and Mann (2000, p. 7) who identify the pressure mothers in particular face in 'presenting themselves to professionals as coping and competent'. They additionally note (2000, p. 4) the challenge of being viewed as a 'special needs family' who, rather than feeling they are free and able to engage in the playful experiences of childhood that are going to support natural development, are encouraged by professionals to undertake focused or packaged 'work' in which they feel 'the focus on the future can interfere with enjoyment of the present'.

Reflective activity: issues around early intervention

Note down what you consider are some of the contentious issues associated with early intervention. Below are the views of two professionals in this area. What do you think?

'On a philosophical level, what comes to mind first is that the best way of supporting them [children] is to listen and watch and to be with them, and not to judge; to hold fast to all the principles of equality and give young children time'. (Teacher)

'Although it's important to give time and watch, and being observant and noticing and not assuming that there is a significant challenge when it may actually just be opportunity and development, in fact it is unhelpful to do nothing. Even if that doing something is observation, that's still doing something. It's really unhelpful to think "Oh they'll grow out of it, and not do anything". To think they may grow out of it is very helpful, because it's true. With opportunity and support, children can overcome challenges, but just to think it's not my concern, they're only little; that's not helpful at all' (Primary SENDCo).

There is a question about whether an early interventionist model should mainly apply when the child exhibits an obvious disability. When development can be seen to be just slightly different or delayed to the 'norm', it may be that more harm than good is done by making parents overly anxious. At a time when parents often hear conflicting views about how to bring up their child, what development to expect when, and the importance of 'school readiness' and not falling behind in the race to attain superior literacy and numeracy skills, it may be that there is a potential for early intervention to impose a certain 'outsider', professional view on their child that is not compatible with the way they wish to engage with their child, as noted above.

Other issues connected with the tensions between intervening early or not include the idea that an early intervention programme can impose a deficit model on the child and parent, with the professional coming in with plans to improve and 'fill the gaps' in the child's learning. Alternative and more enriching approaches advocated by early years specialists would point out that the purpose of assessment should be to enhance learning rather than provide a prescribed checklist of skills against which a child should be measured (see, for example, Carr, 2001). One particularly helpful professional who took this approach was very highly rated by one of the mothers who was interviewed:

> We were supported by the Educational Psychologists and the one that stands out was XXX whom I really rated. She kind of put things in terms that you could understand and related to both parents and child. ... she was kind of common sense in the kind of things that she said, 'We'll try this. What about this?'

A more holistic model for assessing what children can do rather than what they cannot should be more affirming and inclusive overall for both child and parent. However, this view rather conflicts with current policy in the early years that focuses on early identification.

Ultimately, aside from the challenges that arise from professional stances or political positioning and priorities or even labels themselves, as Moore (2004, p. 82) says, 'All I had was George', and, as a parent stated at interview:

> But at the end of the day, you just have to deal with what arises, you deal with your child as you do and try to do the best, regardless of a label. That label does perhaps sometimes help you to access support, assuming people can help and know about the condition ... but you are the one with your child.
>
> (Parent)

Delays in assessment and provision

All the parents interviewed described challenges they faced in trying to get their children what they needed. Delayed assessment and access to resources were two of these. This can cause enormous frustration, as one parent noted:

> You will need a thick skin and grit and determination – because you will have to shout and fight and you will have to try and not care about the impact you are having on others or what they think of you, in order to get what you want and need for your child. I'd like to hope I would be better at that now, but at the time I was too fragile – I

suppose I was grieving **and** I had a naïve faith that the professionals would do the right thing **and** because both my husband and I were 'in the system' we could both see both sides of things – the parent side and the professional constraints, and I think that made me too generous to the professionals for too much of the time when really I should have been shouting and jumping up and down more. I think I tried too hard to see it from their side, to appear reasonable because I thought appearing reasonable would push us through the system quicker. I don't think it did. And actually, appearing to cope is probably counter-productive to getting what you need. On the other hand, I couldn't show myself up to other professionals as someone who **couldn't** cope – so a double bind really.

One of the professionals interviewed expressed her frustration, too, about delays in accessing necessary provisions:

> Sometimes we need to get another professional involved in order to get funding from the borough, and then the waiting times are very frustrating because, actually at the end of the day, the advice they give us is basically what we've been doing all along, but you can't get the funding until you get their report. So, I don't know if that happens everywhere, but certainly in XXX [name of LA] that's the way it's worked. … I just don't think there's the resources. Everybody's stretched. Speech and language are stretched, so it's like a nine-month waiting list. And children in their early years can't afford nine months to wait. And parents can't wait that long to know that there's something. Sometimes parents won't accept or in some sort of denial, and if really they could get another professional to say the same things that we're saying, it might help them to understand that something needs to be done quicker.

Another commented: 'I'd like to see more support within the services and more availability for families'.

Experiences in settings and schools

The relationship between families and professionals in early years settings or schools is obviously crucial in ensuring that young children who experience difficulties of various kinds are included, have their needs met and thrive in all respects.

Reflective activity: importance of home–school relationships

One of the parents interviewed by the current authors recounted her experience of her son's first day at home. Read the account below, and note your responses to the following:

- What are your reactions to this story?
- What principles should teachers and practitioners hold in mind when communicating with parents?
- How might this relationship have been improved?

'The worst day ever was the day my son had his trial day at school. Where we lived, and the fact he had a May birthday, meant that he didn't start school until Year 1 and had spent four terms in a Nursery school and had a 'reception year' there. When I came to collect him, the teacher said: 'Well, we've got a right one here and I can see I'm going to have to keep a very close eye on him', meaning, I think, that she had already marked him out as trouble. Trouble? At that age he wasn't in-your-face disruptive. He was fairly quiet and dreamy and prone to doing his own thing. I suppose she saw this as non-compliance. Whatever, I was so devastated, I just couldn't respond to her. She probably had no idea of the impact of what she said on me. In a way, how could she? And, on the surface, it appears quite an innocuous remark; however, it is **not** so innocuous to a parent who is anxious about their child and a major transition in their lives.

'Perhaps this is a real case in point for professionals to tread quite carefully when they are forging new relationships. There was **no** relationship to be had there after that! If I had my time again I would have asked her to explain herself better. In fact, if I had my time again with nearly **all** of the professionals I have had dealings with about my son, I would challenge them more. But this day, and as with so many other occasions when I've been in formal and less formal meetings about him, I just was unable to express myself. I just went home and cried and worried and prayed about how he would fit in and how he would manage in school. It was such a big thing, and such an inauspicious start. He felt labelled straight away and I felt responsible – and guilty – straight away'. (Parent)

Another parent's story about her son's experience in a Reception class was equally insensitive:

My son had one year at the local mainstream primary. His class teacher, I found was quite judgemental. Admittedly she had an over-large class with kids many from a big estate, and some of them had behavioural difficulties. She was an argumentative woman, and she would kind of come to the door muttering, 'I can't be doing with this. He can't tie his shoelaces. I haven't time with all this'. She was quite negative.

(Parent)

Beveridge (2005) indicates that teachers often seem to view parents as a key part of the problem within the child, ascribing the child's difficulties as a consequence of deficit home support or behaviour management. If so, this can add to an already burdensome sense of guilt ('Is it my fault he's like this?' (Parent)) or frustration as a result of less responsiveness and reciprocity in the child or dealing with their challenging personality, as Randall and Parker (2004) note. Also, anxiety ('Will this be all right?' (Parent)), isolation from 'normal' and the sense of dreams for their child unravelling and going awry can occur.

Of course, while school experiences can be very negative, this is not entirely, and always, the case, as a young woman who had been identified as experiencing SEN attests during an interview with the current authors:

My mum sought help. She really tried to get help. She knew something wasn't right. But her experience was … my head teacher at lower school wanted to have me exorcised because he thought I was evil. What I was lucky about is that in all three of my schools I had at least one teacher who not necessarily understood me but was always there for me.

The need for professionals who are taking charge of a parent's precious child about whom they already may have significant anxieties, is that sensitivity is an essential quality, as illustrated in the following experience of one of the professionals who worked in an early years setting, as related at interview:

> One of our children had quite severe autism and an EAL[1] background. I very rarely saw mum. Dad was the one that did most of the caring. The child couldn't access the nursery at all, really, for the first term. Dad came into the multi-sensory room with us. Gradually, he moved into the hallway so that he could still see his child.
>
> It took us about a whole term for the boy to actually start accessing the nursery provision at all. By the time he left, and he did go to a special school, he was sitting in group time, he was waving hello for his name, he was pointing to photographs of the children that he knew. It was a real complete turnaround, but I suppose the biggest success is that that family were just so overwhelmed with appreciation because we also got them disability living allowance, we filled in the forms for them, we referred them to the children's disabilities team. They had access to none of those prior to this.
>
> Before he came to us they had had this little boy up to the age of three with no understanding that there was anything different and coping with him not sleeping, having to drive him all around the town to get him to sleep every night. Both parents completely sleep deprived. And, so, when his sibling came to us at the age of two, the dad came to see me again and said 'I think I have a similar difficulty'. So, he recognised the difficulty, he trusted us and we started the process straight away. It turns out the second little boy does have similar but not quite as severe difficulties. But dad knew what to do and understood it, and he knew that he could come and talk to us. That was a real success with that whole family.

Meetings with professionals that focus significantly on the child's strengths are more likely to be profitable than those that focus more on difficulties, as Keen and Rodger (2012) amongst others recommend.

Choice of special or mainstream education

Since Warnock in 1978, there has been a significant expectation that children will be included within mainstream settings. The legislation for this has been in place since 1981. The principles of inclusion enshrined in these documents note key benefits of inclusion and the right to access education that gives children the opportunity to achieve their personal potential. Cairns and McClatchey (2013) indicate the positive impact on both social and academic achievement aspects of inclusion for neurotypically developing children, and both they, McConkey (1994) and Mittler (1995), stress that familiarity with disabled and special needs children raises much needed awareness of similarity as well as difference and breaks down some negative attitudes and stereotypes which exist about disability.

The stories related by parents interviewed by the current authors together with those cited by Meyer (1995), Read (2000), Carpenter (2000), Strohm (2002) and others are testimony to the pragmatism of parents, despite their hopes and dreams going awry:

> I must admit there was a kind of horror of snobbery, a hangover of the Special Needs stigma of the special school in our home town where daft kids went to and I couldn't bear the thought of my son going there. ... And I thought, 'That's going to go from bad to worse if he mixes with other kids with learning disabilities', whereas the special school in XX [*another town*] had a very good reputation for kids with both multiple, profound and primarily, I think, for physical disabilities. But I thought, 'Well, he's more likely to get a wider range of peer interaction if there's people with physical disabilities without learning disabilities, if he goes there'. So somehow we made a case.
>
> (Parent)

When this young man transferred to secondary school, it was back in his home town. Here he flourished, partially as a result of the head teacher who thought creatively about problems:

> But kids from F [*secondary special school*] who walked about tended to get bullied and jeered and shouted at. So he was getting upset at that at first. So I talked to the head teacher about it. Instead of saying, 'We told you so', she said, 'Look, there's a couple of lads who live on the estate near you, good lads, I'm going to appoint them as minders for your son. So they came to call for him every morning and walked in with him. And they were kind of rough diamonds but they almost grew into the role of his minder; they were kind of like big brother figures.
>
> (Parent)

The same could always not be said for other children in their mainstream schools, as exemplified by the following story. For some children, continuous low grade bullying is a constant fact of life, and finding ways of managing those situations is not easy for many children with SEND, especially those who lack a voice, the language, social skills or quick wit to rebuff the taunters:

> He did suffer from being bullied at school because he was different and he behaved differently. So, for example, he got into various bits of aggro on the school bus, he just couldn't cope with teasing and brush it off, and so he was banned from the school bus. He then had to have a taxi every day, which marked him out as different again and which is a bit ridiculous. It was only three miles but it would have been easier I would have thought to put in a bit more supervision on the school bus, it would have helped a lot more children, I feel, rather than paying for a taxi.

Role of fathers

The slightly separate issues of fathers and their feelings and ways of accepting their child's difference also appears in the literature and was raised by several of those interviewed by the current authors. Like Meyer (1995) who talks of a father having to go away and reflect in his own way and his own time, before coming to terms with his son's disability, some of those interviewed too noted a range of responses, some which were 'managed' more effectively than others. One mother, for example, recollected:

> He [husband/father] was acutely embarrassed by it [i.e. learning disability and dyspraxia] as the only child of a high-flying father with high expectations. And in fairness to him, he went to the same school where his dad was head of maths and he always had very high expectations so it must have been quite a blow to him to have a son with a learning disability. He tried to kind of play it down, put it on the back-burner, but he didn't like going out in public with our son so from him being very small, that caused tension between us.

This young man's sister commented on the situation as she saw it:

> I don't think my dad coped enormously well with it … I'm sure mum found it really hard as well but I think he particularly found it hard … the pressure that my brother put them under did contribute to them splitting up. Children full-stop put a marriage under strain so I think having a child with learning disabilities would do it. My brother's whole life put a strain on the relationship and especially with my dad's parents. They were always in denial about it.

Some of those interviewed put forward very strongly the case for fathers to be highly included as far as possible from the start in their child's life, their assessments and, as far as possible any ongoing discussions and appointments with other agencies, which McConkey (1994), Meyer (1995) and Strohm (2002) claim is key in helping their own adjustment processes as well as offering support to spouses. They perhaps also highlight the need for fathers to be helped towards reflection on their feelings, views and values, something that would be a helpful step towards greater tolerance and acceptance of difference more generally in society. It brings to the fore again the need for highly skilled listeners, key people, experts, counsellors who can take the time to listen, probe and challenge perceptions and emotions and thus support the journeys parents, including fathers, and grandparents and other involved family members, have to undertake. As Carpenter (2005) notes, these families are often scared, upset, grieving, vulnerable and coming to terms with their changed lives. He says that: 'The role of the professional is to catch them when they fall, listen to their sorrow, dry their tears of pain and anguish, and when the time is right, plan the pathway forward' (2005, p. 181). This asks much of the professional, and highlights again their invaluable support, when offered in a nurturing, timely and empathetic way. It perhaps also raises issues of the training and time allocations of such professionals in a time of ever decreasing budgets and high demand on their time and services. In addition to these practical constraints, the high sensitivity needed to form such trusting relationships with parents and families means that people in these roles must be more highly prized and valued in order to bring all concerned to a deeper and more reflective understanding of themselves, help their marriages or partnerships and quality of life (Kilic et al., 2013; Vasilopoulou and Nisbet, 2016) and for the child.

Siblings' perspectives

While services often talk about a holistic approach that includes the needs of the whole family around the child, in practice this can be complex, for both the professional involved with the child with needs and for the parents and siblings of that child as well. Those in Meyer's (1997) and Strohm's (2002) research note that it can be hard to be the sibling of a child with needs for a range of reasons. These reasons, also endorsed by some of the siblings interviewed, included ideas about doing things together as a family, feeling ignored, dealing with mixed emotions, managing teasing by others and having concern for their parents.

A child in Meyer's study claimed that 'I think brothers and sisters need to be noticed more' (1997, p. 64) whilst another said 'I also don't like it when they [other people] always ask "How's your brother?" and never ask how I am' (p. 63). These are very real issues for children when they sense their equal right to be noticed and may already feel that many aspects of their lives revolve around the priority needs of their sibling. A sibling, interviewed by the authors, wryly made the following observations after meeting a previous teacher in town:

> At school, teachers remember you – well, they always remember my brother and not necessarily for the right reasons – rather than the rest of us and I suppose that it always going to impact on us.

Strohm (2002) additionally notes the mixed emotions that siblings wrestle with. She talks of the upset she felt when others stared at her sister: feelings of sorrow, feeling sorry, seeking approval, anger at herself for not coping or failing at making life better and easier for everyone. Again, however, not all siblings interviewed by the authors reported problems being the brother or sister of a young child with SEND. One commented, for example, when asked if she had had any concerns about bringing friends home when she realised that her brother had difficulties in learning:

> I don't think I did. I think I sometimes thought about it afterwards. But no, I mean my friends have always been great and boyfriends have always been amazing. Yes, very lucky really. I don't know about it, I don't know what they think but, again, you know, I've got a lot of friends who've just known my brother for most of our lives, so it's no.

When asked what advice, from her own experience, she would give to families of young children with difficulties in learning, this sibling expressed strong views about the importance of working from the assumption that everybody learns in the same way albeit some learn more slowly than others:

> … let them live as normal a life as possible. I'd say that's going on my own experience because a lot of my brother's school mates and friends were cosseted and wrapped in cotton wool and I think it seemed to stop them from growing up whereas, hairy as it's been at times, mum's always given my brother a lot of independence and I think it's the best thing she could have done for him. It's amazing. It's really like any of us I suppose, because although he has those difficulties, he still learns in similar ways to us and still develops by trying to get experience of those things. So, yes, just to give people as many opportunities as possible. Really scary to do as a parent, full-stop, I guess, but particularly letting your disabled son use public transport and if he wants to give it a go to try and let him really. So I guess that would be the overriding principle.

Extended family members

There are stories of the power and positive support that friends and family members can provide (for example, Moore, 2004; Read, 2000; Wolman *et al.*, 2001 amongst others). Randall and Parker (1999) note how, overall, the larger proportion of grandparents overall support and accept children with SEND into the family. However, they indicate that between 27 per cent (their estimate from their research) and 33 per cent (a figure they report following the earlier work of DeMyer in 1979) of families experience problems with the responses of grandparents prior to, during, or after diagnosis of a child with special needs in the family. It is obvious that wider families' rejection of a child can cause significant stress and that their attitudes frequently cut off the parents from an important source of support. One of their interviewees talks of how 'We were more or less sent to Coventry' (1999, p. 5).

At interview with the current authors, parents offered mixed stories which possibly also reflect a denial or lack of desire to come to terms with the issues:

> But my in-laws were more kind of, 'You're imagining, he's only slow' and this persisted into his adulthood. My mother-in-law particularly would say, 'If you didn't say he had a learning disability, nobody would know. He doesn't need any extra help'. There was quite a battle on that side, and they were really in denial. It's hard because you tend to be in denial yourself, you kind of hope for the best. This isn't really the best strategy to get the help you need for a child with a learning disability. ... It kind of irritated me a bit and I thought 'She's wrong' but fortunately she lived 114 miles away so she wasn't really around to tell me what I should and shouldn't do.
>
> (Parent)

A further narrative from a parent during interview notes the damage that can be caused by insensitive opinions:

> We were very alone as a nuclear family. Both grandmothers were a long way away geographically **and** emotionally and intellectually. One's view, 'Oh he'll grow out of it', was benign but hardly helpful. However, the other offered a more corrosive and hurtful viewpoint, from which I've never recovered: 'It's your fault, you're a refrigerator mother and he didn't form an attachment'. This was so wrong in fact, and out of touch, and based on no real evidence at all, given that she lived over 250 miles away and she saw us rarely. Bettelheim – I think it's him? - has a **lot** to answer for; will this idea of refrigerator mothers **ever** go away?

The fact that supportive acceptance of a child with special needs or disability by wider family members is common, but not universal, highlights the need for either friends, support groups, a key person and advocate within the LA or a voluntary organisation to provide that crucial listening ear, to hold and contain (Bion, 1961) the range of emotions parents and families might feel.

Importance of support groups

As noted by Kramer *et al.* (2013), the more support networks that parents can gather around them, the easier it can be for many to keep drawing strength to carry on with the supporting role. This is where, critically, the role of the wider friends and family networks and possibly support groups might prove to be invaluable. The use of support groups has been documented widely (see, for example, Giallo and Gavidia-Payne, 2006; Strohm, 2002 or Mittler and Mittler, 1994). Amongst those interviewed by the current authors, there were some mixed reactions to the concept. It is deeply helpful for some to share with others who may have similar experiences and their stories and support can provide enormous reassurance and practical suggestions. For others, however, other parents might be less than helpful, given their own unresolved issues of grief and anger. One, for example, commented:

> The group was full of a miserable, negative group of people. It was almost, um, what's the, was it Seligman's [1975] 'learned helplessness', that kind of, 'Oh what can I do about it, woe is me, oh dear, all full of problems'. Not the kind of group one would want to mix with. It was 'These poor carers' and that's what it was like at these self-help groups, just people kind of sitting round wringing their hands. But perhaps I just had a bad experience.

What has perhaps overall received less attention generally is the potential need for more support groups for siblings, as noted by Naylor and Prescott (2004). Siblings may need the time and safe space to speak their minds, and to open up about their feelings without feeling a sense of disloyalty to their parents or discounting their own feelings or needs. Naylor and Prescott (2004) note how many siblings in the group they set up were initially very reluctant to acknowledge any negative feelings they had about their sibling; indeed many appeared almost habituated to the situation.

Summary

There are many factors that influence a family's adjustment to having a child with special educational needs or a disability. Their cultural background has a key part to play, including their beliefs about what it means to have a child with SEND, along with financial resources, religious beliefs and the social support network within which they nestle. One size does not fit all. Issues such as the type and severity of the disability, and whether it has a greater perceived stigma attached to it by society or whether it seems more socially acceptable (and therefore 'easier' to include the children in social interactions in the outside world) play a part in the complex mix. In addition to these social and structural factors, the temperament of individual family members will affect how they adjust overall. Some people have great inner strength, although it is true that in the adjustment process most families and family members come to recognise their own strengthening core. All may feel vulnerable at times, and some families and family members will feel vulnerable for more of the time than others – vulnerable as a result of guilt, loss of control, isolation, fear for their present circumstances and those that the future might bring. People perceive what is happening around them in different ways. In addition to this, individual reactions in their turn alter the connections outside of the immediate family unit too. Grandparents, for example, and other extended family members and friends will also have their own perceptions on a child seen as having special or additional support needs. Many of these effects will continue over a lifetime. As Russell (2003) notes, many parents' needs are less likely to be met than those of their children. Although, often, parents would rather this than the other way round, it should be increasingly the case that needs are met *together* and holistically and not an either/or situation. Some people will be enriched by the experience, others will struggle to come to terms with it, but all will be touched in some way.

We would like to end this chapter with a request from Russell (1997, p. 79) about how she, as a parent of a child with significant difficulties in learning, would like young children with SEND, or additional learning needs, and their families to be treated – as individual human beings, first and foremost.

- Please accept and value our children (and ourselves as families) as we are.
- Please celebrate difference.
- Please try and accept our children as children first. Don't attach labels to them unless you mean to do something.
- Please recognise your power over our lives. We live with the consequences of your opinions and decisions.
- Please understand the stress many families are under. The cancelled appointment, the waiting list no one gets to the top of, all the discussions about resources – it's our lives you're talking about.
- Don't put fashionable fads and treatments on to us unless you are going to be around to see them through. And don't forget families have many members, many responsibilities. Sometimes, we can't please everyone.
- Do recognise that sometimes we are right! Please believe us and listen to what we know that we and our children need.
- Sometimes we are sad, tired and depressed. Please value us as caring and committed families and try to go on working with us.

Note

1 EAL: English as an additional language.

Chapter 8

Inclusion of young children with SEND

Major questions addressed in this chapter are:

- How can we ensure that children with special educational needs and/or disabilities can be included so that they develop, thrive and make progress in settings and schools?
- How can the assess → plan → do → review cycle described in the *Special Educational Needs and Disability Code of Practice: 0 to 25 years* (DfE, 2015a, pp. 86-7) identify children's needs and help to address barriers to learning and progress?
- What constitutes effective forms of assessment, planning, doing and reviewing?

Introduction

In early years settings and schools, good practice for children who experience SEND will almost invariably mean good practice for all children. The Early Years Foundation Stage (EYFS) Statutory Framework states that every child deserves the best possible start in life and the support that enables them to fulfil their potential (DfE, 2017). The most recent *Special Educational Needs and Disability Code of Practice: 0 to 25 years* in England reiterates that children have the right to an education that enables them to 'achieve the best possible educational and other outcomes' (DfE, 2015a, §5.1). The focus on the needs of the individual child in the early years, with the development of positive relations between staff and families, with learning and development situated in an enabling environment, suggests a blueprint for effective education and care of all children, including those with special educational needs and disabilities.

Teaching includes all of the ways in which adults help young children to learn, as Ofsted (2015) notes. Thoughtful, reflective, responsive teaching forms the basis of any additional or different provision for children with SEND. Both the EYFS (DfE, 2017) and the *SEND Code of Practice* (DfE, 2015a) stress the importance of responsiveness to any cause for concern. Observation, planning and assessment are central to work in the early years, and practitioners need to tune in to the needs of children with SEND even more acutely to ensure their needs are met. Practitioners must discuss any concern regarding a child's lack of progress in any prime area of learning they may have with the parents/carers in a timely manner and agree how to support the child.

Outcomes are important. Indeed, the *Code of Practice* in England advocates the use of the 'Early Years Outcomes guidance tool to assess the extent to which a young child is developing at expected levels for their *[sic]* age' (DfE, 2015a, §5.21). However, ends do not justify means, and it is the practitioner's role in understanding how children are learning, where, why and how their learning is effective or impaired, and the actions they take in relation to this understanding that are crucial in enabling a child to make progress. Observations of young children can inform knowledge of whether they are making typical progress in an area of learning, although we should all acknowledge that very young children learn in an individual, and often uneven, manner. Their progress may well not be linear across all areas of learning. Sometimes this can mean that a rigid use of outcomes can misinform practice and practitioners can fail to see the whole child as a result.

In this chapter we begin by outlining what is meant by the assess → plan → do → review cycle in relation to individual children and their needs in schools and settings. We continue by discussing common assessment tools used in early years settings, observation techniques in particular, and go on to consider how to plan to meet the needs that have been identified, translate plans into classroom activities and review the extent to which plans have been successful. In this we include examples of plans and individual practitioners' reflections on the whole process.

Assess → plan → do → review cycle

Where a child seems to be consistently struggling to make expected levels of development the practitioner must respond sensitively and in an informed manner to support the child's needs, gathering together information on the child from within and beyond the setting. This must include information from the parents/carers as they have a wealth of knowledge of their child in many different contexts. It should also include the child's voice too, a key principle underpinning the *SEND Code of Practice* (DfE, 2015a). There are many ways in which we can actively listen to the child's voice, observing the child and noticing the ways children express themselves in a range of different ways, using photographs and offering other multi-modal ways of representing their views and feelings. Dispositions and attitudes matter here, often more than the academic skills and precise articulation of the level of their attainment.

To comply with statutory guidance in the *SEND Code of Practice* in England (DfE, 2015a), early years settings and schools:

> must have arrangements in place to support children with SEN or disabilities. These arrangements should include a clear approach to identifying and responding to SEN.
>
> (DfE, 2015a, §5.4)

> Where a setting identifies a child as having SEN they must work in partnership with parents to establish the support the child needs.
>
> (ibid., §5.37)

> It is particularly important in the early years that there is no delay in making any necessary special educational provision.
>
> (ibid., §5.36)

The *Code* provides a structure of 'assess → plan → do → review' (DfE, 2015a, pp. 86–7) that mirrors the observation/assessment/planning cycle practitioners use for all children in the Early Years Foundation Stage. All young children are observed and, for some, concerns are identified. Practitioners then reflect on those concerns, assess all of the information that has been collected and plan strategies to support the learning of the child concerned, in close conjunction with the parents and other agencies that might be involved. This can sometimes arise quite naturally from the child's assessment at the age of 2. Once appropriate intervention strategies have been put in place, those in schools and settings can review how well the child is learning with the parents, the child and any other agencies/services that are involved, and support for the child can be adapted accordingly. Figure 8.1 below illustrates this cycle of assess → plan → do → review with the various personnel that may be involved.

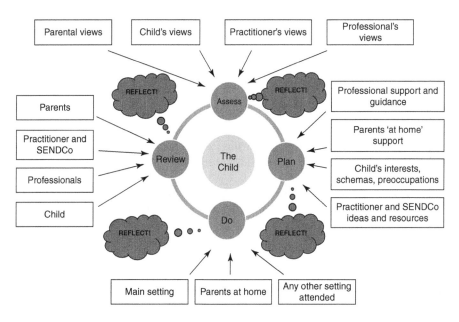

Figure 8.1 Potential participants in assess → plan → do → review cycle

Assessment of young children

The difficulties experienced by some young children will be identified at a very early stage, for example, hearing, sight and/or physical difficulties that may be apparent at the check shortly after birth, and that is outlined in Chapter 6. Different agencies may be involved from this time in a child's life, giving families support in relation to addressing, for example, the challenges in language acquisition for a young deaf child, or the development of motor skills for a child with a serious degree of physical impairment, or a whole range of other issues associated with the outcome of this check. Some difficulties in, for example, poor vision, may also become apparent at the stage of the Integrated Review and identified by specialist professionals, in discussion with families. Again, professionals from different agencies may become involved at this point also. Portage, as discussed in Chapter 7, is a multi-agency service offering targeted support for families of young children with severe special educational, or disability, needs. Other difficulties are less easy to identify clearly when children are very young, however, and may only begin to be noticed when the child makes the transition to formal education.

There is no intention in this chapter to provide an in-depth catalogue on observation, planning and assessment techniques. In Chapters 3 to 6 we have discussed some of the assessment techniques that are appropriate to identifying various kinds of difficulties that may be experienced. Also, settings, schools and LAs may have resources available on their websites that set out expectations for the way in which they expect difficulties to be assessed in the early years. Below we provide a broad overview of some of the tools practitioners can utilise in support of children with SEND.

Observation

The Early Years Foundation Stage, in its various forms since 2008, makes clear that work with very young children most appropriately begins by observing what they know and can do (DCSF, 2008; Early Education, 2012; DfE, 2013a; DfE, 2017). Clear, focused observation, therefore, is crucial in supporting the assessment of young children with SEND (Early Education, 2012). A number of key principles should underpin observational assessment at this stage:

- **Observation and assessment must have a purpose.** Practitioners use this to intervene, support and extend a child's learning as it is happening, to inform planning for the next steps in learning for each child, and in so doing deepening and extending the child's learning.
- **Ongoing observation** of children participating in everyday activities is the most reliable way of building up an accurate picture of what children know, understand, feel, are interested in and can do. These individual pictures will be built up over time … .
- **Practitioners should both plan observations and be ready to capture the spontaneous but important moments.** Everyday experiences and activities will provide an almost complete picture of the child's learning, but particular planning is needed to capture important aspects of learning that may not arise every day. Other opportunities may occur that are unplanned but nevertheless should not be missed.
- **Judgements of children's development and learning** must be based on skills, knowledge, understanding and behaviour that are demonstrated consistently and independently. Assessments cannot be reliable or accurate if they are based on one-off instances or information gleaned solely from adult-directed activities. Observational assessment should be a balance between child-initiated and adult-led activities.
- **Effective assessment takes equal account of all aspects of the child's development and learning.** A holistic approach to assessment is necessary in order to reflect accurately the nature of children's development and to acknowledge the interrelationship between different aspects of learning.
- **Accurate assessments** are reliant upon taking account of contributions from a range of perspectives. These will include all adults who have contact with the child in a range of contexts … .
- **Assessments must actively engage parents in developing an accurate picture of the child's development.** Effective partnership, working with parents, will

ensure that their vital perspective contributes to the overall description of children's development and learning.

- **Children must be fully involved in their own assessment.** Children should be involved in discussing their activities and how they feel about them from the beginning of their time in a setting and from whatever age they start. Encouraging children to respond (using the communication method with which they are most comfortable, including where appropriate their non-verbal response), ask questions, make comments and share their own judgements about what they are learning enables them to take true ownership of their development. It also gives practitioners an invaluable insight into the patterns and process of their learning.

(DfES, 2007a, pp. 9–10)

The principles should act as the bedrock features of observational assessment practice in the setting/school. It is also important to consider ethical issues around observation. Whilst all parents will normally have given permission for their children to be observed as part of the induction process to a setting, it could potentially be more of an issue if the parents are aware that their child may have SEND. With careful and sensitive explanation of the purpose and value of observational evidence, most parents are usually happy to give their consent. It is equally important to request permission from the child to observe them. The United Nations (UN) Convention on the Rights of the Child (UN, 2009) enshrined the notion of listening to the young child's voice as a basic right for all children. Article 12 states:

Parties shall assure to the child who is capable of forming his or her own views the right to express those views freely in all matters affecting the child, the views of the child being given due weight in accordance with the age and maturity of the child

(United Nations, 2009, p. 5)

Even very young children can make their voices heard through a range of participatory strategies, with parents, key workers and other professionals adding their views to create a rich and multi-faceted tapestry of observational assessment.

Observation techniques

As we noted above, some young children will enter a setting with clearly identified SEND issues, whilst others may not yet have been recognised as experiencing challenges in development. It may be useful to consider three levels of increasingly focused observational assessment that will encompass the needs of both sets of children and, indeed, can be used for all young children according to their needs at the time.

Level 1: general observational assessments

Even before a child starts in a setting it is important to begin to learn more about him/her, and this is often achieved by offering a home visit in the child's most comfortable and secure environment. Home visits, usually involving a key person, begin to establish a relationship with the parents and sharing of information from the very outset, and with the child, providing an insight into what the child already knows and can do. General information can be gathered in an 'All about me' observation and shared across the setting to ensure all practitioners are ready to support the child and provision is suitably adapted to ensure the child has a smooth transition into what may be the first experience of learning outside the home environment.

Reflective activity: considering ways to approach 'All about me' activities

A number of examples of formats for 'All about me' observations are available on the internet. You might choose to access some of these, for example, what has been provided by Ealing LA. Consider whether and how you might use what you have accessed directly, or what adaptations you might make for your own setting. The example from Ealing is available at www.egfl.org.uk/topics/early-years/teaching-and-learning-early-years.

Young children with SEND may display very different approaches to learning according to the particular context they are in; their experiences can range from adult-led activities which may or may not require additional levels of self-control and attention, to more playful, child-initiated encounters that very often support a child's own interests more comfortably. It is important, therefore, to observe the young child across a variety of different contexts both inside and outdoors, and at different times of the day. Play is recognised as a key component in the EYFS curriculum and therefore it is important to observe young children's behaviour and learning in playful situations where they display the characteristics of effective learning: playing and exploring, active learning and creating and thinking critically (DfE, 2017, §1.9.). For some young children with SEND, play may look different from that of other children, and practitioners need to be mindful of the alternative representations of it. Children with profound and complex difficulties in learning, for example, may well use toys in a way that is atypical of their peers.

To ensure a holistic understanding of the child's learning and development requires narrative observation as a starting point: planned observations of the child, lasting around 5 to 10 minutes undertaken regularly (monthly/half termly) by the key person but not exclusively so. The observation should not be targeted in any particular way, just provide a set of detailed objective statements on what the child was doing and saying at a moment in time. The observer may be involved in the observation as an active player alongside the child, and be what is known as a participant observer. Alternatively, the observer may just be watching the child from the side-lines, what is known as 'non-participant observation'. Basic information should be recorded within the narrative observation, including:

- date, time and duration of the observation;
- the context (where it is taking place, whether the child is alone or in a group activity and whether the activity is adult-led or child-initiated).

The observer should write down an objective account of what the child does and says. This rich observational data can be shared across the staff team, with parents, with the child and with other professionals beyond the setting who work with the child and family to provide a starting point for reflection and future planning for teaching and learning. Although long narrative observations can be somewhat time-consuming for practitioners and may bring up logistical and management issues, they furnish practitioners with an invaluable insight into the learning of the child, providing evidence for possible future applications for additional funding and support.

Unplanned incidental snapshot observations can be useful to gain a breadth of knowledge of the child's development and are much easier to manage in the setting. Here, all practitioners who see something of note to do with the child should quickly note it down, including the date, time and context. These observations can happen daily/weekly and focus on challenges the child experiences or, more positively, document the small steps the child takes in his/her learning. These snapshots can then be collected with the narrative observations into the Learning Journey and assessment documents to provide ongoing formative assessment to support future practice.

Observation recorded on electronic devices, PCs, tablets and so on, using various apps and programs that can be purchased to facilitate this, is becoming more frequent in early years settings and enables practitioners to record moments instantly in a visual format and to share information with parents and carers more readily. Digital moving images included in observations can offer a very powerful format from which everyone involved can reflect on the child in action (Forman and Hall, 2007). Using a digital recorder can also usefully record a child's speech faithfully and quickly, without having to resort to lengthy transcription, and can be shared easily with others beyond the setting. We should reiterate here, however, that gaining the relevant permissions to record in this way and also safe storage of this information are absolutely crucial considerations.

Level 2: observational assessment in the context of the setting/school

In the next level of observational assessment, practitioners can consider the child with SEND within the context of the early years setting/school, providing a more focused view on the child in relation to other children, to the physical provision and across the time spent in a specific educational context. The first three examples below are useful when more analytial data is needed.

TRACKING

Children in the early years tend to move from one activity to the next in startlingly quick succession. Tracking what a child with SEND accesses over a session and annotating the duration of the visit in minutes onto the sheet can give a useful insight into time spent on an activity of his/her choosing and in adult-led activities. The technique indicates nothing about the reasons behind the choices or the detail of a child's actions. However, it can help to identify if there are any connections between the types of activity chosen, for example, if the child if 'fitting' rather than 'flitting' between unrelated activities. Where there are concerns about a child's physical development, the technique can focus in on the ways in which the child is using physical skills during the session. Children can be encouraged to participate in this type of observation themselves, too, by stamping a card placed next to each activity whenever they access it (see Figure 8.2).

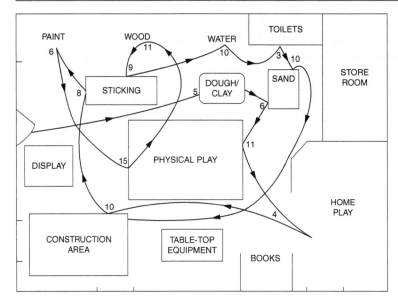

Figure 8.2 Tracking observation of movement

TIME SAMPLING

Time sampling is effectively the recording of a child's activities, and/or interactions and behaviour at pre-determined regular intervals during the day. Typically, time samples are conducted every 5 minutes, 15 minutes or half hourly, but the frequency can be as often or infrequent as is appropriate to the child and situation. In each interval the practitioner writes down what the child is doing and/or whom the child is interacting with. Time samples can be very helpful in monitoring the child's interactions, activities and behaviour across the session. Subsequently, practitioners can reflect on how to support the child in developing social skills or learning from different elements of provision, and/or how to adjust provision to ensure it meets the children's needs (see Table 8.1).

Instead of observing individual children, the focus can be placed on different areas of provision, how many children access each area and for how long, with the intention of fostering increased opportunities for a young child's learning.

Table 8.1 Time sampling of curriculum areas

Date: 1/11/2016
Time: 9:15am–12:15pm
Observer: A
Location: Various
Children: Liam (4.1 yrs); Paul (4.2yrs); Declan (3.9 yrs)

Time	Location	Activities	Interactions
9:15am	Garden	Sandpit/Cooking Pretend Play	Liam
9:45am	Garden	Dinosaur pit (rocks and plastic dinosaurs)	Liam & Paul
10:15am	Garden	Climbing Equipment	Liam
10:45am	Inside	Mobilio	Liam
11:15am	Inside	Blocks	Declan
11:45am	Inside	Dress up	Liam & Paul
12:15pm	Inside	Computer	Liam

EVENT SAMPLING

Event sampling means taking a snapshot of events in which the child is participating. This can often be recorded through the use of time sampling and tracking, outlined above.

SOCIAL MAPS/SOCIOGRAMS

Sociograms are a useful way to illustrate a child's communication and social interactions within a group and play preferences (see Figures 8.3 and 8.4). The key person can represent the information visually with references to indicate the different elements on the 'map'. Sometimes it can be helpful to overlay the interactions with other factors such as the physical layout of an environment, the presence of adults and other relevant influences to see if interactions are affected by these factors, depending on the needs of the child.

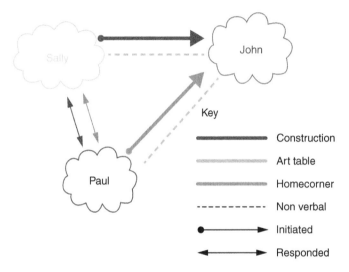

Figure 8.3 Social interactions in a setting

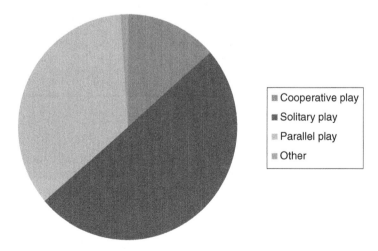

Figure 8.4 Types of play

Level 3: targeted observational assessment

Targeted observations can provide the fine grain detail to understand the unique aspects of the young child's needs. The narrative observations outlined in the previous section can be used very effectively to capture this information. Where a concern has been identified or diagnosed and additional information is required, the observer might target an area to focus in on, for example, recording the child's language, hearing, behaviour and so on, and conduct more detailed observations on the one aspect identified.

OBSERVATIONS OF CHALLENGING BEHAVIOUR

In Chapter 5, we discussed approaches to understanding and addressing behaviour seen as challenging from a behaviourist perspective. We noted how observations of difficult behaviour from this framework should include a record of:

- antecedents (possible triggers, behaviours, actions) immediately prior to the event;
- behaviour (a summary of the observed behaviour);
- consequences (what happened immediately after the behaviour/event).

Below is an example of an event sample using this method of observing a child's aggressive behaviour and associated factors.

Table 8.2 ABC observation of aggressive behaviour

Date: 1/11/2016
Time: 9:15am
Observer: A
Location: Main garden
Children: Dan (4.1 yrs) Liam (4 yrs)

Antecedent	Behaviour	Consequences
Dan and Liam are playing blocks. Dan is building a tower. Liam gets up and asks Dan to come with him to play on the Lego table. Dan does not respond. Liam comes up behind Dan and wraps his arm around Dan. Dan cries 'don't … you hurt me'. Liam says sorry but still pulls at Dan …'come on'. Liam pulls Dan over.	Dan looks up and pushes Liam away. Liam falls over and cries. Liam gets up and runs to a teacher. 'Dan pushed me'.	Dan turns away. 'Liam hurt me'. Dan walks to the book corner on the other side of the room. Liam follows and sits down beside Dan. Two minutes later both boys are smiling again.

RATING SCALES

Rating scales can be used in a number of ways to identify a child's particular difficulties, but they should not be used as the sole method of collecting information and cannot replace the rich evidence found in narrative observations. For example, it can sometimes be useful to use rating scales to identify difficulties in the use of receptive and/or expressive language. The scales can be used over a period of time and progress can be gauged from a baseline measurement. The example below considers receptive language.

Table 8.3 Receptive language rating scale

Behaviours and skills	Circle your level of concern, taking account of the child's age: 1: No concern 2: A little concern 3: Considerable concern 4: Great deal of concern
Can discriminate speech sounds Can recognise common sounds Responds to simple verbal requests Can remember simple verbal instructions Can follow simple three step instructions Requires simple spoken sentences to be rephrased	

When using rating scales it is essential that all those completing them have a common understanding of what each point on the scale represents. The number of points can be increased or reduced as needed in relation to the focus of the assessment. Where there are an equal number of points with positive indicators on one side and negative on the other, the choice is 'forced'. In other words, the rater is forced to choose whether to make a positive or negative rating. If there are an odd number of points, there is a tendency to rate at the centre which may or may not be helpful to an accurate assessment of a child.

Observation rating scales can be adapted to incorporate key indicators for a range of children's difficulties, as outlined in Chapters 3–6.

Preliminary assessment of need

When information from parents, the child and other professionals have been collated, an assessment of the individual needs of the child can begin. Summative assessments of progress taken at a particular point in time, for example, at the Two Year Old Integrated Review, or on entry to school, are compiled from a range of observations and information across the range of adults involved in the child's life, parents, professionals and so on, as well as the child. From these assessments individual support plans can be drawn up, if necessary, and negotiated between families, professionals and support personnel and the child as well, wherever possible. Once the learning plan has been put into effect, it is always important to have a sense of young children's progress through ongoing continuous formative assessment that can provide teachers and others with opportunities to notice what is happening during learning activities, recognise the level and direction of the learning of individuals and see how they can help to support the child in their next steps in learning. Both forms of assessment contribute essential insights into what children are gaining from their experiences in the setting. Practitioners should remember that, for children with SEND, learning may look very different, and they may need to have a heightened awareness of the ways in which learning might be demonstrated.

Depending on their special educational need, children will demonstrate learning and development in different ways. Practitioners observing a child involved in day-to-day activities must be alert to their demonstrating attainment in a variety of ways, including eye pointing, use of symbols or signs. With the exception of ELG03 Speaking [from DfE, 2013a], where the EYFS profile contains the word 'talks' or 'speaks', *Early Years Foundation Stage* Profile Handbook (2016, p.18) children can use their established or preferred mode of communication.

(STA, 2016, p. 18)

Planning individual provision

The planning stage follows on from significant time spent gathering information. The *Code of Practice* defines progress that is less than expected given the child's age and circumstances as progress which:

- is significantly slower than that of their peers starting from the same baseline;
- fails to match or better the child's previous rate of progress;
- fails to close the attainment gap between the child and their peers;
- widens the attainment gap.

(DfE, 2015a, §6.17)

If this is the case, then additional or different provision needs to be made. Personalising learning to the individual child, as a result of observations and discussions, needs to be recorded in a clear plan, shared with others, reflected upon and monitored regularly so progress over time can be evaluated. Key elements that should be considered in planning for young children include:

- learning outcomes, including emotional, social, intellectual and physical;
- adult involvement (or peer engagement) and playful adult-led activities as well as opportunities for children to initiate and explore their own interests in the setting's environment;
- continuous inside and outside provision, and the planning of space, layout and accessibility;
- enhanced resources, either in the environment or for specific activities/outcomes;
- time and pace of activities;
- language development and vocabulary;
- developing thinking through questions and connections to other learning and experiences.

For the children for whom we have identified that there may be a need for some short-term – or longer-term – intervention, planning needs to show clearly how what this child will do and work towards will have some differences from what the other children may do. Planning, therefore, has key equity implications: the idea that in order to promote the opportunity to succeed and achieve, often something different needs to be offered to a young child.

Differentiation and inclusion is all about how the need to support a child's learning takes into account the child's learning strengths and prior achievements as well as the needs of the curriculum and what should be taught. Differentiation can be planned in detail prior to teaching an idea, concept or activity (planned differentiation), or it may occur spontaneously as a practitioner working with a child and scaffolding (Wood, Bruner and Ross, 1976) learning reflects on the child's responses as a task or activity progresses. Many children, with and without an identified need, can be appropriately supported and included in setting activities and experiences through clear differentiation of tasks. This incorporates the planned differentiation concept. Differentiation incorporating a Vygotskian notion of teaching a child within his/her Zone of Proximal Development (Vygotsky, 1978), as noted in Chapter 4, arises as a result of careful listening and attunement on the part of the practitioner to what the child is on the cusp of learning or is interested in learning and to what they recognise as what Drummond (2006) terms a 'teachable moment'. Doing this does require the practitioner to be sufficiently focused on children's *learning* (which at that moment in time might be a different proposition to the practitioner's intended *teaching* and planned-for outcomes). It is at this point that the practitioner needs to make some key decisions, what Schon (1991) terms 'reflection-in-action', regarding whether to pursue a set, generalised, outcome-focused agendum or to follow the child's motivation and interest. Doing the latter may not 'tick the box' to indicate the child has experienced, practised or consolidated a certain concept (indeed, young children need many repeated opportunities to do this in any case), but it may engender in the child a greater sense of personal worth, 'voice' and orientation to learning as a worthwhile and intrinsically motivating pursuit. Helping children's learning orientations to focus on effort, relish learning risks and challenges and develop strategies for autonomy, personal management and a sense of mastery and self-direction is a key part of learning for life and what the Characteristics of Effective Learning in the EYFS (Early Education, 2012) encourage practitioners to enable through their teaching, provision and ethos.

Reflective activity: planning for inclusion

First, please read the following narrative. Then note down your responses to the questions that follow it.

The context for the narrative is an activity led by a teaching assistant (TA) reading *Dinosaurs Love Underpants* to 22 children. Child M is 3 years 9 months old.

After a few hours of free flow, children had been told to tidy away and sit together on the carpet for story time. This was routine every day before lunch was served at 12 o'clock. The book was never the same as the previous story time but could have been read within the past few weeks. Being familiar with the book, some children would get excited and shout things out.

The TA sat down in front of the carpet holding a book.

A child shouted out, 'Can we read another book?'

'No I want to read the *Dinosaurs Love Underpants* today. Now what is this part of a book called?' asked the TA as she pointed up and down one long side of the book.

'The spine!' the majority of the children on the carpet shouted out, a few raised their hands but quickly put their hands back down as other children called out, whilst children in front of the TA watched her quietly.

TA: 'Very good, now what is the writing on the back of the book?'
         The class shouted, 'The blurb!'

TA: 'Yes, but what are the words across the front of a book?'
               Some children answered, 'The title'.
TA: 'Who writes the story?'
Children: 'The author!' The majority of the children shouted the answer together,
               although two children quickly said the answer a few seconds after the
               rest of the class.
TA: 'And, finally, who draws the pictures in our books?'
               Again the class shouted out the answer: 'The illustrator!'

As the TA was reading the book and changing her voice for different characters
Child M began to start shouting, 'ROAR!' from the back of the carpet.

The TA took no notice and continued to read the book as some children looked
towards the child who shouted out. Again Child M shouted, 'ROAR!' She then
shouted again and got up on her feet and started stomping at the back of the carpet
as children began to turn around and stare at her.

The TA stopped reading the story and looked at Child M as she said, 'Child M,
sit back down, please, and stop shouting out. Other children want to read the story'.

Child M, however, stared at the TA, then walked off.

Questions for reflection:

- How was this planned session successful? How was it less successful?
- How do you think Child M was feeling at the end of this session?
- What were Practitioner A's focus and intentions for this session?
- How might the TA build on Child M's contribution in a more sensitive and
  inclusive way that would connect with her interest and needs?
- How might this be turned into a vibrant learning opportunity for *all* of the
  children?

Let us further consider the adult's role in terms of acting more spontaneously to support
learning.

Reflective activity: including Jess

Read the scenario below, and then note down your responses to the questions that
follow:

Jess often plays on her own. She can often be found watching the other children,
but it has been noted and discussed within the team that she rarely joins in, and it
could be that she lacks some strategies to create 'opening' into play with others.
Although there does not seem to be a specific problem with her speech and language, she has been slow to make requests and ask for what she needs or to offer
ideas or opinions.

One day you see a group of children playing an imaginative game with monsters
and chasing and catching. It is a game which is not heavily reliant on sophisticated

language, but the children involved are highly engaged and having fun. Jess is close by watching them, and she looks interested.

Can and should the practitioner do anything at this point? What do you think? How far might it be appropriate to:

- Provide a way for her to join in, for example, 'Oh Jess, look! A monster! Sophie is a monster. Let's go and chase her!'
- Once involved, consider suggesting a specific role either for yourself (and perhaps have Jess alongside you) or a role for Jess alone – for example, a guard to stop the monsters going to a certain place, or alternately helping the monsters escape.
- Look for ways to name the children involved in the game so that Jess is clear who they are. This may give her future strategies to be able to say: 'X, can I play?' Offer a commentary on what is happening in the game, too, to help any possible misunderstandings if the play moves along at a fast rate, as children's free flow play invariably does!
- Be alert for opportunities to leave the play, either because Jess has sustained her involvement for as long as she seems to want, in which case leave together and just watch or find quieter activities for Jess, or because Jess seems happy to remain involved without your support.

Practitioners should be alert to seeing opportunities as they arise as well as following through planned support. In the instances outlined above, valuing the child, showing an interest, modelling an open and curious disposition and helping them to engage are all important strategies. The following ideas might specifically help communication when children are engaged in play or playful activities. They might well also further support understanding of play, attention to roles, belonging in groups and ultimately well-being and confidence. Practitioners might:

- expand, so a child gets a fuller understanding of an idea;
- interpret, for example, other children's intentions;
- repeat directly back to the child, so s/he is clear about an idea;
- simplify, breaking down an idea or activity;
- slow down, so children can process ideas and events;
- bridge, helping children to move on from one idea or play mode to another.

Planning outcomes, SMART targets and small steps

Some children may require significantly differentiated plans which need to be more formally documented. This may happen as a result of whole group teaching that includes some differentiation but is insufficiently differentiated for individual learning needs. Other children may already arrive at the setting with an identified need and already be the recipient of an EHC plan. One of the SENDCos interviewed by the current authors explained how she conceptualised planning in small steps for children who need that level of support:

So let's just say you have a child on the autistic spectrum disorder and they're not using any language at all. A parent might say, 'Well I'd like them to be able to talk in sentences and communicate with me'. So you have to be able to break that right down back to the very, very basics and have some sort of starting point because there's no point in giving a parent the hope that in three weeks' time that child is going to be able to talk in sentences. So what you have to do is work back the way and find a solution to children communicating and helping parents to understand that there's many, many steps to that. If having a child use a sentence is the result of 15 steps then how do you backtrack that to the first step? What is the first step going to be?

There is no set format for these plans, but settings and some LAs may have a preferred style that they wish practitioners to use. Regardless, there are key elements that should be addressed in each child's plan in order to make clear to all concerned how individual needs should be addressed, including:

- the nature of the difficulty(ies);
- short term targets/outcomes set for (and sometimes by) the child;
- strategies to be used;
- provision of resources, including adults, to be put in place;
- success criteria – how you know how your intervention will have achieved its aim;
- a space for reviewing outcomes.

With young children in particular, given that collaboration with their parents should be close, regular, respectful and informed, it is essential to discuss interventions with them further so that, wherever possible, their 'at home' contributions to support their child complement what goes on in the setting, as, for example, this nursery SENDCo noted at interview:

> So, PECs [Picture Exchange System] – we tend to model that for parents so that they understand how to do it at home.

A key notion connected to individual plans is that they are working documents. They should not be solely seen as paper exercises to 'tick the box' for paperwork and that takes both practitioners and SENDCos away from valuable contact and involvement with the children, actively making a difference. A further important point to make, and endorsed by the *Code of Practice* (DfE, 2015a) is that it is preferable to set only a small number of targets but to make these achievable, both for the child and in terms of the practitioners' time and resources. Therefore, Specific, Measurable, Achievable, Realistic, Time-related (SMART) targets are important in order to be able to evaluate how well children are doing. Clearly, it can be challenging to the practitioner to be able to meet all these requirements, and especially when a child's difficulty seems so significant that it is hard to be sure how to break a larger need into more manageable, smaller steps and feel confident that these are the 'right' steps in the 'right' order. This idea was reflected in an interview with an educational psychologist. She expressed concerns about the pace of the curriculum and the drive to move onto new knowledge that may create tensions between what practitioners' professional knowledge tells them about children needing time to repeat and consolidate learning through different activities, and what the evidence before their eyes shows regarding children's need to do this.

Reflective activity: concerns about curricular requirements

Read the following opinion about the current early years curriculum. To what extent do you agree with the comments that were made?

'But the current pace of the curriculum is such that it doesn't allow people to break those things down into smaller steps. This is an impression on my part that they struggle to find the time to break things down to suit individual children because they have to move on to the next thing. Which is crazy because when you look at anything that any of us learned, until you've got those basics consolidated and secure, there is no point moving on to the next step, because by the time you get five steps down the thing, if you think about learning to drive, unless you've learnt how to do that pedal clutch control and accelerate in a synchronised way, there is no point talking about going on the motorway driving at 70 miles an hour if you can't even do that basic control. It's the same with learning. That's the bit that as a psychologist is very frustrating because what we see now, particularly in schools and I dare say I see it in settings as well, this urgency about children being moved on to the next bit before they've consolidated what they've learnt. Infants, very young children, need to repeat experiences but the way in which some of the early years curriculum is being interpreted is that you can't repeat it because they should've moved on, and it's the same, it's mirrored within the school curriculum. If you don't get it first time, that's it. Whereas actually learning doesn't really happen like that. The neurology tells us that as well. It shows us that'.

These concerns aside, it is the role of the practitioner, sometimes aided by the SENDCo, to develop sensitive and supportive plans for the child to show what they know and can do, and using resources flexibly in order to do so. For example, one of the school SENDCos that was interviewed discussed how she used Pupil Premium (DfE, 2015d):

> So, for example, we might use it to employ an extra member of staff or to buy certain pieces of equipment which we think will enhance learning. For example, we've used it this year to pay for a practitioner who is trained in a children's activity to do with yoga and involves singing. She comes into school once a week and works with small groups of children to develop their physicality and their listening and attention skills in that way. And they have so much fun too. We can record this on several children's learning plans and so many have benefitted from this, I'm so glad we did it.

The sample plans below demonstrate ways in which young children's needs might be formally recorded and addressed:

Table 8.4 Sample plan 1

Setting:	Name of Child:	D.O.B.:	Key support person:
Start Date:			
Planned Review Date:			

Area of Concern	Target (What to Teach)	Strategy (How) Resources / Frequency of Support	Progress on review date
Language: S uses very little language in school, other than a few words. Speech and Language therapist is concerned that his language is severely delayed.	**S will:** 1. Increase word vocabulary to 75 words.	P to use books and ipads as well as activities that support S's interests and the topics that the school are focusing on. Ratio: 1:1 Duration: 15 minutes Frequency: daily (pm)	
	2. Begin to use positional language in his speech (adult supported).	Using small world, books, ICT, large apparatus to transfer S's knowledge of positional language explicitly into his speech. Correct language structures and positional vocab put into the context of a sentence modelled by adult and repetition by child. Ratio: 1:1 Duration: 10 minutes Frequency: daily	
	3. Speak in sentences of 3–4 words using correct grammatical phrasing e.g. 'He is running'. 'The boy is painting'.	P to support S during session time, using picture dictionaries, action cards, photo books, 'What's wrong?' cards Ratio: 1:1 Duration: 10 minutes Frequency: daily	
	4. Participate with turn-taking and following rules in a structured game with up to 3 other children.	P to support S in a small group, focusing on language and maths games including Lotto, dominos and sorting activities. Ratio: 1:4 Duration: 20 minutes Frequency: twice weekly	

Parental/carer contribution:

Play Lotto, dominoes. Focus on participating and turn-taking. Name the pictures on the cards, and extend to sentences, e.g. 'It's a red car'; 'The dog is brown'; 'There are six spots'.

Table 8.5 Sample plan 2

Setting: Name of Child: D.O.B.:
    Key support person:
Start Date:
Planned Review Date:

Area of Concern	Target (What to Teach)	Achievement criteria	Resources	Class strategies	Support from TA
Physical and motor skills	**Child will:** 1. be able to hold a pencil effectively to make marks with an even and appropriate pressure;	Pencil hold correct without reminder 2 out of 3 times. Even pressure seen in work samples 2 out of 3 times.	Triangular pencil grip.	Range of fine motor opportunities: painting; marks in dough; chalk; crayon; cornflour; shaving foam.	Drawing, writing, painting, dough activities inside and outside, pegs and washing line, games using paper clips. Ratio: 1:1 10 mins daily
	2. be able to use a correct scissor grip to snip and to cut out simple shapes;	Correct scissor grip without reminder 2 out of 3 times.	Try spring loaded scissors.	Encourage activities in workshop area whenever possible.	Snipping paper, cutting catalogues, cutting different thicknesses of paper and card, holding paper while he snips, snipping Playdough, snipping Sellotape to join boxes and bits of paper together. Ratio: 1:1 10 mins daily
	3. be able to complete leg, heel and toes exercises in school provided on physio sheet.	Exercises completed as advised on sheet provided by external specialist describes.			Ratio: 1:1 10 mins daily

Parental/carer contribution:
Practise physio exercises at home 3 times per week (if possible, alternate days to school)
Progress on review date
Target 1:

Target 2:

Target 3:

Reflective activity: conceptualising SMART targets

Many areas of the curriculum lend themselves to devising targets that are Specific, Measurable, Achievable, Realistic, and Time-related where measurement of progress can be achieved through changes in behaviour or progress in new learning. However, this is not the case in all areas. For example, it is hard to see how emotions and feelings such as sadness, confidence, anger, concentration and so on can be measured except through observable behaviours that we assume are indicative of those feelings. We might call these proxy measures. Nevertheless, practitioners are expected nowadays to create targets for learning and behaviour in all areas against which progress can be measured.

We would like you to read through the targets below that have been written in a way that is not SMART and turn them into SMART targets:

- Joanne will recognise some letters of the alphabet.
- Smita will be able to catch a ball.
- To improve Ryan's concentration.
- Lauren will draw some shapes.
- To understand that a story has a beginning, middle and end.
- Daniel will follow instructions.
- To put on his coat.
- To improve Ravi's concentration.
- To encourage Connor's listening skills.

How did you get on?

One issue in creating SMART targets is that, in focusing on measurement, these targets may sometimes lack meaning. For example, the targets above might be re-written as:

- Joanne will recognise the first letter of her name, J, used in her name and 5 other words (5 successes over the period of a month).
- Smita will catch a large beach ball when thrown to her from a distance of one metre (5 times per session).
- Ryan will participate in an adult chosen activity for 1 minute. Sand timer to be used. 3 times per day.
- Lauren will draw a recognisable circle (square, and so on) on three occasions.
- Amir will listen to a story for 3 minutes and make a response to it.
- Daniel will follow a visual programme to enable him to concentrate on an activity for 3 minutes.
- Sam will take the coat off the peg, put his arms in the sleeves and come to an adult for help before pulling the last part up by himself.
- Ravi will sit at an activity for 2 minutes without an adult.
- Connor will select and match the correct pictures to the corresponding sounds at least 5 times in a listening game.

We do not, however, know what kind of stories engage Amir's interest, or what sort of activities motivate Ravi, but we do know that interest and motivation are important factors in holding a child's attention. Target-setting can therefore only be part of the story in supporting young children to make progress.

Planning the environment

The plans above are designed for short term (6–8 week) interventions. They make substantial use of adult support, clearly identified and timetabled in; however, they also rely on a rich environment in which children are given multiple opportunities to absorb and practise the foundation of skills and dispositions they will need. As with the pre-schools of Reggio Emilia in Italy (Rinaldi, 2001), the environment needs to be regarded as a third teacher, rich in potential and affordances (Claxton and Carr, 2004; Gosling, 2016). Careful and reflective planning and resourcing of areas will help to ensure that children can inter-act at their own developmental level. One Nursery SENDCo describes her setting and her setting's approach at interview in this way:

> We have lots of sign language and visual prompts and that helps all our children, not just the children with special educational needs. We have quiet spaces for children who find the whole busy environment overwhelming. And we find that our approach is that it's inclusive in the first instance, and then where children are struggling, they tend to get withdrawn in small groups to a small space where they do much more intense work. And that seems to work well for the majority of the day if they're accessing the same thing as everybody else, but for small bits of the day, 10/15 minutes they have for maybe quite intense turn-taking in a smaller environment or language work, that kind of thing.

There are, however, always going to be some children for whom this kind of rich and often busy environment is not appropriate, as this SENDCo notes, and therefore quiet spaces are essential. Furthermore, there are other children who may need other adjustments and consideration. For example, the child who has sensory sensitivity may be overloaded by high noise, bright or flickering light, smells which we barely notice but are highly irritat-ing to the child or the scratchy texture of the carpet where s/he is required to sit for group times. There may be children who are highly distracted by bright and colourful displays, or objects which spin around. There are children whose vision is impaired and so clear spaces and pathways through the setting need to be ensured, and variation or moving of key equipment should be avoided. There may be children whose gross motor movements and gait may be impeded and who also need clear pathways or space for their standing frame. The needs of these children and their presenting difficulties have been discussed in Chapters 3–6, with some clear strategies for specific support and intervention. For these children, their specific requirements regarding the learning environment might appear contradictory to what we might regard more generally as effective practice, but neverthe-less their needs need to be incorporated into planning and consideration of the material provision indoors and out. Time spent observing these children, talking with their parents and with the children themselves, as well as any existing support personnel, will help to find ways to take account of their needs whilst not diminishing other children's access to an environment that excites, motivates and supports them in their learning.

Summary of planning

Plans should clarify the arrangements to be made for specific children to achieve suc-cess. They will contain short term and longer term targets, meaningful activities based on observations of the child's current stage of development and comprising SMART targets and small steps to enable progress and a sense of achievement. Adult time will be planned carefully in order to ensure that what is planned for the child happens. Regular reflection, monitoring and evaluation are needed, both formally and informally, in order to recognise and acknowledge what children can do and the ways and contexts in which they work well. In this case here, then, a team approach to feeding back information, monitoring the child's progress and their interaction and engagement with both tasks and resources/environment (the 'what' and the 'how') and forward planning as a result of this further information is a vital component to success.

A number of questions should be borne very clearly in mind when planning to meet children's needs and, subsequently, observing children's responses to the planning and activities carried out, consider the following questions:

- How is the task developmentally appropriate for the child/ren?
- How does the task challenge the child?
- How does the task incorporate strengths in learning as well as difficulties?
- How does the task take into account possible differences in learning style for the child?
- How is the pace and sequence of learning organised to enable optimal child engagement?
- How do the resources support high engagement?
- Is cooperative and collaborative learning enabled – and is this an effective strategy for the task and the child?
- Is the child enabled to be independent and to have a growth mindset about their capacity to achieve?
- How transparent and clear is the process of differentiation?
- How do you know whether processes of learning and outcome have been successful? What evidence do you have?

A final word on planning for different needs comes from the transcript of an interview with an educational psychologist. Her words are timely reminders of a key consideration that practitioners should keep at the forefront of their minds when thinking about the special needs of children in the early years:

> Rather than looking for the gaps, you look for the brilliances with infants and people with special educational needs. Let's look for the brilliances, the strengths rather than the fact, oh they can't do that and can't do that. I know we do need to manage those gaps, and in some ways the problem with the assessment systems we have, it's about identifying the things you can't do and you've got to make sure they can't do them well enough to secure funding or extra resources. But these young children - let's try to enjoy and celebrate what they can do too.

Implementing the plan ('Do')

Once the plans are made, incorporating the best knowledge practitioners have of the child from the range of sources which have given information, it is time to put plans into action. In order to do this, flexibility, adaptation, communication across different players in the process is required, along with a strong team understanding of what the presenting issues for the child are and how these can be sensitively and creatively addressed.

The SENDCo might have a key liaison role to play here, as his or her knowledge and experience can be of significant help here in ensuring that all practitioners working

Table 8.6 Phonics session Year 1 (Beams, unpublished)

Phase: 3[1]
New Sound: /ear/
Revisit and review sounds: from Phase 2
Tricky words to introduce : said, so, have, like, some, come, were, there

Introduction	Revisit and Review	Teach	Practise	Apply	Assessment Opportunity	Resources
Learning outcome: to recognise and write the grapheme for the /ear/ sound.	Review all phase 2 sound sets. Use phase 2 sounds ppt. and sand timer. Use flashcards for sounds. MT: sit with CS, Visiobook and CS prompts.	Teach the new sound /ear/ recap the diagraph sound button and ask children to write and repeat the sound. Practise using lead ins. MT focus: simple letter formation MT supported by CS.	Play sound buttons Words: /ear/Children to sound out and read: 1. dear 2. fear 3. beard 4. year 5. clear MT: with CS. CS to clearly point out the repeated graphemes via Visiobook.	Children to use pictures to write /ear/ words on lined WOWO[2] soundtalk boards. Use sound buttons to show graphemes and diagraphs. Use lines for correct letter formation MT focus: simple letter formation MT to use thick lines WOWO board and pen, supported by CS RDF to support OC.	Children observed during writing and reading activities	WOWO boards Phase 2 phonics ppt and phoneme cards Sand timer VisioBook MT to use VisioBook to access IWB materials alongside CS.

[1]These Phases are set out in DfES (2007b) Letters and Sounds. Available online at: www.gov.uk/government/publications/letters-and-sounds
[2]WOWO: 'write on, wipe off'

with the child are fully briefed. It can sometimes happen that practitioners placed with children to do intervention or support work have relatively low or few direct qualifications or experience with the specific needs of the child with whom they are engaged to support, and in these instances, the SENDCo has a responsibility to offer informal training on the presenting needs, why the child might act in the way that they do and strategies which might help. S/he should also try to seek more formalised training and professional development opportunities for their staff, as well as opportunities for team meeting of all staff involved in special needs support. Then knowledge and practice, both general to different needs and specific to different children, can be shared between all concerned, including LA networks. Carrying out the plans, therefore, needs the commitment to see it happen along with good time management, creativity and enthusiasm that is infectious and helps to instil a sense of self belief in the children and a sense of good feeling among the team members working effectively together in the interests of the children.

The following table shows a plan for a phonics session for a Year 1 class and an observation to exemplify how this plan was carried out. This class has a child with visual impairment (VI) in it. The plan identifies the role for the learning support assistant (LSA) who regularly supports the child (identified here as MT). Note here the use of the VisioBook (a portable electronic magnifier and distance viewing aid) as a key support to enabling MT to take part in all the activities the adult has planned. The shaded sections indicate the way the activity is differentiated for the individual child.

Translating the plan into action

Below we have described the way in which the plan above has been translated into classroom activities. We can see the way in which:

- the VisioBook is used;
- in the context section, the child is included in other ways, for example, through the use of the thick black marker pen (context section);
- in section 9
  - the way the teacher helps him to know where there is a space where he can safely walk to get to the board at the front;
  - how she moves an obstruction so he can place his feet and body without fear of tripping;
- in section 4 and elsewhere, the way in which the LSA mediates with warmth and sensitivity for him throughout, taking some of the strain of the range of things he has to consider, for example, in the use of the sand timer, enabling him to focus on the learning;
- in sections 3 and 11, MT shows his understanding with clever humour. Nevertheless, we can still also see how his attention could wander as a result of the intense concentration that this session requires of him, given that he has to balance the learning with the extra strain his impairment puts him under, even though this is a relatively short and pacy session that appears within his capabilities;
- in section 12, the discussion afterwards between LSA and class teacher, to assess progress and consider successes, strengths and any amendments for future sessions.

Reflective activity: inclusion in the classroom

The text below relates to the discussion of translating plans into action above. First read this text, and then note down your responses to the questions that follow.

Context: adult-led activity led by the class teacher. The LSA (CS) is present to support child (MT) in a class of 24 children.

All the children enter the classroom from assembly. They sit down on the floor, the child with VI sits on a chair, and the LSA sets up the VisioBook in front of him. The child was ill the previous day, so today is his first day of the week at school. The class teacher sets up the board and all the children are handed WOWO boards (lined whiteboards around A4 sized). The child has a thick black marker to use alongside his WOWO board.

Section 1: The LSA (CS) sits next to MT and turns on the VisioBook.

LSA:	'Come on machine, it doesn't want to come to school this morning'.
Class teacher:	'We are going to start with our word race'.
MT:	'What's a word race?'
LSA:	'If we listen we will find out'.
Class teacher:	'More like a sound race'.

Section 2: A variety of letters come up on the board and all the children as a class call out the sounds, MT calls out the sounds slightly after the rest of the class.

Class teacher:	'Are you ready to start?'
MT:	'I thought we were doing the race?'

MT begins singing to himself; the LSA places a WOWO board on a plastic tray right in front of the VisioBook in the MT's line of sight.

Section 3: The class teacher begins to check the children's understanding.

Class teacher:	'What's the name of the sound with 3 letters? I'm going to write the sound. Using my links, first *eh*, second *ay* and last *rr*. What's my sounds?' All the children sound out 'ear' with MT slightly delayed. Another child in the classroom says: 'ear'. MT, giggling: 'I can't ear you'.

Section 4: The class teacher sets a written activity.

Class teacher:	'Can we practice three times on our boards? I want you all done by the time the sand gets to the bottom'. The class teacher turns the sand timer over.
MT:	'How long do we have?'
LSA:	'I'll keep an eye on the time and you concentrate on writing. Make sure you do it on the line'. MT writes 'ear'.

LSA:	'Fantastic, can you do another one for me?'
	MT continues looking down under his glasses at the WOWO board.

Section 5: The class teacher begins a group activity to practise the new sounds.

Class teacher:	'Shall we find some words which might have these sounds in?'
	A variety of pictures come up on the board with red lines underneath, one for each letter of the word. All the children, except MT put their hands up and suggest: 'Earring', 'beard'.
	After children in the class say the words, MT repeats them to himself.

Section 6: The class teacher points to pictures whose names contain the given sounds.

Class teacher:	'You have five minutes to write these words. Remember tall, small and tail letters'.
LSA:	'Let's start with beard'.
	MT comes very close to the WOWO board, looking under his glasses. MT begins talking to himself whilst writing.
LSA:	'What's the next letter?'
MT:	'ear'.
	LSA, pointing at letters on the VisioBook screen says 'eh, ay, rr'.
LSA:	'What's next? If we are doing bear**d** (emphasis on d), what do we need at the end?'
MT:	'Bear**d**'.

Section 7: MT begins writing sound bars underneath the word.

LSA:	'When we do the lines we do it straight across, underneath the sound'.
	MT begins pushing his chair backwards and gazing around the room.
LSA:	Okay, MT! Let's concentrate now.

Section 8: The class teacher checks the children's knowledge of letter sounds.

Class teacher:	'Okay, what's this one?'
All children:	'ear, eh ay rr'. MT's responses are delayed.
Class teacher:	'Who wants to put the sound bars on?'
	A child from the class underlines the 'ear' in the word 'year'. The class teacher moves on to the next picture which is a ghost scaring a person.
	All children, except MT: 'Fear'.
	MT, looking at LSA, says: 'ff, ear'.
	MT points at the word 'fear' on the VisioBook, and repeats the sounds in the word 'fear', pointing to them on his screen.

Section 9: The class teacher points to pictures showing a man with a beard.

Class teacher:	'What's this one?'

	All children, including MT in unison: 'Beard! B ear d'. A child writes the word 'beard' on the board.
Class teacher:	'MT would you like to come and do the sound bars?'
	MT gets up from his chair and walks towards the board.
Class teacher:	'There is a space between E and A [two of the children] for you to come through'.
	MT stands in front of the board.
MT:	'B ear d'.
	MT draws a line underneath the 'ear' of beard. The class teacher moves a green plastic tray from under the board as MT steps away.
Class teacher:	'MT can you help me point to the sounds?'
	MT, pointing to each sound: 'B ear d'.
	MT walks back to his chair and sits down.

Section 10: The class teacher puts a game on to the screen, with a yellow blob called Obb and a blue blob called Bob.

Class teacher:	'If it's a real word we put our thumbs up and it goes to Bob. If it's a made up word we put our thumbs down and it goes to Obb'. The Class teacher clicks on the board and the word 'green' appears on screen.
	The LSA points at the word 'green' on the VisioBook screen.
MT:	'Gerh rr eeeee nn'.
Class teacher:	'What's the word?'
	All children, together with MT: 'Green'.
Class teacher:	'Show me those thumbs. MT show me yours'.

Section 11: Consolidation of new learning.

All the children put up their thumbs in the air. A child comes and clicks on the word green and drags it onto Bob. Bob the characters burps. The class teacher clicks for a new word and they continue in this way for several more words, many with /ear/ sounds in them, all which go to Bob.

   MT, looking at LSA: 'Obb must be starving'.

Section 12: Conclusion of lesson.

Class teacher:	'Well done everyone. Put your coats on. Time to go out'.
	All the children get up from the floor, MT gets up from his chair and they walk over to their pegs. The class teacher walks over to the LSA and discusses MT's work and interaction during the activity.

Questions for reflection:

- If you were the LSA in this classroom, what would you be reporting back to the class teacher?
- How would you assess MT's progress in this session?
- What recommendations would you make for future sessions?

Review

The review stage of the process is the point when there is a systematic consideration of the progress made by the child in relation to the plan(s) that was drawn up for him/her. Reviews may be informal and ongoing, involving formative assessment and feedback, or more formal, for example, at regular reviews of progress involving a range of professionals as well as the child and the family. As we have seen in the above case study of MT in his setting, his LSA and the class teacher met almost immediately after the phonics session to review, informally, how successful it had been for the child. Either the LSA or the class teacher would do well here to make some brief written notes of the session at this point, in order to inform any more formal meetings about MT's progress in due course. These informal discussions, then, help to form part of a more formal review of a child's progress which will then in turn help to develop objectives for the next few weeks of support. In addition, however, this information also is required by the setting or school SENDCo, who has the overall responsibility for monitoring not only children's needs and progress but also how to map adult resources and staff skills to children, targeting these key resources to provide the most effective way of meeting children's needs in the whole setting.

One of the issues at formal review meetings is the degree to which all involved feel comfortable in sharing and disclosing essential information about a child. One of the SENDCos interviewed notes how her

> role has become much more strategic rather than being hands-on, which it used to be. So, people are quite comfortable now with meeting parents at the key worker stage. And this works with parents because they get approached by their key worker in the first instance, and they have those low level discussions about their child and their progress before I get involved.

The SENDCo, therefore, needs to plan in time for informal as well as more formally time-tabled discussions that should include parents and the child as well, and sometimes where possible any other agencies connected to the child and their learning. Key questions that a SENDCo might ask at these meetings with practitioners include:

- How well is this intervention/strategy helping this child to achieve their targets?
- How do we know this – what evidence of progress and achievement is there?

Answers to these questions might then go on to form the basis of a SENDCo's actions regarding what might be needed regarding continued support for the practitioner or LSA in their role as well as what information will be taken forward to subsequent and more formal meetings about the child.

Formal reviews of progress

Holding formal reviews with all involved parties is a time consuming process and requires significant skills in order to ensure that all involved have a voice, have time to express their views and that clear targets for future action arise from the discussions that take place. Such meetings, therefore, should focus clearly on the progress the child has made, the effectiveness of the planned support and next steps. For some children, sometimes it is deemed that intervention has been successful, especially if a shorter term issue for the child had been identified and therefore, substantially differentiated planning can be reduced. However, for some other children the review will identify that the child's needs are not being met within the setting's present resources and so, further support and assessment may be required and, for some children, this might extend as far as referral for an EHC assessment.

Reflective activity: discussion of sensitive issues at review meetings

Please read the narrative below. As you do so, consider the following:

- Should children's choice of key worker be honoured, and if so, why?
- What are the emotive concerns around children biting? Why does it happen and how might we find a way of preventing this happening in the setting?
- Revisit the chapter on social, emotional and mental health needs for the section on attachment theory (pp. 97–8) and nurture groups (pp. 98–100). How might a knowledge and understanding of these and this type of provision have supported the child?
- How important is it that practitioners have training and understanding and that this is similarly extended to parents and families?

An educational psychologist writes:

High needs funding was being used to employ a key worker who was able to work one to one with one child to provide the support and also to provide guidance to other people in the setting. She was the one to whom he turned and she was the one who had her antennae attuned to notice when he might spark off and when he was calmer. He went into school, a big, busy open plan setting at reception and he was overwhelmed, and when he's overwhelmed he throws and he bites. So I was asked to come in and because he was biting and he's biting adults as well and I'm saying, 'Well, that's because your arm is there. That's his way of saying, "I'm really distressed but I've got so distressed that I can't hold it in"'.

Unfortunately, it just accelerated, staff becoming more emotive and he picked up that they were anxious. They were rightly worried; it's not okay to bite but they were also expecting him to do things that he didn't know how to do, like sit on the floor for 20 minutes. It's a long time in any child's life, particularly if you're quite restless. ... This child definitely had a need that was an emotional need about being overwhelmed by having too many demands made on him, and the school struggled because they became afraid of him.

What happened was that I was brought in and was asked to do formal cognitive assessment; fine I did that. However, there was a lot of other stuff going on. It was clear that this child needed more nurture than challenge. He needed more relationship building than some of the other things. He also struggled during free time, unstructured time and there was a lot of that in this particular big, big reception class. Not all children thrive with unstructured 'do your own thing and move along and learning by osmosis'. He needed structure and guidance.

What then happened was that we had a series of meetings, I did some training with staff around their own emotional containment about helping them read his facial expressions to anticipate when he might be overwhelmed so they could get in there to do a bit more nurturing rather than sit down and do this, or remove him from the situation. What I also needed to do was stuff around attachment with mum, because when the mum came in to get her little boy, and it was really hard because she just heard all the awful stuff, he was looking at her like this, 'Oh mummy', and when she picked him up she thought he was going to bite her so she pulled away. I looked at her and said, 'He just wants to give you a kiss'. So she needed help with that too. But I couldn't do it, because the school ran out of money. That's quite hard as a service provider, a commissioned provider, because funding suddenly stops. I think the child might be on a part time timetable now.

As this educational psychologist noted, as an employee of a commissioned service, SENDCos and schools need to manage their budgets carefully in order to ensure support can continue where needed.

Annual reviews for children with Education, Health and Care (EHC) plans

The *Code of Practice* (DfE, 2015a §9.1666–9.176) notes the full details of annual review procedures. All EHC plans statutorily must be reviewed at least annually. These formal reviews must focus on the child's progress towards achieving the objectives that their EHC plan specifies. Children, their parents and key parties should attend, and advance preparation is essential in terms of obtaining and then circulating written advice about the child from all who should provide input, often based on the more regular review meetings that the setting has held over the year as noted above.

Review meetings can be very stressful, and particularly, often, for parents who may want some support in preparing their written information prior to the meeting or putting it across once the meeting takes place. In fact, the recent *Study of Early Education and Development* (SEED) document (Griggs and Bussard, 2017, p. 30) quotes a setting SENDCo as terming it 'daunting', but recognising that changes in systems create some stress as new systems such as the EHC bed in. In addition, Griggs and Bussard (2017) also noted from their research that awareness of EHC plans and review processes are generally low among parents, and so the onus should therefore be on the school or setting to ensure that their knowledge is raised and stress reduced. Cowne *et al.* (2015) recommend that the following points are considered:

- how the room is set up to put the parent and child at ease;
- at the start, inviting those present to place strengths and positive points for progress on a flipchart for all participants to see;
- reflecting on what is working as well as what is not, and ensuring that what is important to the child remains central;
- ensuring that there may be differing perspectives, however, drawing together a workable plan that all can agree to and work with;
- recording any unanswered questions, with some responsibilities attached as to who might follow these through and seek some answers.

Reflective activity: review of personal skills

Please consider the following:

- How confident are you in your skills of observation, scaffolding, planning?
- What could help you to become even better?
- The educational psychologist noted the challenges in breaking concepts or actions down into small steps. How skilled and experienced are you in doing this?

Summary

This chapter has briefly examined the key role that observations, planning and assessment have in determining and organising support for children in general, and individual children with particular needs, in order to ensure they thrive within a setting/school. It raises issues about how important it is for children and their families to feel they have enough genuine opportunities to offer their voice and have it heard and to retain sufficient control over what is happening to them and their child. Observations, planning and carefully judged assessment inform practice and benefit the child through ensuring provision is as close a match to the child's needs and current capabilities as possible, with some additional challenge in order to move the child forward to new and enhanced possibilities for experiences and learning. What has been seen is that a thorough knowledge of child development, a thorough knowledge of *this* child's development, a good understanding of the barriers that might impede this child's progress and performance and a high commitment to overcoming those barriers is essential for all concerned with the child. An indication of some key people involved with the 'assess, plan, do, review' process has been raised in this chapter. More about some of their key roles and responsibilities and ways in which they should work together for the benefit of the child are noted in Chapter 9.

Collaboration with other professionals

Major questions addressed in this chapter are:

- What is the range of people who may be involved in support for young children in the early years who experience some sort of difficulty, and what is their likely role?
- What is the role of external agencies supporting provision for SEND in early years contexts?
- What might be some of the issues in multi-agency working, and how might these be addressed?
- What does effective multi-agency working 'look like' in practice?

Introduction

It is very likely that a young child who experiences more complex and severe difficulties (as well as some medical conditions associated with learning problems) and his/her family will be involved with other agencies in addition to the school, especially if these have been identified before school age. Indeed, the *Code of Practice* (DfE, 2015a, §1.2) specifically comments on an expectation of 'collaboration between education, health and social care services to provide support'. For teachers, parents and families, knowing when and how to interact with the range of professionals, inside and outside the school, who may become involved with a particular child can be crucial in sorting out the complex interaction of factors which result in difficulty in learning, and knowing how they might begin to address this. As one SEN(D) Co in a pre-school setting commented when interviewed by the authors of this book:

> Families having support from a range of different professionals helps the child, and the parents, to see the issues from a number of different perspectives, and that helps them to really know what is going on with the difficulties their child, and themselves, are facing.

In support of this view, an Area SENDCo remarked:

> together we have a toolbox of experiences that parents can draw on in order to support their family as they grow and develop ... working in harmony with social

services and with health professionals has formed the basis of the education, health and care plans we now develop.

This chapter first considers the history of collaborative working across agencies and reasons why this collaboration is seen as so important. It goes on to outline the roles of the range of people who might have an interest in supporting children who experience some sort of difficulty, and possible roles: the special educational needs and disability co-ordinator inside the school, outside agencies and so on. It then discusses challenges in relation to this kind of partnership work with examples of what might be considered good practice.

History of, and rationale for, collaborative working

Collaborative working is not a new concept. In a number of respects, early childhood education has been positioned at the forefront of practice. Educating and ensuring the welfare of young children with varied and complex needs has often necessitated the support of services from a range of different areas: education, health, welfare and so on. Indeed, we saw collaborative working in the work of Owen and the McMillan sisters in Chapter 1. In the first part of the twentieth century, more formal collaborative working can be identified in the Hadow Report (1933, p. xviii) which comments on 'the work of the school medical service', and expresses 'appreciation of the triumphs which it has won'.

Collaborative working was recognised as being important within the field of social work after World War Two. Tilda Goldberg, for example, a social work researcher, was concerned with the practice of inter-agency working and advocated the need for 'complex statutory bodies to collaborate flexibly with other social agencies' (Goldberg et al., 1956, p. 76). She was aware of the challenges this would bring with it, articulating how sometimes 'ignorance and misconception of each other's functions' (ibid., p. 76) affected co-operation. Her advocacy for the co-location of 'general practitioners, social workers, nurses and psychiatrists' in health centres, where they would be 'easily accessible to each other and the patient' (ibid., p. 38), reflects later working practices in the Children's Centre programmes at the beginning of the twenty-first century.

In 1973, the death of 7-year-old Maria Colwell at the hands of her stepfather triggered legislation and child protection procedures that have evolved since that time. The 1977 inquiry identified that there had been a failure in communication between agencies and services. She had been seen at various times by an NSPCC inspector, social services, a doctor and an education welfare officer. Gradually, following the 1977 enquiry, guidance and protocols were established to co-ordinate the provision of child protection services.

In the context of provision for special educational needs, the Warnock Report (DES, 1978, §9.40) makes the point that multi-agency 'support, however and wherever given, must be seen as taking place within a partnership between parents and the members of the different services'. The point here is that this support should enable 'parents more effectively to help their children at home and at school'.

The concept of 'special educational', or 'additional support' needs covers a wide area that may go well beyond school and the conventional realm of 'education' into, sometimes, health and welfare. Multi-agency collaborative working practices have been encouraged by various governments as paramount for the safety of children since the 1980s, with subsequent recommendations about training in joint working practices for health professionals, social workers, teachers and others (Dunhill, 2009). Despite the move towards greater inter-agency collaboration over a long period of time, however, as Nethercott (2015) notes, reports from many child protection reviews within the UK over the past 20 years (Brandon *et al.*, 2008; Brandon *et al.*, 2009; Laming, 2003; Reder and Duncan 2003; Rochdale Borough Safeguarding Children Board (RBSCB), 2012) have concluded that a lack of communication between agencies has contributed to the death or serious abuse of a child. The three primary care agencies, Education, Health and Social Services, have tended to operate to different legislative frameworks with different priorities and definitions of what constitutes a need (Roaf and Lloyd, 1995). Lack of clear structure to determine responsibilities in inter-agency working could also generate considerable tension, especially when resources were under pressure.

System failure is illustrated in recent years, in the case of the tragic death of Victoria Climbié, a child known to be at risk by both educational and social services. In 2003, alongside the formal response to the report into the death, the Government published a Green Paper, *Every Child Matters* H.M. Treasury, 2003) followed by the Children Act (2004) that gave legal force to five interdependent outcomes (DfES, 2004). The clear failure re-emphasised the need for closer co-operation between agencies which exist to support children in difficulties and their families or carers. The Every Child Matters agenda (DfES, 2004) sought to resolve these difficulties by unifying the range of children's services.

The early years outcomes provisions in sections 1–4 of the Childcare Act 2006 placed a duty on English LAs, working with their NHS and Jobcentre Plus (JCP) partners, to improve the five Every Child Matters (ECM) outcomes of all young children (0–5) in their area and reduce inequalities between them, through integrated early childhood services. The programme of SureStart Children's Centres supported collaborative, holistic working from one centre. The aim was for every neighbourhood to have a Children's Centre by 2010, which was shaped around the unique needs of the communities who lived there. However, with the change of government in 2010, ring-fenced funding was removed, national funding reduced and many LAs restricted or closed the services. Many Children's Centres lost their funding with money being diverted elsewhere after the advent of the Early Intervention Grant allowed LAs to decide where to spend the money.

With the introduction of the *Early Years Foundation Stage* in 2008 (DCSF, 2008), the distinction between education and care was removed and both came together in the Statutory Framework. One of the key themes was positive relationships, recognising the need to work with families and children alongside multi-disciplinary teams. This was further enhanced by the Early Years Professional (EYP) programme, which gave a professional status to practitioners working with the very young children across health, social care and education (Lumsden, 2014). However, the EYP has since been replaced by the Early Years Teacher status, with a distinct focus on teaching and learning, mirroring the Teacher's Standards (DfE, 2011b), thus representing a shift away from a multi-disciplinary status.

After the election of the Coalition government in 2010, a joint DfE/DoH document 'Supporting Families in the Early Foundation Years' was issued (DfE/DoH, 2011, p. 5) which set out the government's intention on how to encourage:

> partnerships between health and early years services, leading to stronger integrated working; clarifying how information-sharing in the foundation years can work better; a continuing important role for local authorities in addressing disadvantage and

inequalities by securing sufficient early years provision and championing the needs of vulnerable children and families.

More recently, the Children and Families Act (2014, section 1.22) requires education, health and social care services to work together to ensure all children receive appropriate support. Section 25 places a legal requirement on LAs to ensure integration between services for children and young people with SEND. Thus, LAs continue to have an important role in supporting the organisation, provision and funding for the needs of children with SEND and their families (Griggs and Bussard, 2017). There is a similar emphasis in the Care Act (2014) which places a legal duty on LAs to co-operate and promote integration of care, support and health services.

Range of services

Since 2014, LAs in England have been required to publish their 'Local Offer'. This means the publication, in one place, of information about provision available in their area for children and young people from 0 to 25 who have SEND. The local offer must include both local provision and provision outside the area that the LA expects is likely to be used by children and young people with SEND for whom they are responsible. This can cover education, health and care services. Table 9.1 below outlines some of the different individuals that practitioners and families might expect to work with and gives an indication of their job role.

Pivotal to effective collaborative working across agencies in the early years is often the SENDCo, a required role in settings and schools in England, Wales and Northern Ireland.

Role of SENDCo

In England, Wales and Northern Ireland the role of the SENDCo developed in response to the introduction of legislation related to the identification of children with SEN and a statutory requirement to meet their needs in schools. In the most recent *Code of Practice* in England (DfE, 2015a, §5.54), for example, the responsibilities in early years settings are defined as:

- ensuring all practitioners in the setting understand their responsibilities to children with SEND and the setting's approach to identifying and meeting SEND;
- advising and supporting colleagues;
- ensuring parents are closely involved throughout and that their insights inform action taken by the setting; and
- liaising with professionals or agencies beyond the setting.

In many places the role of the SENDCo has developed considerably since the role was first envisaged in the publication of the (2001) Code. It may be allocated to members of the school senior management team or practitioners. SENDCos may have responsibilities both at the level of the individual children and the whole setting or school. They may take charge of budgeting, resource allocation, timetabling and other managerial and administrative roles. They may also work with individual children, as well as advising, appraising and training staff and liaising with outside agencies, professionals and parents.

Table 9.1 Professional roles in supporting children in the early years

Title	Job Role	Aspects of the work
Education **SEN advisory teacher/** **Area SENDCo**	The Area SENDCo helps make the links between education, health and social care to facilitate appropriate early provision for children with SEN and their transition to compulsory schooling.	Typically, the role of the Area SENDCo includes providing advice and practical support to early years providers about approaches to identification, assessment and intervention within the SEN Code of Practice and providing day-to-day support for setting-based SENDCos in ensuring arrangements are in place to support children with SEN. They support the links between the settings, parents, schools, social care and health services by developing and disseminating good practice, supporting the development and delivery of training both for individual settings and on a wider basis and developing links with existing SENDCo networks to support smooth transitions to school nursery and reception classes. They inform parents of and work with local impartial Information, Advice and Support Services, to promote effective work with parents of children in the early years.
Educational **Psychologist**	Educational psychologists (EPs) have knowledge and understanding of children's development.	Their role is to find solutions to difficulties in early years settings (and schools) and at home, to enable children to get the best from their educational opportunities. They do this through the assessment of an individual child's learning and/or behavioural needs and providing training for staff working in early years provision.
Education Health **and Care plan** **co-ordinator**	Education, Health and Care Plan co-ordinators are responsible for case management for children and young people who are having a needs assessment for an EHC plan and those who currently hold statements of special educational needs (SEN).	They make sure that parents/carers of children and young people with SEN are provided with support and advice about the needs assessment process, the statement/EHC plan and the annual review processes. They ensure the child receives suitable educational provision in line with what is set out in the statement or EHC plan.
SENDCo	The early years framework requires early years providers to have a designated person to act as special educational needs co-ordinator (SENDCo). In maintained nursery schools this will be a qualified teacher.	The role of the SENDCo involves advising and supporting colleagues to adopt a graduated approach with four stages of action: assess, plan, do and review. Early action to help children is very important and settings will work in partnership with parents to establish the support their child needs. This doesn't necessarily need to be an Education, Health and Care plan but the special educational provision should be matched to the child's identified special educational needs.

Teacher for the hearing impaired (HI)/ Teacher for the visually impaired (VI)	The teacher for hearing impaired children assesses and advises settings and practitioners and teaches deaf children and young people.	They work closely with health and social care and other agencies (where appropriate) following diagnosis and collaborate with voluntary agencies to provide services e.g. National Deaf Children's Society, Royal National Institute for the Blind. They also work with hospital departments to ensure children and young people receive the most appropriate assessment.
Learning Support Assistants/Teaching Assistants	A learning support assistant (LSA) or teaching assistant (TA) is someone who works in the classroom under the direction of a qualified teacher.	TAs/LSAs support individual children or small groups to help them learn and take part in activities in schools or nurseries.
Portage and Early Support	Portage is a home based education service for families with a child or children from birth to 5 with complex additional needs.	Portage works closely with a wide number of other professionals from Social care, Health and the voluntary sector. Portage will offer advice and support to the pre-school setting where the child is attending and may support the child through the transition process into pre-school or school when the time comes.
Health		
Designated clinical officer (DCO)	The designated clinical officer is the key point of contact between the local NHS and the LA, and should help facilitate the Education Health and Care Plan (EHC Plan) process and navigate the local health systems.	The DCO provides the point of contact for LAs, early years, schools and colleges seeking health advice on children and young people who may have SEND. The role also provides a point of contact for clinical commissioning groups and health providers so that processes are in place to ensure that appropriate notification can be given to the LA of children who they think may have SEND.
Paediatrician	A paediatrician is a specialist doctor who looks after babies and children. They are often involved, particularly early on, when there are concerns a child may have an impairment or disability.	A paediatrician is able to refer for further medical investigations and diagnosis. They are able to direct children to other paediatric specialists e.g. therapists, psychologists and specialist nursing services as needed.
Health Visitor (HV)	A Health Visitor is a qualified nurse or midwife who has special training in child health. They give help, advice and practical support to families about the care of children under 5.	The health visitor will check that the child is growing and developing as expected as part of the Integrated Review at 2. Where a child has additional needs they may be part of a team of professionals working to support the child and family.

(Continued)

Table 9.1 (Continued)

Title	Job Role	Aspects of the work
Speech and Language Therapists (SLT)	Speech and language therapists (SLT) assess and treat speech, language and communication problems in people of all ages to help them better communicate. They'll also work with people who have eating and swallowing problems.	The speech and language therapist works in homes, early years settings and schools providing specialist assessments, support and advice to parents/carers and professionals. They work closely with health and social care and other agencies (where appropriate) following diagnosis and can collaborate with voluntary agencies to provide services.
Physiotherapists	Physiotherapists are health care professionals registered with the Health and Care Professions Council (HCPC). They work with parents and professionals, aiming to help children and young people to reach their physical potential, to achieve improved independence and quality of life.	Children's physiotherapists provide specialist assessment and intervention to children and young people who have a range of conditions involving physical and movement difficulties which limit their mobility, function, and/or independence. They work in a range of locations, including clinics, school and pre-school settings, homes and respite or voluntary care settings. Children's physiotherapists may be employed by NHS, LA, private or charitable sector providers.
Occupational therapists (OTs)	Occupational therapists are health professionals, registered with the Health and Care Professions council (HCPC). Occupational therapists aim to help children and young achieve their full potential in their ability to play, learn and look after themselves.	They can work with a variety of children with special educational needs, disability and complex health difficulties, and work in the setting that is most appropriate for the child, young person or their family/carers, including home, clinic, education setting or respite care.
Clinical psychologists	Clinical psychologists offer a range of services for children and young people, when there are concerns about their development, their behaviour, their mental health and their relationships.	Clinical psychologists can do different things to help such as assessments (neuropsychological, diagnostic, behaviour) of the challenges they face, and of their mental health. Sometimes clinical psychologists work directly with the child but sometimes it is better to work with other people to help them to enable the child. This might include nurses, psychiatrists, early years practitioners, teachers, social workers, assistant psychologists, to support them in supporting children and young people.
Child mental health teams	Children's Mental health nurses offer counselling and support to children and using a variety of therapeutic approaches.	They provide advice and support for behaviour management, signpost children and young people to other agencies as appropriate and can be called in by Critical Support Team to provide support to settings.
Children's community learning disability nurse (CCLDN)	CCLDNs are specifically trained learning disability nurses registered with the Nursing and Midwifery Council.	They work with children, families and staff within settings to help manage behaviour, communication and mental health difficulties, using a variety of skills and techniques. Work may include training for parents using specific training approaches.

Social Care **Social worker**	Social workers tend to specialise in either adult or children's services.	A social worker's work with children with special educational needs (SEN) includes: Informing the County Council of any children who they think may have SEN Ensuring that schools have a contact for seeking social work advice on children who may have SEN Co-ordinating social services advice for any statutory assessments, transition reviews and annual reviews as appropriate Ensuring social services provision is made for any children with SEN where appropriate Attending annual reviews for 'Looked After Children' who hold statements
Parent Support Advisor (PSA)	Parent support advisers (PSAs) are employed by a school or group of schools. They provide information and support to parents/carers of a child at the school(s).	Their role includes providing information to parents about the school and local services which may be of help, including those provided by education, social care, youth justice, childcare providers and the voluntary sector.
Voluntary sector **Voluntary support agencies**	A range of charitable and other support services that will focus on one or more area of need.	Provide information and support. This varies considerably from service to service

The new (2015a) *SEN and Disability Code of Practice* that operates in England highlights the strategic nature of the role at the level of the senior management team in a school or college:

> The SENDCo has an important role to play with the headteacher and governing body, in determining the strategic development of SEN policy and provision in the [setting or] school. They will be most effective in that role if they are part of the school leadership team.
>
> (DfE, 2015a, §6.87)

The day-to-day responsibility of the SENDCo is outlined as:

> ... the operation of SEN policy and co-ordination of specific provision made to support individual pupils with SEN, including those who have EHC plans.
>
> (DfE, 2015a, §6.88)

The SENDCo is therefore often at the very centre of collaborative working in practice (see Figure 9.1 below) and is the lynchpin drawing together the different services, and the wider community, to support the child's needs.

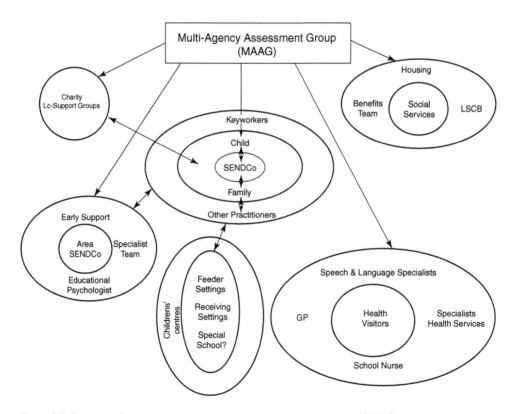

Figure 9.1 Example of multi-agency assessment group working with the SENDCo

Inter-agency collaboration and assessment in the early years

Assessment of children's progress and/or special or additional educational needs and/or disabilities in the early years is most usually carried out through a number of different specialist agencies. These assessments may relate to the Early Years Foundation Stage progress check and the health visitors' assessment that is part of the Healthy Child Programme, and Early Help Assessment (EHA) plan if the child has one, and statutory assessment of SEND through, for example, Co-ordinated Support Plans in Scotland, and Education, Health and Care Plans in England.

Common Assessment Framework (CAF) and Early Help Assessments (EHA)

As part of the ECM agenda, a Common Assessment Framework (CAF) for use across the children's workforce was developed to provide a shared framework for enabling decisions 'about how best to meet [children's] needs, in terms of both what the family can do and also what services could be provided' (CWDC, 2009, para. 1.11). As a result of the common assessment discussion, concerns about the child might be resolved, or particular actions for the professional undertaking the CAF and his/her service might be agreed with a date for review and monitoring progress. Alternatively, actions might be identified for other agencies. This involves sharing the assessment with these agencies, subject to the appropriate consent of the child or young person/family, and forming a team around the child (TAC) or team around the family (TAF) to support the child or young person. The actions needed would be agreed with the other agencies and a plan and responsibilities for delivering the actions would need to be recorded on the CAF form (CWDC, 2009).

Clearly, in the attempt to ensure the 'joined-up thinking' that was required by the 2004 Children Act and the ECM agenda, in schools and settings there was a potential overlap between assessment associated with provision for special educational needs and that carried out for the CAF. However, the CAF was not intended to replace other statutory assessments, but to complement or be integrated with them. Nor was it for assessment of a child where there is any suggestion of harm. Guidance given by the CWDC (2009, para. 1.4) states 'The CAF is not for a child or young person about whom you have concerns that they might be suffering, or may be at risk of suffering, harm. In such instances, you should follow your Local Safeguarding Children Board (LSCB) safeguarding procedures without delay'.

More recently, in response to Government challenge to simplify procedures, LAs have been developing Early Help processes that use shortened assessments such as an Early Help Assessment (EHA) that are designed to speed up access to services. Modelled on CAF procedures, these are being co-ordinated through Multi-Agency Safeguarding Hubs (MASHs), where key agencies (police, social care, education, health) are physically in one team, thus reducing the distinction between each agency's procedures in arriving at safeguarding or family support decisions. As with the CAF, these are not intended as a replacement for other statutory assessments or for children who already have the engagement of services who already support their identified need.

The two-year-old integrated review

The Early Years Foundation Stage (EYFS) progress check became a statutory requirement for all providers offering childcare to two year olds within the EYFS Framework in

September 2012. As the *Code of Practice* (DfE, 2015a) notes, there is another assessment also that health visitors carry out to check children's physical development milestones between 2 and 3 years of age as part of the universal Healthy Child Programme. From 2015, an integrated review has been introduced to cover the development areas in the Healthy Child Programme two-year review and the EYFS two-year progress check. The integrated review (DfE, 2015a, §5.25) is proposed to:

- identify the child's progress, strengths and needs at this age in order to promote positive outcomes in health and well-being, learning and development;
- enable appropriate intervention and support for children and their families, where progress is less than expected; and
- generate information which can be used to plan services and contribute to the reduction of inequalities in children's outcomes.

This implies practitioners in settings, health professional and parents coming together to discuss a child's progress. Indeed, it may well be the return to more cohesive collaborative working with which to support the additional needs of children with SEND. Certainly a SENDCo in a nursery setting seemed to feel this might be the case:

> But talking about the positives going forward, I think the two-year-old check, the Integrated Review, is a very positive thing. I think it opens that door to have conversations with parents and practitioners' understanding of child development and getting that over to parents, how their child is within the normal development, I think that will really help.

Statutory assessment of individual support needs

Across the UK, statutory assessment of young children's special educational needs and disabilities and/or additional support needs requires effective inter-agency collaboration in order to ensure that they are supported with the special/additional provision that they need to engage with the school or college curriculum and make good progress. In Scotland, the individual plan that results from statutory assessment is termed 'a co-ordinated support plan':

> … a number of children and young people have additional support needs arising from complex or multiple factors which require a high degree of co-ordination of support from education authorities and other agencies in order that their needs can be met. This support is co-ordinated through the provision of a co-ordinated support plan under the Act.
>
> (Scottish Government, 2010, p. 74, §1)

To achieve the level of effective inter-agency collaboration that is required, the *Code* in Scotland (2010, p. 30, §8) reads:

> Education authorities need to play their part in ensuring that there is effective communication, collaboration and integrated assessment, planning, action and review when other agencies are involved.

In England, the new Education, Health and Care plans introduced by the Children and Families Act, 2014, by definition also require a similar degree of collaboration, however problematic the history of such collaboration may have been in previous years.

Challenges in developing Education, Health and Care Plans

A number of 'Key challenges and enabling factors' were identified during the piloting of EHC plans in England (DfE, 2014b, p. 14). In some cases these issues were interpreted as 'fundamental to the new process' (ibid.). The first identified challenge was 'ensuring sufficiency and consistency of multi-agency working that might be addressed by:

- Increased levels of strategic and operational commitment to contribute to the new process.
- Provision of clear guidance to all professionals detailing expectations of how, when and why they should be involved.
- Creation of 'champions' or 'spearheads' for individual agencies (and services within these) to act as the point of contact for the EHC planning process.
- Introduction of proportionate approaches to multi-agency working e.g. use of multi-media to enable capacity constrained professionals to input to meetings.

Other challenges related to multi-agency working included 'meeting the reduced 20-week statutory timeframe', potentially to be addressed by:

- Alignment of early years and school paper work to enable efficient translation of pre-referral information into the EHC planning process.
- Creating efficiencies between agencies through sharing of assessments and reports.
- Introduction of proportionate approaches to multi-agency working, e.g. use of multi-media to enable capacity constrained professionals to input to meetings.
- Development of integrated resourcing and funding mechanisms.

In addition, the 'sharing of information between agencies and with families might be achieved by (DfE, 2014b, p. 15):

- Having the family as the holder of all information and paperwork and relying on them to give permission and transfer it from place to place.
- Development of an integrated technology system that enables all relevant professionals and families to access the 'live' EHC plan and grants differing levels of permissions for distinct parties to edit the plan.

Essential factors in multi-agency partnerships

Collaborative working means different services, agencies, teams of professionals and other staff working together to provide services that meet the needs of children, young people, and their parents or carers (DfE, 2015c, p. 21). It embraces two key concepts of partnership and integration:

- Partnership working is characterised by a shared sense of purpose, which can only really be successful if there is mutual respect across all the relationships forged around the child and family, and a willingness to negotiate to ensure their needs are met.

- An integrated model of service provision aims to meet the holistic needs of the child and their family.

Two SENDCos interviewed by the authors noted the key importance of communicating these concepts. One stated:

So it's about creating that consistency between family and consistency between an early years setting.

The other noted:

We have a responsibility to try and communicate in a way that allows the parent's voice to be heard, where possible allows the child's voice to be heard, but that can be really difficult sometimes.

If multi-agency partnerships are to be effective in developing, resourcing and maintaining statutory assessment and provision for special, or additional, educational needs, then

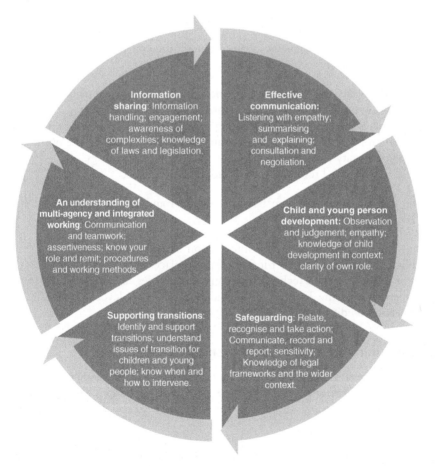

Figure 9.2 Six key areas of common core skills required for working with children and families

(Adapted from Common Core Skills and Knowledge for the children's and young people's workforce (DfE 2010))

it is patently obvious that what constitutes good practice in such relationships should be developed and maintained.

Effective collaborative working across agencies

The government recognised the importance of working collaboratively and republished guidance of Common Core Skills and Knowledge (DfE, 2015c), which outlined six areas of expertise in the 'common core' offer (see Figure 9.2). The document also outlines a number of tools and processes that make integrated working more effective in meeting the needs of children and families who experience collaborative working and is well worth using in settings to help guide collaborative working.

Communication

> Good communication is central to working with children, young people, families and carers. It helps build trust, and encourages them to seek advice and use services. It is key to establishing and maintaining relationships, and is an active process that involves listening, questioning, understanding and responding.
>
> (DfE, 2015c, p. 6)

Understanding of the differing terminologies used across the professionals, listening skills and the ability to negotiate and compromise are essential for collaborative working to be effective. Communication is vital on a number of different levels. In a busy early years setting it can be very challenging to find the time and space (sometimes literally a free space to use) to listen and talk with parents about their child's additional needs. It is often the first time a parent may begin to articulate, or hear, that their child may be experiencing difficulties or issues in their development. It is even more challenging, then, to communicate across disciplines and services with the child and parent firmly at the centre of the discourse and possibly getting very confused, emotional and worried about what is going to happen. Careful use of language, empathy and clarity are then essential prerequisites, as one Area SENDCo confirmed:

> I take a non-judgemental approach. I think I am very open with people. I try to be very honest without being judgmental and I think I'm probably quite good at holding people's hands without being … I suppose I take maybe perhaps a bit of a friendly approach. I think it's more to do with the type of personality that I have. So although I maintain a professional approach I think there's a big lump of my personality in there in terms of, 'I'm here to help you and I'm here to be a support to you. I'm not here to judge'.

A SENDCo in a nursery setting agreed with this approach to parents:

> What do I avoid? I always try to be really, really honest with people but that would be something I would always do with people. I think parents sometimes expect us to make a diagnosis or for me to make a diagnosis and I certainly will always be very, very clear that that's not my role. I think every time I meet families I am probably a little bit guarded and being careful in not saying the wrong thing in terms of, perhaps, presenting with a hope. I try to be very honest and very straight and actually talk through more about the process of support, because every child is individual and the development process is very, very individual to the support given.

Choice of language

It is important that everyone involved, particularly the children and families, understand the terms used by different professionals so that they feel that they have full cognisance about what is going on. The clarity of communication and terminology needs to be addressed at all levels from the strategic lead to the practitioners in settings (Atkinson *et al.*, 2002). Pietroni (1992) identified the professional language and discourses that practitioners use goes deeper than just the words; it reflects the attitudes, values and culture of the profession. This can lead to significant misunderstandings and confusion affecting the provision and effectiveness of care for children. It is therefore vital that there is openness, questioning and reflection on established practices in order for successful collaboration to be established. Several of the parents quoted in Chapter 7 noted that the best relationships with professionals were characterised by clarity of language, action and plans and empathy.

Roles and responsibilities

Communication on roles and responsibilities within the collaboration is equally important. Each spoke in the wheel of support around the child must be clear on their area of responsibility of support in order for the work to be carried out in an effective way. This may require the professional to give up some autonomy in their area and allow another professional to direct and undertake work that might have originally been part of their area of expertise. It is also vital that all professionals involved are ready and willing to share their knowledge of the child and the support they can offer clearly and in a timely fashion, something noted by setting SENDCos, school SENDCos and educational psychologists in their interviews. This is not always as easy as it sounds and requires an equality of power, what Jones (2004) calls a moving away from professional imperialism: letting go of the knowledge and distinctness of our own professional role for the benefit of the child and family. With this come lots of feelings around professional status and standing that can be very hard to let go of. What is really needed here is a set of shared aims, values and visions across the collaborators that will guide the practice to counterbalance the separateness of the individual professionals and agencies involved.

Reflective activity: personal experience of challenges in collaborative working

Note down your responses to the following questions:

- What, in order of importance, would you say are the challenges in partnership working?
- What difference do you think professional background is likely to make?
- What attitudes and approaches will those involved need to have for successful partnership working?
- What will successful partnership require of leaders in an early years setting (both the SENDCo and the lead practitioner or manager)?

Information sharing

> Sharing information in a timely and accurate way is an essential part of delivering better services to children, young people, their families and carers. Sometimes it can help to save lives. Practitioners at different agencies should work together and share information appropriately for the safety and well-being of children. It is important to understand and respect legislation and ethics surrounding the confidentiality and security of information.
>
> (DfE, 2015b, p. 24)

If we are to support children and families with SEND, indeed all children and their families, we need to ensure that we are in full possession of the relevant information. Barnes (2008, p. 231) has outlined how this is far from the case and 'fragmentation between agencies and the subsequent failure to share information' has undermined collaborative working. Indeed, as Griggs and Bussard (2017) commented, parents have sometimes been left to pass on information to other settings and agencies which, almost inevitably, creates '… problems that impact on the setting's ability to provide additional support'.

Reflective activity: taking account of information provided by families

Read the narrative below.

- Note down your reactions to the situation that is described here.
- How might the practitioners have behaved in a way that would have enabled the needs of the children in the family to have been met more quickly and effectively?

A family has three children aged, 7, 4 and 2 years of age who attend a local primary school, nursery school and children's centre which are co-located but separately governed and managed.

The oldest child entered the primary school having attended an early years setting onsite and it was noted by the teachers at the nursery school that she was experiencing significant speech and language difficulties. The process of collecting observations and information began and information had been sent to the primary school at the time.

The children at the nursery school and children's centre were both being identified with some speech and language issues. The nursery and children's centre were working collaboratively with their Speech and Language Therapist (SaLT) and this was being shared with the parent. In addition, the parent had been targeted to join an 'Early Explorers' group, designed for parents and children in their final term in the children's centre to support transition into the nursery. Run over 6 weeks, this enabled children's physical and emotional acclimatisation to their new setting. An activity pack was provided to extend the experiences in the home – for example, this pack included the key nursery rhymes sung in the nursery. This had the dual impact for this family of supporting the 2-year-old and the 4-year-old.

The nursery setting had given the school full records and observations in the form of the Learning Journey and assessment information matched to the EYFS outcomes.

> However, the school setting decided to make its own assessments of the child, starting from scratch. Staff stated their inclination to ignore the prior information they had received. They wanted to give the child a 'fresh start' and also preferred to use their own systems and data collection. Additional concerns were expressed by the school around data protection, despite the parents' willingness to have key information shared.
>
> The nursery and children's centre expressed the opinion that they did not want the two younger children to experience any further delay in intervention.
>
> The SaLT assigned to the children's centre and nursery was prevented by her remit with the local health organisation from supporting any children above the age of 5, i.e. statutory school age.
>
> In this situation, parties felt disempowered to act; the 7-year-old's needs had not been met as quickly as would have been ideal, and the 4 year old might potentially experience a similar occurrence.

Challenges in collaborative working

One of the aims of collaborative working is to support the integration of services; when it works effectively, as we have seen on page 189, it can lead to greater understanding and knowledge of other professional roles (Whiting, Scammell and Bifulco, 2008), yet this can sometimes be a slippery concept and prove challenging in practice. The CWDC (2010) identified there was a consensus questioning the assumption that integrated working was a good thing. Indeed, Siraj-Blatchford and Siraj-Blatchford (2009), in their review on improving developmental outcomes through integrated early years provision, make the point that there is little direct evidence of effectiveness. Different services are organised in diverse ways, with legislative requirements, funding and competition between services getting in the way of collaboration (Atkinson *et al.*, 2002). It is vital that practitioners are aware of the potential pitfalls of collaboration and reflect on how they can be overcome for the benefit of all involved. There are many potential areas of concern that can arise but here we focus on those that are particularly relevant to the early years sector.

Challenges around the culture and values of a professional

Professional boundaries

Despite the desire to provide a more effective service to meet the needs of the child, professionals working closely together with different visions of the child and family and diverse working practices can lead to them 'unconsciously endeavouring to preserve a professional boundary around the group' (Nethercott, 2015, p. 40). An early years practitioner may look at the needs of a young child in a very different way to a health professional, stemming from their knowledge and understanding of that child's needs from the underlying philosophy from their training and experiences within an educational setting. A health professional's perspective might focus on very different elements relating more narrowly to, say, physiological development stemming once again from their training and experiences within a medical setting. Each might feel their perspective is the most important, and an invisible tussle for their viewpoint to be paramount can ensue. Moreover, putting professionals together can reinforce boundaries (Lee and Stead, 1998), as it can bring a sense of threat and a need to protect the individual's sense of professional identity. All those involved in the collaborative work need to be mindful of this: all need to be valued and their differing perspectives respected to enable their training and experiences to contribute collectively to the support of the child.

Status and power

The issue of power relationships can be a knotty problem for collaborative working. Qualifications, and indeed disciplines, attract a certain status and authority, however, Aubrey (2010, p. 210) suggests that in such situations authority should 'rest on knowledge and expertise rather than on status'. Many early years practitioners working in pre-school settings have level three qualifications, fewer have level four or above. In an inter-disciplinary team they may be working alongside other professionals who are more highly qualified than they are, and many feel daunted and reluctant to share their views. A level three practitioner who has worked closely with a SEND child and her family may very well be the expert – having a comprehensive knowledge of the child in a diverse set of experiences to draw on to inform the assessment and planning for the child. If we firmly place the needs of the child at the centre of our work we should ensure that all professionals have an equal opportunity to share their knowledge and understanding of the child freely and safely, and be respectfully listened to.

Practical challenges

We have already considered how collaborative working can be hindered in a number of different ways. The practical challenges that practitioners in the early years sector might encounter are clearly identified by Wall (2011) and confirmed by Griggs and Bussard (2017):

- Time, money and resources will always be an issue. Those interviewed by the authors with many years of experience working with several different frameworks over time raised and recognised these challenges. However, it is also up to practitioners and settings to be proactive and creative, sharing practice and ideas within their networks and carefully planning and prioritising their time and resources.
- Burdensome bureaucracy and barriers to efficiency are often present. As a SENDCo in an infant school noted:

And we had one child come to us in April who does have quite significant social and communication difficulties, and he's going into reception in September, and I've put in the application for the Education, Health and Care plan, but the funding won't have come through for September. So, in that case I've made an argument for the school to cover the cost of some of that but we won't be able to, I'm anticipating that he will have quite a high level of funding through the plan. There's a six week limit from the time I put in the request, but you have to have a paediatrician's report and a speech and language therapist's report. But sometimes ... well, I had another child's application turned down for assessment yesterday, because the autism support teacher's report hadn't reached the panel before they did. So there was all the evidence from the school, evidence from the paediatrician, evidence from speech and language therapy, but the autism advisory teacher's report hadn't got there in time, so it was deemed to be insufficient evidence. And that's frustrating – because children don't get what they need.

• No system is ideal. Much relies on the will of practitioners to make systems work for the children and families they deal with, as far as possible.
• We acknowledge that face to face training has been reduced in this current climate of austerity. However, SENDCo training remains available and expected, and LAs offer regular networking opportunities, critical for sharing information and practice, and in this digital age there is a vast array of resources and knowledge for practitioners to access. We would particularly recommend the following websites:

  • www.foundationyears.org.uk
  • www.councilfordisabledchildren.org.uk
  • www.ncb.org.uk
  • www.nasen.org.uk
  • www.sendgateway.org.uk

Summary

With regard to the essentials of effective multi-agency practice to ensure the needs of children and young people who experience difficulties are assessed and met, these may be summed up from the findings of a systematic literature review 'Multi-agency working and its implications for practice' (Atkinson, Jones and Lamont, 2007):

• 'clarifying roles and responsibilities';
• 'securing commitment at all levels … engendering trust and mutual respect';
• 'fostering understanding between agencies (e.g. through joint training and recognition of individual expertise)';
• 'developing effective multi-agency processes: ensuring effective communication and information sharing';
• securing the 'necessary resources for multi-agency work and … securing adequate and sustained funding (e.g. through pooled budgets …)';
• 'ensuring continuity of staffing … and an adequate time allocation';
• 'ensuring effective leadership … although also dependent on effective governance and management arrangements … and an effective performance management system';
• 'providing sufficient time for the development of multi-agency working';
• 'the provision of joint training';
• 'agreement of joint aims and objectives'.

We close this chapter here with the views of an Area SENDCo at the heart of the collaborative triangle between child, parents and other services, and with a view to how we can continue to collaborate effectively in the support agenda for children and families:

I think I'd like to see more support within the services and more availability for families. I would absolutely love to see the key working principles and practice and that's very, very much about keeping the family at the very heart of what you do and actually working from what they want, rather than getting tied up in what professionals want of families. … The only agenda that we should be working to is the family's agenda.

Afterword

For children in the early years, the kind of education they experience is fundamentally important because it is the opening of their identities as learners and as members of the wider society. This does not mean that every child will achieve the same as any other, but that every child has an entitlement to be valued, respected, believed in and cared for as a human being in his/her own right.

Practitioners may well feel tension in the system that requires identification of negative difference to 'prove' a need for additional resources, that increasingly focuses on high stakes assessment that marginalises and often demoralises some young children, and at the same time expounds a rhetoric of inclusion and inclusive practices. However, the process of education in the early years is enacted by people.

> Each child wants to know immediately if he is a worthy person in your eyes. You cannot pretend, because the child knows all the things about himself that worry him.
> Gussin Paley (2000, p. 28)

Belief in young children's potential to become confident, capable learners, irrespective of difficulties they may experience, must therefore be at the heart of practice and in the hearts and minds of those practitioners.

References

Adams, C. and Lloyd, J. (2007) 'The effects of speech and language therapy intervention on children with pragmatic language impairments in mainstream school', *British Journal of Special Education*, 34(4), pp. 226–233.

Adult Literacy and Basic Skills Unit (1992) *The ALBSU Standards for Basic Skills Students and Trainees*, Adult Literacy and Basic Skills Unit, London.

Aitken, S. (2000) 'Understanding deafblindness' in S. Aitken, M. Buultjens, C. Clark, J.T. Eyre and L. Pease (eds) *Teaching Children Who are Deafblind*, London: David Fulton Publishers, 1–34.

Aitken, S. and Millar, S. (2002) *Listening to Children with Communication Support Needs*, Glasgow: Sense Scotland.

Alexander, R. (2011) *Children, Their World, Their Education: Final Report and Recommendations of the Cambridge Primary Review*, Abingdon: Routledge.

Allen, G. (2011) *Early Intervention. The Next Steps*, available at http://media.education.gov.uk/assets/files/pdf/g/graham%20allens%20review%20of%20early%20intervention.pdf (accessed 6 March 2017).

Allenby, C., Fearon-Wilson, J., Merrison, S. and Morling, E. (2015) *Supporting Children with Speech and Language Difficulties*, London: Routledge.

American Psychiatric Association (1994) *Diagnostic and Statistical Manual of Mental Disorders*, 4th edn *(DSM-IV)*, Arlington, VA: American Psychiatric Association.

American Psychiatric Association (2015) *Diagnostic and Statistical Manual of Mental Disorders, Fifth Edition (DSM-V)*, Arlington, VA: American Psychiatric Association.

Armitage, M. (2009) *Play Pods in Schools An Independent Evaluation Project 43,* available at: www.play pods.co.uk/PlayPods%20in%20schools-an%20independent%20evaluation%202009.pdf (accessed 27 February 2017).

Asperger, H. (1944/1991) translated as 'Autistic psychopathy in childhood' in U. Frith (ed) *Autism and Asperger syndrome*, Cambridge: Cambridge University Press.

Athey, C. (2007) *Extending/thought in Young Children: A Parent-Teacher Partnership*, London: Sage Publishers.

Atkinson, M., Jones, M. and Lamont, E. (2007) *Multi-Agency Working and Its Implications for Practice: A Review of the Literature.* Slough: CfBT Education Trust.

Atkinson, M., Wilkin, A., Stott, A., Doherty, P. and Kinder, K. (2002) *Multi Agency Working: A Detailed Study* (LGA Research Report 26). Slough: NFER.

Aubrey, C. (2010) 'Leading and working in multi-agency teams' in G. Pugh and B. Duffy (eds) *Contemporary Issues in the Early Years*, 5th edn. London: Sage, 209–224.

Baldock, P., Fitzgerald, D. and Kay, J. (2013) *Understanding Early Years Policy*, 3rd edn, London: PCP.

Ball, C. (1994) *Start Right Report: Start Right: The Importance of Early Learning*, London: Royal Society for the Encouragement of Arts.

Ballard, P.B. (1915/16) 'Norms of performance in reading', p.154, cited by Carroll, J.A., K. Barger, K. James, and K. Hill (2017) *Guided by Meaning in Primary Literacy: Libraries, Reading, Writing, and Learning*, New York: Praeger.

Barnes, P. (2008) 'Multi-agency working: What are the perspectives of SENCos and parents regarding its development and implementation?' in *British Journal of Special Education*, 35(4), pp. 230–240.

Beattie, R. (2006) 'The oral methods and spoken language acquisition' in P. Spencer and M. Marshark (eds) *Advances in the Spoken Language Development of Deaf and Hard-of-Hearing Children*, New York: OUP.

Beaumont, H. (2016) *Hole in the Heart. Bringing up Beth*, Brighton: Myriad.

Bell, D. (1967) *An Experiment in Education. The History of Worcester College for the Blind, 1866–1966*, London: Hutchinson.

Benn, C. and Chitty, C. (1996) *Thirty Years On: Is Comprehensive Education Alive and Well or Struggling to Survive*, London: David Fulton.

Bennathan, M. (2000) (2nd ed.) 'Children at risk of failure in primary schools' in Bennathan, M., and M. Boxall (2012) *Effective Intervention in Primary Schools: Nurture Groups*, London: Routledge, pp. 1–18.

Bennathan, M. and Boxall, M. (2000) *Effective Intervention in Primary Schools: Nurture Groups*, 2nd edn, London: Routledge.

Bentley, L., Dance, R., Morling, E., Miller, S. and Wong, S. (2016) *Supporting Children with Down's syndrome*, London: David Fulton.

Berryman, M. and Glynn, T. (2001) *Hei Awhina Matua: Strategies for Bicultural Partnership in Overcoming Behavioural and Learning Difficulties*, Wellington: Specialist Education Service.

Beveridge, S. (2005) *Children, Families and Schools: Developing Partnerships for Inclusive Education*, London: RoutledgeFalmer.

Bion, W. (1961) *Learning from Experience*, London: Heinemann.

Bird, G. and Thomas, S. (2002) 'Providing effective speech and language therapy for children with Down syndrome in mainstream settings: A case example', *Down Syndrome News and Update*, 2(1), pp. 30–31.

Bishop, D. V. M. (2000) 'Pragmatic language impairment: A correlate of SLI, a distinct subgroup, or part of the autistic continuum?' in Bishop, D.V.M. and L. Leonard (eds) *Speech and Language Impairments in Children: Causes, Characteristics, Intervention and Outcome*, Hove: Psychology Press.

Blairmires, G., Coupland, C., Galbraith, T., Parker, J., Parr, A., Simpson, F. and Thornton, P. (2016) *Supporting Children with Sensory Impairment*, London: David Fulton.

Bloch, M.H. and Leckman, J.F. (2009) 'Clinical course of Tourette syndrome', *Journal of Psychosomatic Research*, 6, pp. 497–501.

Board of Education (1905) *Reports on Children Under Five Years of Age in Public Elementary Schools, by Women Inspectors. Cd2726*, London: HM Stationery Office.

Board of Education (1908) *Report on School Attendance of Children Below the Age of Five (Acland Report)*, London: HM Stationery Office.

Board of Education (1910) *Annual Report for 1910 of the Chief Medical Officer. Cd5952*. London: HMSO.

Board of Education (1933) *Report of the Consultative Committee on Infant and Nursery Schools (Hadow Report, 1933)*, London: HM Stationery Office.

Board of Education (1938) *Report of the Consultative Committee on Secondary Education with Special Reference to Grammar Schools and Technical High Schools (Spens Report)*, London: HM Stationery Office.

Bowlby, J. (1944) 'Forty-four juvenile thieves: Their character and home life', *International Journal of Psychoanalysis*, 25, pp. 19–52.

Bowlby, J. (1952) 'A two-year-old goes to hospital', *Proceedings of the Royal Society of Medicine*, 46, pp. 425–7.

Bowlby, J. (1988) *A Secure Base*, London: Routledge.

Boxall, M. (2002) *Nurture Groups in School: Principles and Practice*, London: Paul Chapman.

Bradburn, E. (1966) 'Britain's first nursery-infant school', *The Elementary School Journal*, 67(2), pp. 57–63.

Brandon, M., Bailey, S., Belderson, P., Gardner, R., Sidebotham, P., Dodsworth, J., Warren, C. and Black, J. (2009) *Understanding Serious Case Reviews and their Impact. A Biennial Analysis of Serious Case Reviews 2005–07*, London: Department for Children, Schools and Families.

Brandon, M., Belderson, P., Warren, C., Gardner, R., Howe, D., Dodsworth, J. and Black, J. (2008) 'The preoccupation with thresholds in cases of child death or serious injury through abuse and neglect', *Child Abuse Review*, 17(5), pp. 313–330.

Brewster, S. J. (2004) 'Putting words into their mouths? Interviewing people with learning disabilities and little/no speech', *British Journal of Learning Disabilities*, 32(4), pp. 166–169.

Bridle, L, and Mann, G. (2000) 'Mixed feelings – A parental perspective on early intervention', originally published in *Supporting Not Controlling: Strategies for the New Millennium: Proceedings of the Early Childhood Intervention Australia National Conference*, July 1–23, 2000, pp. 59–72.

British Psychological Society (BPS) (1999) *Dyslexia, Literacy and Psychological Assessment*, Leicester: BPS.

Broadfoot, P. (2011) *Assessment, Schools and Society*, London: Routledge.

Brooker, L., Rogers, S., Ellis, D., Hallett, E. and Guy Roberts-Holmes, G. (2010) *Practitioners' Experiences of the Early Years Foundation Stage (RB029)* London: Department of Education.

Bruner, J. (1966) *Toward a Theory of Instruction*, Cambridge, MA: Harvard University Press.

Burman, D, Nunes, T. and Evans, D (2006) 'Writing profiles of deaf children taught through British Sign Language', *Deafness and Education International*, 9, pp. 2–23.

Burnett, J. (1994) *Destiny Obscure*, London: Routledge.

Cairns, B. and McClatchey, K. (2013) 'Comparing children's attitudes towards disability', *British Journal of Special Education*, 40, pp. 124–129.

Campbell, C. (2011) *How to Involve Hard to Reach Parents: Encouraging Meaningful Parental Involvement with Schools*, Nottingham: National College of Teaching and Learning.

Carpenter, B. (2000) 'Sustaining the family: Meeting the needs of families of children with disabilities', *British Journal of Special Education*, 27(3), pp. 135–144.

Carpenter, B. (2005) 'Early childhood intervention: Possibilities and prospects for professionals, families and children', *British Journal of Special Education*, 32(4), pp. 176–183.

Carr, M. (2001) *Assessment in Early Childhood: Learning Stories*, London: Paul Chapman.

Carreiras, M., Seghier, M. L., Baquero, S., Estévez, A., Lozano, A., Devlin, J. T. and Price, C. J. (2009) 'An anatomical signature for literacy', *Nature*, 461(7266), pp. 983–986.

Central Advisory Council for Education (CACE) (1967) *Children and Their Primary Schools. A Report of the Central Advisory Council for Education (England)*, (The Plowden Report), London: CACE.

Children's Workforce Development Council (CWDC) (2009) *The Common Assessment Framework for Children and Young People. A Guide for Practitioners*, London: CWDC.

Children's Workforce Development Council (CWDC) (2010) *Common Core of Skills and Knowledge*, Leeds: CWDC.

Children's Workforce Development Council (CWDC) (2010) *Common Core of Skills and Knowledge for the Children's and Young People's Workforce*, London: CWDC.

Children's Workforce Development Council (2010) *The Common Assessment Framework for Children and Young People: A Practitioners' Guide*, Leeds: CWDC.

Clark, C., Dyson, A., Millward, A. and Skidmore, D. (1997) *New Directions in Special Needs*, London: Cassell.

Claxton, G., and Carr, M. (2004) 'A framework for teaching learning: The dynamics of disposition', *Early Years: Journal of International Research and Development*, 24(1), pp. 87–97.

Cole, T. (1989) *Apart or a Part? Integration and the Growth of British Special Education*, Milton Keynes: Open University Press.

Cole, T. (1990) 'The history of special education: Social control of humanitarian progress'?, *British Journal of Special Education*, 17(3), pp. 101–107.

Cooper, P., Arnold, R, and Boyd, E. (2001) 'The effectiveness of Nurture Groups: Preliminary research findings', *British Journal of Special Education*, 28(4), pp. 160–166.

Cooper, P. and Lovey, J. (1999) 'Early intervention in emotional and behavioural difficulties: The role of Nurture Groups', *European Journal of Special Needs Education*, 14(2), pp. 122–131.

Coulter, S., Kynman, L., Morling, E., Grayson, R. and Wing, J. (2015) *Supporting Children with Dyspraxia and Motor Co-ordination Difficulties*, London: David Fulton.

Council of Europe (1966) *European Convention on Human Rights (Rome, 1950) and Its Five Protocols*, Strasbourg: Council of Europe.

Couture, C., Cooper, C. and Royer, E. (2011) 'A study of the concurrent validity of the Boxall Profile and the Goodman Strengths and Difficulties Questionnaire', *The International Journal of Emotional Education*, 3(1), pp. 20–29.

Cowne, E., Frankl, C. and Gerschel, L. (2015) *The SENCo Handbook*, 6th edn, London: David Fulton.

Crozier, G. and Reay, D. (2005) (Eds) *Activating Participation: Parents and Teachers Working Toward Partnership*, Stoke-on-Trent: Trentham.

Davis, P. (2003) *Including Children with a Visual Impairment in Mainstream Schools: A Practical Guide*, London: Fulton.

Dehaene-Lambertz, G., Hertz-Pannier, L., Dubois, J., Meriaux, S., Roche, A., Sigman, M. and Dehaene, S. (2006) 'Functional organisation of perisylvian activation during presentation of sentences in preverbal infants', *Proceedings of the National Academy of Sciences*, 103(38), pp. 14240–14245.

Department for Children, Schools and Families (DCSF) (2008) *Statutory Framework for the Early Years Foundation Stage*, Nottingham: DCSF.

Department for Education (DfE) (1994) *The Code of Practice for the Identification and Assessment of Special Educational Needs*, London: DfE.

Department for Education (DfE) (2010) *Common Core Skills and Knowledge for the Children's and Young People's Workforce*, London: DfE.

Department for Education (DfE) (2011a) *Review of Best Practice in Parental Engagement*, London: Institute of Education.

Department for Education (DfE) (2011b) *Teachers' Standards*, London: DfE.

Department for Education (DfE) (2012) *Statutory Framework for the Early Years Foundation Stage (EYFS)*, London: DfE.

Department for Education (DfE) (2013a) *The National Curriculum in England Key Stages 1 and 2 Framework Document*, London: DfE.

Department for Education (DfE) (2013b) *Early Years Outcomes*, London: DfE, available at: /www.foundationyears.org.uk/files/2012/03/Early_Years_Outcomes.pdf. (accessed 22 May 2017).

Department for Education (DfE) (2014a) *Special Educational Needs and Disability (SEND) – A Guide for Parents and Carers*, London: DfE.

Department for Education (DfE) (2014b) *Special Educational Needs and Disability Pathfinder*, London: DfE.

Department for Education (DfE) (2015a) *Special Educational Needs and Disability Code of Practice: 0 to 25 Years*, London: DfE.

Department for Education (DfE) (2015b) *Information Sharing: Advice for Practitioners*, London: DfE.

Department for Education (DfE) (2015c) *Common Core of Skills and Knowledge for the Children's and Young People's Workforce*, London: DFE.

Department for Education (DfE) (2015d) *Pupil Premium 2015 to 2016: Conditions of Grant*, London: DfE.

Department for Education (DfE) (2016a) *Phonics Screening Check: Scoring Guidance*, London: DfE.

Department for Education (DfE) (2016b) *Mental Health and Behaviour in Schools*, London: DfE.

Department for Education (DfE) (2017) *Early Years Foundation Stage Statutory Framework*, London: DfE.

Department for Education and Employment (DfEE) (1996) *Desirable Outcomes for Children's Learning on Entering Compulsory Education*, London: DfEE.

Department for Education and Employment (DfEE) (1996) *Nursery Education: Desirable Learning Outcomes for Children's Learning on Entering Compulsory Education*, London: DfEE.

Department for Education/Department of Health (DfE/DoH) (2011) *Supporting Families in the Early Foundation Years*, London: DfE/DoH.

Department of Education and Science (DES) (1977) *A New Partnership for Our Schools (Taylor Report)*, London: HM Stationery Office.

Department of Education and Science (DES) (1978) *Special Educational Needs, Report of the Committee of Enquiry into the Education of Handicapped Children and Young People, Cmnd. 7212 (Warnock Report)*, DES: London, HM Stationery Office.

Department of Education and Science (DES) (1990) *Starting with Quality. The Report of the Committee of Inquiry into the Quality of the Educational Experience Offered to 3 and 4 Year Olds (The Rumbold Report)*, London: HM Stationery Office.

Department for Education and Skills (DfES) (2001) *Special Educational Needs Code of Practice*, London: DfES.

Department for Education and Skills (DfES) (2002) *Birth to Three Matters*, London: DfES.

Department for Education and Skills (DfES) (2004) *Every Child Matters: Change for Children*, London: DfES.

Department for Education and Skills (DfES) (2006) *Primary Framework for Literacy and Mathematics*, Norwich: DfES.

Department for Education and Skills (DfES) (2007a) *Creating the Picture*, London: DfES.

Department for Education and Skills (DfES) (2007b) *Letters and Sounds*, London: DfES, available online at: www.gov.uk/government/publications/letters-and-sounds. (accessed 22 May 2017).

Department of Education and Science and the Welsh Office (1989) *Discipline in Schools/Report of the Committee of Enquiry Chaired by Lord Elton* (Elton Report); London: HM Stationery Office.

Department of Education, Northern Ireland (DENI) (2005) *Supplement to the Code of Practice on the Identification and Assessment of Special Educational Needs*, Bangor: DENI.

Department of Education, Northern Ireland (DENI) (1998) *The Code of Practice for the Identification and Assessment of Special Educational Needs*, Bangor: DENI.

Desforges, C. and Abouchaar, A. (2003). *The Impact of Parental Involvement, Parental Support and Family Education on Pupil Achievement and Adjustment: A Literature Review*, Nottingham: DfES.

Dewey, J. (1902) *The Child and the Curriculum*, Chicago: University of Chicago Press.

Dickens, C. (1910) *Hard Times and Sketches by Boz*, London: Caxton.

Dixit, R. (2006) *Child Development: Birth to Adolescence*, Bhopal: Indra.

Donaldson, M. (1984) *Children's Minds*, London: Fontana.

Donnachie, I. (2000) *Robert Owen: Owen of New Lanark and New Harmony*, Edinburgh: Tuckwell Press, Brilinn Ltd.

Donnachie, I.L. and Hewitt, G. (1993) *Historic New Lanark: The Dale and Owen Industrial Community Since 1785*, Edinburgh: Edinburgh University Press.

Douglas, G. and McLinden, M. (2005) 'Visual impairment' in Norwich, B. and A. Lewis, (eds) *Special Teaching for Special Children? Pedagogies for Inclusion*, Maidenhead: Open University Press, pp. 26–40.

Down, J.L.H. (1866) 'Observations on an ethnic classification of idiots', *Clinical Lecture Reports*, London Hospital 3: pp. 259–62, available at www.neonatology.org/classics/down.html (accessed 22 May 2017).

Drummond, M.J. (2006) 'How teachers engage with assessment for learning: Lessons from the classroom', *Research papers in education*, 18(4), pp. 119–132.

Dunhill, A. (2009) *What is Communication? The Process of Transferring Information*, Exeter: Learning Matters.

Dykens, E.M. and Kasari, C. (1997) 'Maladaptive behavior in children with Prader-Willi syndrome, Down syndrome, and nonspecific mental retardation', *American Journal on Mental Retardation*, 102(3), pp. 228–237.

Early Education (2012) *Development Matters in the Early Years Foundation Stage*, Early Education: London.

Education Department (1898) *Report of the Departmental Committee on Defective and Epileptic Children (Sharpe Report)*, London: HMSO.

Enquire (2014) *The Parents' Guide to Additional Support for Learning*, Edinburgh: Enquire.

Equality and Human Rights Commission (2016) *Private and Public Sector Guidance: Reasonable Adjustments*, available at www.equalityhumanrights.com/private-and-public-sector-guidance (accessed 9 March 2016).

Exner, C.E. (2005) 'Development of hand skills' in Case-Smith, J. (ed) *Occupational Therapy for Children* 5th edn, St. Louis: Mosby, pp. 304–355.

Farroni, T., Csibra, G., Simion, F. and Johnson, M.H. (2002) 'Eye contact detection in humans from birth', *PNAS*, 99(14), pp. 9602–9605.

Field, T. M. (1979) 'Games parents play with normal and high-risk infants', *Child Psychiatry and Human Development*, 10, pp. 41–48.

Firth, C. and Venkatesh, K. (1999) *Semantic Pragmatic Language Disorder: Part 1*, Milton Keynes: Speechmark Publishing.

Fisch H., Hyun G., Golden R., Hensle, T.W., Olsson, C.A. and Liberson, G.L. (2003) 'The influence of paternal age on down syndrome', *Journal of Urology*, 169(6), pp. 2275–2278.

Forman, G. and Hall, E. (2007) 'Wondering with children: The importance of observation in early education', *Early Childhood Research and Practice*, 7(2), pp. 1–11.

Frederickson, N. and Cline, T. (2015) *Special Educational Needs, Inclusion and Diversity*, 3rd edn, Maidenhead: Open University Press/McGraw Hill.

Freeman, S.B., Taft, L.F., Dooley, K.J., Allran, K., Sherman, S.L., Hassold, T.J., Khoury, M.J., Saker, D.M. (1998) 'Population-based study of congenital heart defects in Down syndrome', *Am J Med Genet*, 80(3), pp. 213–217.

Froebel, F. (1826/2005) *The Education of Man*, translation by W.N. Hailmann, Mineola, NY: Dover.

Furlong, V.J. (1985) *The Deviant Pupil: Sociological Perspectives*, Milton Keynes: OU Press.

Gallagher, A.L. and Chiat, S. (2009) 'Evaluation of speech and language therapy interventions for pre-school children with specific language impairment: A comparison of outcomes following specialist intensive, nursery-based and no intervention', *International Journal of Language & Communication Disorders*, 44(5), pp. 616–638.

Galloway, D.M. and Goodwin, C. (1987) *The Education of Disturbing Children: Pupils with Learning and Adjustment Difficulties*, London: Longman.

Galloway, D.M., Armstrong, D. and Tomlinson, S. (1994) *The Assessment of Special Educational Needs: Whose Problem?*, Harlow: Longman.

Garner, R. (2010) 'Here's to the early years: The Pre-school Learning Alliance's playgroups are facing an uncertain future', *Independent*, (16 December 2016).

Gee, J. (2000) 'New people in new worlds: Networks, the new capitalism and schools' in Cope, B. and M. Kalantzis (eds) *Multiliteracies: Literacy Learning and the Design of Social Futures*, London: Routledge.

Gerhardt, S. (2010) *The Selfish Society: How We All Forgot to Love One Another and Made Money Instead*, London: Simon & Schuster.

Gerhardt, S. (2015) *Why Love Matters* 2nd edn, London: Routledge.

Giallo, R. and Gavidia-Payne, S. (2006) 'Child, parent and family factors as predictors of adjustment for siblings of children with a disability', *Journal of Intellectual Disability Research*, 50(12), pp. 937–948.

Gillard, D. (2011) *Education in England: A Brief History*, available at: ww.educationengland.org.uk/history (accessed: 13 July 2016).

Glynn, T. (1982) 'Antecedent control of behaviour in educational contexts', *Educational Psychology*, 2, pp. 215–229.

Goldberg, E.M., Irvine, E.E., Lloyd Davies, A.B. and McDougall, K.F. (eds) (1956) *The Boundaries of Casework: A Report on a Residential Refresher Course Held by the Association of Psychiatric Social Workers*, London: APSW.

Goldberg, L.R. and Richberg, C.M. (2004) 'Minimal hearing impairment: Major myths with more than minimal implications', *Communication Disorders Quarterly*, 24, pp. 152–160.

Goldschmeid, E. and Jackson, S. (2004) *People Under Three: Young Children in Day Care*, Hove: Psychology Press.

Gosling, A. (2016) 'Quality early years environments' in Slaughter, E. (ed) *Quality in the Early Years*, London: OUP, pp. 30–49.

Goswami, U. (2008) *Cognitive Development. The Learning Brain*, Hove: Psychology Press.

Goswami, U. (2015) *Children's Cognitive Development and Learning* (CPRT Research Survey 3), York: Cambridge Primary Review Trust.

Grandin, T. (1995) *Thinking in Pictures*, New York: Bantam Doubleday Dell.

Grandin, T. and Panek, R. (2013) *The Autistic Brain: Thinking Across the Spectrum*, Boston: Houghton Mifflin Harcourt.

Grauberg, E. (2002) *Elementary Mathematics and Language Difficulties*, London: Whurr.

Greenhalgh, P. (1994) *Emotional Growth and Learning*, London: Routledge.

Gregory, E. (1996) *Making Sense of a New World*, London: Paul Chapman.

Griggs, J. and Bussard, L. (2017) *Study of Early Education and Development (SEED): Meeting the Needs of Children with Special Educational Needs and Disabilities in the Early Years*, London: DfE.

Griscom, J. (1832/2013) *A Year in Europe*, Kingston, Ontario: Legacy Books Press.

Groos, K. (1898) *Die Spiele der Tiere* translation by E. L. Baldwin as *The Play of Animals*, New York: Appleton.

Gussin Paley, V. (2000) *White Teacher*, Cambridge: Harvard University Press.

Hage, C. and Leybaert, J. (2006) 'The effect of cued speech on the development of spoken language' in Spencer, P. and M. Marshark (eds) *Advances in the Spoken Language Development of Deaf and Hard-of-Hearing Children*, New York: OUP.

Hall, J. (2008) 'Looking back. Mental deficiency – changing the outlook', *The Psychologist*, 21(11), pp. 1006–1007.

Hallgarten, J. (2000) *Parents Exist, ok!? Issues and Visions for the Parent-School Relationship*, London: IPPR.

Hanko, G. (1994) 'Discouraged children: When praise does not help', *British Journal of Special Education*, 21(4), pp. 166–168.

Harlow, H.F. (1958) 'The nature of love', *American Psychologist*, 13, pp. 673–685.

Harlow, H.F. (1962) 'Development of affectional patterns in infant monkeys' in Foss, B. M. (ed) *The Determinants of Infant Behavior, vol. II*, New York: Wiley, pp. 75–88.

Harlow, H.F. and Harlow, M.K. (1962) 'The effect of rearing conditions on behaviour', *Bulletin of the Menninger Clinic*, 26(5), pp. 213–224.

Harris, M. and Moreno, C. (2006) 'Speech reading and learning to read: A comparison of 8-year-old profoundly deaf children with good and poor reading ability', *Journal of Deaf Studies and Deaf Education*, 11, pp. 189–201.

Harris, A., Andrew-Power, K. and Goodall, J. (2010) *Do Parents Know They Matter? Raising Achievement Through Parental Engagement*, London: Continuum.

Harris-Hendriks, J. and Figueroa, J. (1995) *Black in White: The Caribbean Child in the UK*, London: Pitman.

Hebden, J. (1985) *She'll Never Do Anything Dear*, London: Souvenir Press.

Higashida, N. (2007/2014) *The Reason I Jump*, New York: Random House.

Hirschorn, L. (1998) *The Workplace Within: Psychodynamics of Organisational Life*, Cambridge, MA: MIT Press.

Holmes, J. (1993) *John Bowlby and Attachment Theory*, London, Routledge.

House, R. (ed) (2011) *Too Much, Too Soon?*, Stroud: Hawthorn Press.

Howard-Jones, N. (1979) 'On the diagnostic term "Down's disease"', *Medical History*, 23(1), pp. 102–104.

Hughes, M. (1986) *Children and Number. Difficulties in Learning Mathematics*, London: Blackwell.

Isaacs, S. (1929) *The Nursery Years, the Mind of the Child from Birth to Six Years*, London: Routledge.

Isaacs, S. (1952) *The Educational Value of the Nursery School*, London: Headly Brothers.

Jackson, J. (2004) *Multicoloured Mayhem*, London: Jessica Kingsley.

Jackson, L. (2002) *Freaks, Geeks and Asperger Syndrome*, London: Jessica Kingsley.

James, M. and Pollard, A. (n/d) 'TLRP's ten principles for effective pedagogy: rationale, development, evidence, argument and impact', available at http://eprints.ioe.ac.uk/7044/1/James2011TLRP%27s275.pdf (accessed 23 March 2017).

Jones, C.A. (2004) *Inclusion in the Early Years* 3rd edn, Maidenhead: McGrawHill.

Jones, H. (2000) Partnerships: A common sense approach to inclusion? Paper presented at the SCUTREA 30th Annual Conference, University of Nottingham, 3–5 July, available at: www.leeds.ac.uk/educol/documents/00001456htm (accessed 27 August 2016).

Jordan, R. (1999) *Autistic Spectrum Disorders: An Introductory Handbook for Practitioners*, London: David Fulton.

Jordan, R. (2001) *Autism with Severe Learning Difficulties*, London: Souvenir Press.

Kanner, L. (1943) 'Autistic disturbances of affective contact', *Nervous Child*, 2, pp. 217–250.

Keen, D. and Rodger, S. (2012) *Working with Parents of a Newly Diagnosed Child with an Autism Spectrum Disorder*, London: Jessica Kingsley.

Kilic, D., Gencdogan, B., Bag, B. and Arican, D. (2013) 'Psychosocial problems and marital adjustments of families caring for a child with intellectual disability' *Sex Disability*, 31, pp. 287–296.

Kirby, A.H.P. (1914) *Legislation for the Feeble-Minded*, London: John Bale.

Klin, A., Sparrow, S., Marans, W.D., Carter, A. and Volkmar, F.R. (2000) 'Assessment issues in children and adolescents with Asperger syndrome' in Klin, A., F.R. Volkmar, and S. Sparrow (eds) *Asperger Syndrome*, New York: Guilford Press, pp. 309–339.

Kozulin, A. (2003) 'Psychological tools and mediated learning' in Kozulin, A., B. Gindis, V.S. Ageyev and S.M. Miller (eds) *Vygotsky's Educational Theory in Cultural Context* Cambridge: Cambridge University Press, pp. 15–38.

Kramer, J., Hall, A. and Heller, T. (2013) 'Reciprocity and social capital in sibling relationships of people with disabilities', *Intellectual and Developmental Disabilities*, 51(6), pp. 482–495.

Kwon, Y.I. (2002) 'Changing curriculum for early childhood education in England', *Early Childhood Research and Practice*, 4(2), available at http://ecrp.uiuc.edu/v4n2/kwon.html (accessed 18 March 2017).

Lamb, B. (2009) *Report to the Secretary of State on the Lamb Inquiry Review of SEN and Disability Information*, London: DCSF.

Laming (2003) *The Victoria Climbié Inquiry. Report of an Inquiry by Lord Laming*, London: Crown.

Law, J., Lindsay, G., Peacey, N., Gascoigne, M., Soloff, N., Radford, J. and Band, S. (2002) 'Consultation as a model for providing speech and language therapy in schools: A panacea or one step too far?', *Child Language Teaching and Therapy*, (18), pp. 145–163.

Le Couter, A., Lord, C., and Rutter, M. (2007) *Autism Diagnostic Interview-Revised (ADI-R)*, Los Angeles: Western Psychological Services.

Lee, M. and Stead, V. (1998) 'Human resource development in the United Kingdom', *Human Resource Development Quarterly*, 9(3), pp. 297–308.

Leinonen, E. and Letts, C. (1997) 'Why pragmatic impairment? A case study in the comprehension of inferential meaning', *European Journal of Disorders of Communication*, 32, pp. 35–51.

Lewis, S. (1996) 'The reading achievement of a group of severely and profoundly hearing-impaired school leavers educated within a natural aural approach', *Journal of the British Association of Teachers of the Deaf*, 20, pp. 1–7.

Littleton, K. and Mercer, N. (2013) *Interthinking. Putting Talk to Work*, London: Routledge.

Lloyd, G., Stead, J. and Kendrick, A. (2001) *Interagency Working to Prevent School Exclusion*, York: Joseph Rowntree Foundation.

Lorenz, L. (1952) *King Solomon's Ring*, London: Methuen.

Lorenz, S. (1998) *Effective In-Class Support*, London: David Fulton.

Lowenfeld, M. (1935) *Play in Childhood*, Oxford: Blackwell.

Lumsden, E. (2014) 'Joined-up thinking in practice' in Waller, T. and G. Davis (eds) *An Introduction to Early Childhood* 3rd edn, London: Sage, pp. 286–304.

McConkey, R. (ed) (1994) *Innovations in Educating Communities About Learning Disabilities*, Chorley: Lisieux Hall.

Macintyre, C. (2014) *Identifying Additional Learning Needs in the Early Years* 2nd edn, London: Routledge.

Mair, M. (1988) 'Psychology as storytelling', *International Journal of Personal Construct Psychology*, 1, pp. 125–132.

Mason, H. (2001) *Visual Impairment*, Tamworth: NASEN.

Mason, H., McCall, S., Arter, C., McLinden, M. and Stone, J. (1997) *Visual Impairment: Access to Education for Children and Young People*, London: Fulton.

Mehan, H. (1996) 'The politics of representation' in Chaiklin, S. and J. Lave (eds) *Understanding Practice: Perspectives on Activity and Context*, Cambridge: Cambridge University Press.

Mencap (n.d.) *About Profound and Multiple Learning Disabilities*, London: Mencap.

Mental Deficiency Committee (1929) *Report of the Mental Deficiency Committee (WoodReport)*, London: HM Stationery Office.

Merrett, F. (1985) *Encouragement Works Better than Punishment: The Application of Behavioural Methods in Schools*, Birmingham: Positive Products.

Mesibov, G. (2015) *What is TEACCH?*, available at ://www.autismuk.com/training/what-is-teech/ (accessed 22 May 2017).

Mesibov, G.B., Shea, V. and Schopler, E. (2004) *The TEACCH Approach to Autism Spectrum Disorders*, London: Springer.

Meyer, D. (ed) (1995) *Uncommon Fathers: Reflections on Raising a Child with a Disability*, USA: Woodbine House.

Meyer, D. (ed) (1997) *Views from our Shoes*, Lakewood, NJ: Woodbine House.

Miller, O. and Ockleford, A. (2005) *Visual Needs*, London: Continuum.

Ministry of Education (MoE) (1945) *The Nation's Schools*, London: MoE.

Ministry of Education (1946) *Special Educational Treatment*, Ministry of Education Pamphlet no 5, London: HM Stationery Office.

Mittler, H. (1995) *Families Speak Out*, Cambridge, MA: Brookline.

Mittler, P. and Mittler, H. (eds.) (1994) *Innovations in Family Support for People with Learning Disabilities*, Chorley: Lisieux Hall.

Moeller, M.P., Tomblin, J.B., Yoshinaga-Itano, C., Connor, C. and Jerger, S. (2007) 'Current state of knowledge: Language and literacy of children with hearing impairment', *Ear and Hearing*, 28, pp. 740–753.

Montessori, M. (1913) *Pedagogical Anthropology*, Michigan: Frederick A. Stokes Publisher.

Moore, C. (2004) *George and Sam*, London: Penguin.

Moores, D. (2001) *Educating the Deaf*, Boston: Houghton Mifflin.

Moores, D. (2008) 'Research in Bi-Bi instruction', *American Annals of the Deaf*, 153, pp. 3–4.

Morris, J. K., Wald, N.J., Mutton, D. E. and Alberman, E. (2003) 'Comparison of models of maternal age-specific risk for Down syndrome live births', *Prenatal Diagnosis*, 23(3), pp. 252–258.

Morris, M. and Smith, P. (2008) *Educational Provision for Blind and Partially Sighted Children and Young People in Britain: 2007*, London: RNIB.

Mosley, J. (1996) *Quality Circle Time in the Primary Classroom: Your Essential Guide to Enhancing Self-Esteem, Self-Discipline and Positive Relationships*, Cambridge, LDA.

Moyles, J. (2010) *The Excellence of Play*, Maidenhead: Open University Press/McGraw Hill.

National Assembly of Wales (2004) *Special Educational Needs Code of Practice*, Cardiff: NAW.

National Assembly of Wales (NAW) (2012) *Forward in Partnership for Children and Young People with Additional Needs*, Cardiff: NAW.

National Autistic Society (2016) 'About autism', available at www.autism.org.uk/about/diagnosis.aspx (accessed 9 March 2016).

National Children's Bureau (2012) *A Know How Guide: The EYFS Progress Check at Age 2*, London: National Children's Bureau.

National Children's Bureau (2012) *The EYFS Progress Check at Age Two*, London: DfE.

National Deaf Children's Society (NDCS) (2008) *Acoustics Toolkit*, London: NDCS.

National Deaf Children's Society (NDCS) (2010) *Communicating With Your Deaf Child*, London: NDCS.

National Deaf Children's Society (NDCS) (2015a) *Communicating With Your Deaf Child*, London: NDCS.

National Deaf Children's Society (NDCS) (2015b) *Supporting the Achievement of Hearing Impaired Children in Early Years Settings*, London: NDCS.

National Deaf Children's Society (NDCS) (2016) 'Supporting your deaf baby or toddler's listening and speech development', available at http://soundingboard.earfoundation.org.uk/downloads/supporting_your_deaf_baby_or_toddler%252592s_listening_and_speech_development.pdf (accessed 24 May 2016).

National Health Service (NHS) (2015) 'Hearing loss – Diagnosis', available at www.nhs.uk/Conditions/Hearing- impairment/Pages/Diagnosis.aspx (accessed 9 March 2016).

National Institute for Health and Care Excellence (NICE) (2011) *Autism in Under 19s: Recognition, Referral and Diagnosis*, London: NICE.

National Institute of Neorological Disorders and Stroke (NINDS) (2005) *Tourette Syndrome Fact Sheet*, Bethesda, MD: NINDS.

Naylor, A. and Prescott, P. (2004) 'Invisible children? The need for support groups for siblings of disabled children', *British Journal of Special Education*, 31(4), pp. 199–206.

Nethercott, K. (2015) 'Understanding the use of the Common Assessment Framework exploring the implications for frontline professionals', unpublished PhD thesis, Luton: University of Bedfordshire.

Nicholson, S. (1971) 'How not to cheat children: The theory of loose parts', *Landscape Architecture Quarterly*, 62(1): pp. 30–4.

Nind, M. (1999) 'Intensive interaction: A useful approach? *British Journal of Special Education*, 26(2), pp. 96–102.

Norbury, C. F. and Bishop, D.V. M. (2003) 'Narrative skills in children with communication impairments', *International Journal of Language and Communication Impairments*, 38(2), pp. 87–313.

Nurture Group Network (2016) *History*, available at https://nurturegroups.org/about-us/history (accessed 9 March 2016).

Office for Standards in Education (Ofsted) (2015) *School Inspection Handbook*, Manchester: Ofsted.

Oliphant, J. (2006) 'Empowerment and debilitation in the educational experience of the blind in nineteenth-century England and Scotland', *History of Education*, 35(1), pp. 47– 68.

Open University (2000) *Audio Interview in E831 Professional Development for Special Educational Needs Co-ordinators*, Milton Keynes: Open University.

Owen, R. (1816) *A New View of Society*, available at www.marxists.org/reference/subject/economics/owen/ch01.htm (accessed 1 March 2017).

Owen, R. (1841) *Address on Opening the Institution for the Formation of Character at New Lanark, Delivered on 1st January, 1816, Being the First Announcement of the Discovery of the Infant School System*, London: Home Colonization Society.

Owen, R. (1857) *The life of Robert Owen Written by Himself, Vol 1, Pt 1*, London: Effingham Wilson.

Owen, R. (1920) *The Life of Robert Owen by Himself*, London: Bell.

Owen, R. D. (1824) *Outline of the System of Education at New Lanark*, Glasgow: University Press.

Padden, C. and Gunsals, D. (2003) 'How the alphabet came to be used in a sign language', *Sign Language Studies*, 4, pp. 1–13.

Paige-Smith, A. and Rix, J. (2006) 'Parents' perceptions and children's experiences of early intervention – inclusive practice?' *Journal of Research in Special Educational Needs*, 6(2), pp. 92–98.

Palaiologou, I. (2016) *The Early Years Foundation Stage: Theory and Practice* 3rd edn, London: Sage.

Paley, V.G. (2005) *A Child's Work: The Importance of Fantasy Play*, Chicago: University of Chicago Press.

Paley, V.G. (2009) *The Kindness of Children*, Boston: Harvard University Press.

Panksepp, J. (1998) *A Textbook of Biological Psychiatry*, New York: Wiley.

Park, K. (1997) 'How do objects become objects of reference?' *British Journal of Special Education*, 24(3), pp. 108–114.

Parker-Rees, R. and Willan, J. (2006) *Early Years Education, Major themes in Education. Volume 1 Histories and Traditions*, London: Routledge.

Pavey, B. (2016) *Dyslexia and Early Childhood*, London: David Fulton.

Peeters, T. and Gilberg C. (1999) 'The autistic spectrum: From theory to practice.' in Brace N. and H. Westcott (eds) *Applying Psychology*, Milton Keynes: Open University, pp. 243–315.

Perry, B.D. (2002) 'Childhood experience and the expression of genetic potential: What childhood neglect tells us about nature and nurture', *Brain and Mind*, 3, pp. 79–100.

Pestalozzi, J. H. (1801/1894) *How Gertrude Teaches her Children* translated by Lucy E. Holland and Frances C. Turner, Edited with an introduction by Ebenezer Cooke, London: Swan Sonnenschein.

Piacentini, J., Woods, D.W., Scahill, L., Wilhelm, S., Peterson, A.L., Chang, S., Ginsburg, G.S., Deckersbach, T., Dziura, J., Levi-Pearl, S. and Walkup, J. (2010) 'Behavior therapy for children with Tourette disorder', *Journal of the American Medical Association*, 303(19), pp. 1929–1937.

Piaget, J. (1954) *Construction of Reality in the Child*, New York: Basic Books.

Piaget, J. (1964) 'Cognitive development in children', *Journal of Research in Science Teaching*, 2(3), pp. 176–186.

Piaget, J. (1969) *The Child's Conception of Time*, London: RKP.

Piaget, J. and Inhelder, B. (2016) *Memory and Intelligence*, London: Psychology Press.

Pietroni, P.C. (1992) 'Towards reflective practice: Languages of health and social care.' *Journal of Interprofessional Care*, 6(1), pp. 6–16.

Pohlschmidt, M. and Meadowcroft, R. (2010) *Muscle Disease the Impact: Incidence and Prevalence of Neuromuscular Conditions in the UK*, London: Muscular Dystrophy Campaign.

Poulou, M. and Norwich, B. (2002) 'Cognitive, emotional and behavioural responses to students with emotional and behavioural difficulties: A model of decision-making', *British Educational Research Journal*, 28(1), pp. 111–138.

Previc, F.H. (2009) *The Dopaminergic Mind in Human Evolution and History*, Cambridge: CUP.

Price, C.J. (2012) 'A review and synthesis of the first 20 years of PET fMRI studies of heard speech, spoken language and reading', *NeuroImage*, doi:10.1016/j.neuroimage.2012.04.062

Primary National Strategy (PNS) (2005) *Speaking Listening Learning: Working with Children Who Have Special Educational Needs*, London: QCA.

Randall, P. and Parker, J. (1999) *Supporting the Families of Children with Autism*, Chichester: John Wiley and Sons.

Rapin, I. and Allen, D. (1983) 'Developmental language disorders: Neuropsychological considerations', in U Kirk (ed) *Neuropsychology of Language, Reading and Spelling*, New York: Academic Press, pp. 155–184.

Rapin, I. and Allen, D.A. (1998) 'The semantic-pragmatic deficit disorder: Classification issues', *International Journal of Language and Communication Disorders*, 33(1), pp. 82–87.

Read, J. (2000) *Disability, the Family and Society: Listening to Mothers*, Buckingham: OUP.

Reder, P. and Duncan, S. (2003) 'Understanding communication in child protection networks', *Child Abuse Review*, 12(2), pp. 82–100.

Reid, G. (2017) *Dyslexia in the Early Years*, London: Jessica Kingsley.

Research Autism (2016) 'Improving the quality of life', available at http://researchautism.net/autism-interventions/types/alternative-and-augmentative-communication (accessed 1 November 2016).

Riddick, B. (1996) *Living with Dyslexia*, London: Routledge.

Riddick, B. (2010) *Living with Dyslexia: The social and Emotional Consequences of Specific Learning Difficulties/disabilities*, London: Routledge.

Riddick B., Wolfe J. and Lumsdon D. (2002) *Dyslexia. A Practical Guide for Teachers and Parents*, London: David Fulton.

Rinaldi, C. (2001) 'Documentation and assessment: What is the relationship?' in Giudici, C., C. Rinaldi and M. Krechevsky (eds) (2001) *Making Learning Visible: Children as Individual and Group Learners*, Italy: Reggio Children.

RNID, (2004) *Inclusion Strategies*, London: RNID.

Roaf, C. and Lloyd, C. (1995) 'Multi-agency work with young people in difficulty', *Social Care Research Findings*, No. 68, June 1995, York: Joseph Rowntree Foundation.

Robinson, M. (2003) *From Birth To One: The Year of Opportunity*, Maidenhead: Open University Press.

Robinson, M. (2008) *Child Development from Birth to Eight: A Journey Through the Early Years*, Maidenhead: Open University Press.

Rochdale Borough Safeguarding Children Board (RBSCB) (2012) *Review of Multi-agency Responses to the Sexual Exploitation of Children*, Rochdale: RBSCB.

Rogers J. (2007) 'Cardinal Number and its representation: Skills, concepts and contexts', *Early Childhood Education and Care*, 178(2), pp. 211–225.

Rogers, B. (2013) 'Communicating with children in the classroom' in Cole, T., H. Daniels and J. Visser *The Routledge International Companion to Emotional and Behavioural Difficulties*, London: Routledge, pp. 237–245.

Rosch, E. (1978) 'Principles of categorisation' in Rosch, E. and B.B. Lloyd (eds) *Cognition and Categorisation*, Hillsdale, NJ: Lawrence Erlbaum, pp. 27–48.

Rose, J. (2009) *Identifying and Teaching Children and Young People with Dyslexia and Literacy Difficulties*, London: DCFS.

Royal National Institute for the Blind (RNIB) (2008) *See it Right Checklist*, London: RNIB.

Royal National Institute for the Deaf (RNID) (2004) *Inclusion Strategies*, London: RNID.

Russell, F. (2003) 'The expectations of parents of disabled children', *British Journal of Special Education*, 30(3), pp. 144–149.

Russell, P. (1997) 'Parents as partners: Early impressions of the impact of the Code of Practice' in Wolfendale, S. (ed) *Working with Parents After the Code of Practice*, London: Fulton.

Rutter, M. (2005) 'Incidence of autism spectrum disorders: Changes over time and their meaning', *Acta Paediatrica*, 94, pp. 2–15.

Rutter, M., Tizard, J. and Whitmore, K. (1970) *Education, Health and Behaviour*, London: Longman.

Salmon, P. (1998) *Life at School*, London: Constable.

Sarbin, T. (1986) *Narrative Psychology: The Storied Nature of Human Conduct*, New York: Praeger.

Schön, D. (1991) *The Reflective Practitioner*, London: Ashgate.

Schopler, E. (1997) 'Implementation of TEACCH philosophy' in Cohen, D.J. and F. R. Volkmar (eds.) *Handbook of Autism and Pervasive Developmental Disorders*, New York: Wiley, pp. 767–795.

Schopler, E., Reichler, R.J., and Lansing, M.D. (1980) *Individualized Assessment and Treatment for Autistic and Developmentally Disabled Children*, Baltimore: University Park Press.

Scottish Executive Education Department (SEED) (2004) *Curriculum for Excellence*, Edinburgh: Scottish Executive.

Scottish Government (2010) *Supporting Children's Learning Code of Practice* (revised), Edinburgh: Scottish Government.

Scottish Government (2014) *Planning Improvements for Disabled Pupils' Access to Education*, Edinburgh: Scottish Government.

Seligman, M. E. P. (1975) *Helplessness: On Depression, Development, and Death*, San Francisco: W. H. Freeman.

Selikowitz, M (2008) *Down Syndrome*, Oxford: OUP.

Shah, M. (2001) *Working with Parents*, Oxford; Heinnemann Educational Publishers.

Sheehy, K. (2004) 'Approaches to autism' in Wearmouth, J., R.C. Richmond and T. Glynn (eds) *Addressing Pupils' Behaviour: Responses at District, School and Individual Levels*, London: Fulton, pp. 338–356.

Silber, K. (1965) *Pestalozzi: The Man and His Work* 2nd edn, London: Routledge.

Simon, B. (1974) *The Two Nations and the Educational Structure 1780–1870*, London: Lawrence and Wishart.

Siraj-Blatchford, I. and Siraj-Blatchford, J. (2009) *Improving Children's Attainment Through a Better Quality of Family-Based Support for Early Learning*, London: C4EO.

Siraj-Blatchford, I., Sylva, K., Muttock, S., Gilden, R. and Bell, D. (2002) *Researching Effective Pedagogy in the Early Years (RR 356)*, London: Institute of Education.

Skinner, B.F. (1938) *The Behavior of Organisms*, New York: Appleton Century Crofts.

Smedley, M. (1990) 'Semantic-pragmatic language disorders: A description with some practical suggestions for teachers', *Child Language Teaching and Therapy*, (5), pp. 174–190.

Snowling, M. J. (2000) *Dyslexia* 2nd edn Oxford: Blackwell.

Somerset Educational Psychology Service (n.d.) *Supporting Young Children Through Bereavement and Loss. Information and Advice for Staff in Early Years Settings*, available at www.somerset.gov.uk/EasySiteWeb/GatewayLink.aspx?alId=52787 (accessed 1 March 2017).

Spencer, P. and Marshark, M. (eds) (2006) *Advances in the Spoken Language Development of Deaf and Hard-of-Hearing Children*, New York: OUP.

Spencer, P.E. and Marschark, M. (2010) *Evidence-based Practice in Educating Deaf and Hard-of-Hearing Students*, Oxford: OUP.

Standards and Testing Agency (STA) (2016) *Early Years Foundation Stage Profile 2017 Handbook*, London: DfE.

Stanovich, K.E. (1986) 'Matthew effects in reading: Some consequences of individual differences in the acquisition of literacy', *Reading Research Quarterly*, Fall, pp. 360–406.

Stansfield, J. (2014) 'Early identification' in D. Llewellyn-Jones, J. Carroll, J. and K. Saunders, K. (eds.), *The Dyslexia Handbook*, Bracknell: British Dyslexia Association, pp. 107–112.

Strohm, K. (2002) *Being the Other One*, Boston, MA: Shambhala Publications.

Strouse Watt, W. (2003) *How Visual Acuity Is Measured*, available at /www.mdsupport.org/library/acuity.html (accessed 22 May 2017).

Sunderland, M. (2016) *What Every Parent Needs to Know* 2nd edn, London: Penguin Random House.

Sylva, K., Melhuish, E., Sammons, P., Siraj-Blatchford, I., Taggart, B. and Elliot, K. (2004) *Effective Provision of Pre-school Education (EPPE)*, London: Institute of Education.

Tai, Y.F., Scherfler, C., Brooks, D.J., Sawamoto, N. and Castiello, U. (2004) 'The human premotor cortex is "mirror" only for biological actions', *Current Biology* 14: pp. 117–120.

Tammet, D. (2006) *Born on a Blue Day: The Gift of an Extraordinary Mind*, London: Hodder and Stoughton.

Tate, R., Smeeth, L., Evans, J., and Fletcher, A. (2005) *The Prevalence of Visual Impairment in the UK; A Review of the Literature*, available at www.vision2020uk.org.uk/the-prevalence-of-visual-impairment-in-the-uk-a-review-of-the-literature/ (accessed 28 February 2016).

Taylor, K. (2007) 'The participation of children with multi-sensory impairment in person-centred planning', *British Journal of Special Education*, 34(4), pp. 204–211.

Tew, M. (1998) 'Circle time: A much neglected resource in secondary schools', *Pastoral Care*, (Sept 1998), pp. 18–27.

Thomas, G. and Loxley, A. (2007) *Deconstructing Special Education and Constructing Inclusion*, Maidenhead: Open University Press.

Thomson, M. (1998) *The Problem of Mental Deficiency: Eugenics, Democracy and Social Policy in Britain, c.1870–1959*, Oxford: Clarendon Press.

Tickell, C. (2011) *Tickell Review: The Early Years: Foundations for Life, Health and Learning*, London: HM Stationery Office.

Treatment and Education of Autistic and Related Communication Handicapped Children (TEACCH) (1998) 'Treatment and education of autistic and related communication handicapped children', available at //www.teacch.com/ (accessed 1 March 2017).

Underwood, J.E.A. (1955) *Report of the Committee on Maladjusted Children*, London: HMSO.

United Nations (UN) (2007) *Convention on the Rights of Persons with Disabilities 61/106*, Geneva: UN.

United Nations (UN) (2009) *Convention on the Rights of the Child*, Geneva: UN.

Vasilopoulou, E. and Nisbet, J. (2016) 'The quality of life of parents of children with autism spectrum disorder: A systematic review', *Research in Autism Spectrum Disorders*, 23, pp. 36–49.

Verschueren, K., Doumen, S. and Buyse, E. (2012) 'Relationships with mother, teacher and peers: Unique and joint effects on young children's self-concept', *Attachment and Human Development*, 14(3), pp. 233–248.

Vygotsky, L.S. (1962) *Thought and Language*, Cambridge, MA: MIT Press.

Vygotsky, L.S. (1978) *Mind in Society. The Development of Higher Psychological Processes*, Cambridge, MA: Harvard University Press.

Wall, K. (2011) *Special Needs and Early Years: A Practitioners' Guide* 3rd edn, London: Sage.

Watkins, C. and Wagner, P. (2000) *Improving School Behaviour*, London: Paul Chapman.

Wearmouth, J. (1986) *Self Concept and Learning Experiences of Pupils with Moderate Learning Difficulties*, Unpublished Masters thesis, Institute of Education, London University.

Wearmouth, J. (1997) *Prisoners' Perspectives on What Constitutes a 'Good' Education*, paper presented to the British Psychological Society Annual Conference (Education Section), Warwicks, England.

Wearmouth, J. (1999) 'Another one flew over: 'Maladjusted' Jack's perception of his label', *British Journal of Special Education*, 26(1), pp. 15–23.

Wearmouth, J. (2004) 'Learning from 'James': Lessons about policy and practice for literacy difficulties in schools' special educational provision', *British Journal of Special Education*, 31(2), pp. 60–67.

Wearmouth, J. (2009) *A Beginning Teacher's Guide to Special Educational Needs*, Buckingham: Open University Press.

Wearmouth, J. (2016a) *Effective SENCo: Meeting the Challenge*, Maidenhead: McGraw Hill.

Wearmouth, J. (2016b) (2nd ed.) *Special Educational Needs and Disability: The Basics*, London: Routledge.

Wearmouth, J. (2017) *Special Educational Needs and Disability: A Critical Introduction*, London: Bloomsbury.

Wearmouth, J. and Berryman, M. (2011) 'Family and community support for addressing difficulties in literacy' in Wyatt-Smith, C., J., Elkins and E.Gunn (eds.), *Multiple Perspectives on Difficulties in Learning Literacy and Numeracy*, London: Springer.

Wearmouth, J., Glynn, T. and Berryman, M. (2005) *Perspectives on Student Behaviour in Schools: Exploring Theory and Developing Practice*, London: Routledge.

Whiting, M., Scammell, A. and Bifulco, A. (2008) 'The health specialist initiative: Professionals' views of a partnership initiative between health and social care for child safeguarding', *Qualitative Social Work: Research and Practice*, 7(1), pp. 99–117.

Widgit (2016) 'Symbols', available at www.widgit.com/symbols/index.htm (accessed 11 November 2016).

Wilkins, M. and Ertmer, D.J. (2002) 'Introducing young children who are deaf or hard of hearing to spoken language', *Language, Speech and Hearing Services in Schools*, 33, pp. 196–204

Wilkinson, E. (1947) *The New Secondary Education*, London: HM Stationery Office.

Wing, L. (1996) *The Autistic Spectrum: A Guide for Parent and Professionals*, London: Constable.

Wing, L. and Gould, J. (1979) Severe impairments of social interaction and associated abnormalities in children: Epidemiology and classification, *Journal of Autism and Developmental Disorders*, 9, pp. 11–29.

Winnicott, D.W. (1984) *Deprivation and Delinquency*, London: Tavistock.

Wolf, M. (2007) *Proust and the Squid: The Story and Science of the Reading Brain*, New York: HarperCollins.

Wolman, C., Garwick, A., Kohrman, C. and Blum, R. (2001) 'Parents' wishes and expectations for children With chronic conditions', *Journal of Developmental and Physical Disabilities*, 13(3), pp. 261–277.

Wood, D., Bruner, J. and Ross, G. (1976) 'The role of tutoring in problem solving', *Journal of Child Psychology and Psychiatry*, 17, pp. 89–100.

Woodhouse, J. (1982) 'Eugenics and the feeble-minded: The Parliamentary debates of 1912–14', *History of Education*, 11(2), pp. 127–137.

World Health Organization (WHO) (1994) *International Statistical Classification of Diseases* – ICD-10, WHO: Geneva.

World Health Organization (WHO) (2016) *The International Statistical Classification of Diseases* – ICD-10, WHO: Geneva.

Wright, D. and Digby, A. (1996) *From Idiocy to Mental Deficiency*, London: Routledge.

Yoder, P. J. (1990) 'The theoretical and empirical basis of early amelioration of developmental disabilities: Implications for future research', *Journal of Early Intervention*, 14, pp. 27–42.

Yoshinaga-Itano, C. (2003) 'From screening to early identification and intervention: Discovering predictors to successful outcomes for children with significant hearing loss', *Journal of Deaf Studies and Deaf Education*, 8, pp. 11–30.

Yurdakul, N.S., Ugurlu S., and Maden, A. (2006) 'Strabismus in Down syndrome', *Journal of Pediatric Ophthalmology and Strabismus*, 43(1), pp. 27–30.

Index

Gower College Swansea
Library
Coleg Gŵyr Abertawe
Llyrfgell